THE WRONGS

OF

THE CAFFRE NATION;

A NARRATIVE,

BY

JUSTUS.

WITH AN APPENDIX,

CONTAINING

LORD GLENELG'S DESPATCHES TO THE GOVERNOR
OF THE CAPE OF GOOD HOPE.

Auferre, trucidare, rapere falsis nominibus imperium,
atque ubi solitudinem faciunt pacem appellant.

TACITUS.

LONDON:
JAMES DUNCAN, PATERNOSTER ROW.

MDCCCXXXVII.

PREFACE.

THAT narrative, which displays a colony of the British nation systematically oppressing the aboriginal inhabitants by harsh and unrelenting injustice, and enlarging its boundaries by acts of violent spoliation, ought to be fortified with more than ordinary proofs, for without such proofs it would be difficult to believe the astonishing accusations of our colonial history. These proofs now exist in abundance, and there has been nothing wanting but the labours of a compiler to set before the public " the wrongs of the Caffre nation." In undertaking this work, the author has chiefly acted as a compiler, either selecting passages from books written on South Africa, or from parliamentary documents and evidence, which the orders of the House of Commons, or the investigations of its committees, have put within the reach of the inquirer; and though this sort of *documentary narrative*, may be less inviting to the general reader, it is assuredly more valuable, as it furnishes proofs of statements, which, from their startling nature, could hardly otherwise be credited.

It is certainly no agreeable task thus to unveil the disgrace of England; we would willingly have another story to tell: we would willingly declare, if the truth would allow, that our vast power, our great resources, and our almost boundless mastery of the physical world, had been turned to honourable and useful purposes in South Africa; that our strength and wisdom had conquered evil rather than augmented it, and that after thirty years' possession, we had, by our superiority in justice and virtue, brought into a cheerful and friendly obedience those barbarian neighbours, who have expected to find in us examples of moral pre-eminence. But such is not the case; the government of South Africa has been steadily advancing from bad to worse, from one act of impolitic injustice to another, till the last Caffre war, by its enormities in crime, compelled the British government to arrest at last the madness of the colony.

History, therefore, has in her annals of the British rule in South Africa to record all that is disgraceful, tragic, and disheartening; it must be written against us, and never can be erased, that up to the present hour, we have been a scourge to the Aborigines, that we have, at a very great cost to ourselves, stretched out the arm of oppression against our neighbours, and with shameless dupery made dishonest treaties, which we have dishonestly broken, and by sheer robbery seized on a vast extent of territory, which our ignorance of good government has rendered unavailing for any useful purposes, and which even now is thinly inhabited by a scanty population of unquiet settlers.

The whole population of the colony of the Cape of Good Hope, does not[*] equal the population of the town of Manchester, but even to this handful of inhabitants, the immense domain of our South African territory appears too small, and several hundred Boors have lately marched northwards beyond the Orange River, where, unchecked by the feeble and foolish government of the Cape, they are, by private commandos and associations of plunder, spreading havoc and destruction amongst the northern tribes. Within the colony discontent and dissatisfaction prevail, society there is divided into parties of contending interests, which can agree in nothing but a taste for tyranny. A population which has been long accustomed to the demoralizing habits of slavery, will not forego the sweets of oppression without violent reluctation ; and hence the Boors and settlers are not preparing them-

---

[*] The consequence of the rapid and exorbitant increase of territory by the colony, has been dispersion on our side, and condensation on that of the natives. At this moment the population of the colony exhibits not quite so much as *one* on the square mile, whilst the Caffre population, between the Keishkamma and the Kei, by a census recently taken, exceeds ten; had Sir B. D'Urban's late conquest been retained by the home government, the disproportion would have been fearfully increased.

selves for an abolition, but a fraudulent perpetuation of slavery. The attempt to evade the emancipating act was made by the promoters of the vagrant bill in 1834, and though that crooked scheme failed, yet the colonists consider themselves only temporarily defeated, and anticipate the success of some more artful legislation; whilst many of the Boors have decamped northwards, and taken their slaves with them to avoid the approaching year of jubilee.

In the meantime the first principles of justice are unacknowledged at the Cape, and society there is tainted with a moral disorder such as can scarcely be conceived in England. To comprehend fully the extent of this disorder, the reader should peruse attentively some of the colonial newspapers of the government party, in which the most frightful political immorality is advocated without shame or disguise; but as such evidence is necessarily within the reach of few in this country, it will be here acceptable to give a portion of a speech delivered on a very solemn occasion at Graham's Town in the presence of his Excellency the governor, in Sept. 1835. The speaker was Dr. Murray of the Medical Staff, who had accompanied his Excellency in the Caffre war, and who stood so high in favor with his Excellency, that one of the forts in the new province was named after him. At a public dinner given to the governor at Graham's Town, and to which his Excellency came in vice-regal pomp, drawn in a coach with six horses, with guards of state, chaplains, and other officials; Dr. Murray thus uttered the vulgar and savage sentiments of the colony :—" He would say that the Caffre, *Parthis mendacior*, is born and notoriously bred a cattle-stealer and a rogue. Detected in a lie, in a theft, or in cheating, he is never disconcerted ; in fact, lying, cattle-stealing, and cunning are esteemed the greatest accomplishments amongst this treacherous race of savages; they hate the colonists, and would have butchered you all at any former period, the same as they would now if they could ; and assuredly they are only to be kept in subjection and order by the iron rod of power. He would take a professional view of late events, and on probing the sore to the bottom, he might say he had found a *cancerous set-fast at the core,* * which was the true cause he looked to, and which the faculty had been trying to cure by various modes of treatment, but without effect. Some of the most eminent surgeons had recommended strong remedies, such as *firing*, scarifying, &c., which were used at first with much advantage ; but the plan was decried as being inhuman, and only fit for tigers and wolves, and it was left off. In lieu thereof *a plaister* had been recommended by a new staff-surgeon, who had just arrived, which he called the ' *Hue and cry*,' or ' *Catch-'em-if-you-can plaister ;*' and this was tried for some time, but without any advantage whatever ; on the contrary, the sore was increased by it. *The con-*

---

* N.B. The italics are those of the colonial newspapers.

stitution is different here to what it is in England.
At this time some quacks who had been for a long time
intruding their advice, and had got the ear of the patient, and of the medical board at home by professing
that they had a mild and effectual remedy for the disease, obtained leave to try their *patent specific*, which
was nothing more or less than to give the patient *sugar-
plums*, (Hear, hear, hear ; loud applause), and a large
bag of them had actually arrived in Cape Town from
England, and the government waggon was preparing
to bring them up, and the patient had been told to expect them daily ; but in the interim, before their arrival,
it so happened that a pretty strong *catch-'em-if-you-
can plaister* had been applied to the sore by some young
surgeons, in consequence of some bad appearances in
it, which made the patient very angry, and *he refused
to submit to any more plaistering, as he had been promised the sugar-plums and would have them;* and it
made him so obstreporous, and fretted him so much,
that he broke out into an eruption all over his body,
and the sore over the cancerous set-fast put on a
very malignant appearance.   The general doctor, (*i.e.*
Sir B. D'Urban the governor), upon this came up, and
took the treatment into his own hands.   He discarded
the quacks and their charlatanerie, which he saw to be
stark-staring nonsense, and had immediate recourse to
phlebotomy, firing, lead pills, and low diet, by which
means the eruption soon disappeared, and the patient
assumed a healthy condition.

" But mark me, gentlemen, take care that no more *placebo plaisters* be tried, and that the patient be not again tampered with by benevolent theorists and Caffre maniacal quacks. The *cancerous set-fast* must be cauterized and thoroughly subdued, and strong *in terrorem* measures, such as firing, with bandaging and spare regimen will for a long time be required to prevent a recurrence of what has happened."

This speech was received with enthusiastic acclamations. The Chairman, Dr. Atherstone, proposèd a toast of " Dr. Murray's radical cure of the Caffre set-fast," and the military band played, by desire, " The Rogues' March."

Any where else such pot-house trash would certainly be unworthy our notice ; but when we remember on what occasion the speech was delivered, and before whom, even the representative of the British crown, sitting there in vice-regal state, surrounded with officers of the army, and officials of the colony, it is worthy our most serious consideration, as setting forth, in a striking manner, the state of society at the Cape.

But if these things stand unreproved, if the reign of violence is not terminated, and if our colonial misdeeds are not speedily and permanently prevented, surely it must be a mockery to class England amongst Christian nations? " A Christian people" must mean a people who are under the control* of Christian precepts,

---

* It is, alas! too true, that some writers, even in this country, have, without shame, published such sentiments as one would have

and in a nation, whose pre-eminent boast is, that the
Church is united to the State, we must expect to see
the influence of the doctrines of the Church in the
practice of the State.   Viewing England, therefore, as
a Christian country, we may safely say, that if it could
be proved, that after a thirty years' dominion we had

hoped could only have made their appearance in the slave-states of
North America, or our own wretched South African colony.

  The editor of the journal of the Royal Geographical Society, a
work in much repute, thus unveils his morality in reviewing a
work on South Africa. "The greatest difficulty is in tracing a
boundary between the colonists and their restless neighbours, as
shall easily admit of peaceful communication, and yet be such as
to afford few facilities to marauders—and it is to be observed,
that the acquisition of such a frontier should be as much an object
of desire to the Caffres as to the colonists, for with a little more or
less suffering on both parties, *the uncivilised must give way to
the civilised, and better sooner than late.*"—(Vol. v. pt. ii. 1835, p.
315.)

  But what shall we say to the following passage in Sir John
Ross's second voyage to the Artic Regions? "Our brandy was
as odious as our pudding to our Esquimaux visitors, and they
have yet therefore to acquire the taste which has, in ruining the
morals, hastened the extermination of their American neighbours
to the Southward. If, however, these tribes must finally disappear, as seems their fate, it is at least better that they should
die gradually by the force of rum, than that they should be exterminated in masses by the fire and sword of the Spanish conquest,
since there is some pleasure, such as it is, in the mean time, while
there is also a voluntary but slow suicide in exchange for murder
and robbery? Is it not the fate of the savage and the uncivilized
on this earth to give way to the more cunning and the better informed, to knowledge and civilization? *It is the order of the world,
and the right one;* nor will all the lamentations of a mawkish philanthropy, with its more absurd or censurable efforts, avail one jot
against an order of things as wise as it is assuredly established."
—(Vol. i. p. 257.)

done nothing at all, as far as the government is concerned, to bring the barbarian tribes under the mild and
transforming power of the Gospel—that the government had in no way advanced the civilization, or improved the condition of the Aborigines of its colonies—
then are we weighed in the balance and found wanting;
but when we advance beyond this, and prove that our
Christian sway has been applied to purposes of spoliation, wrong, and cruelty, how shall we find words to
express our guilt and degradation? The Author of our
religion " went about doing good," but in what respect
have we, as a Christian nation, imitated that excellent
example? Nay, rather, have we not, with all zeal and
diligence, taken him for our pattern " who goeth about
like a roaring lion seeking whom he may devour?"

It is chiefly owing to the ignorance of colonial matters which prevails in this country, that the misdeeds of
the colonists have hitherto been unrestrained. If the
editors of the English newspapers had taken any interest in the politics of the Cape, or had thought it worth
while to inquire into these matters, which they could
not understand without a little trouble, and had from
time to time directed the attention of the public to the
riotous tyranny in this distant part of the British
dominions, much of the evil could have been prevented,
and we should not now, in the year 1837, be called
upon, with no little toil, to lay the first stone of a new
edifice of national justice. Information is largely
wanted, and it is to be hoped that the facts explained

in the following narrative, may supply the reader with
such information as may enable him to understand the
true state of affairs in the Cape of Good Hope.

In the meantime, however, many thanks are due to
those who have already raised their voice against oppression, for if some few had not been found faithful to the
cause of humanity, there is no saying what would not
have been done in South Africa by this time. Our
thanks are due to Messrs. Barrow, Bannister, Thompson, Pringle, and Kay, who, at different times, and by
different publications, have drawn the attention of the
British public to the wrongs of the Hottentots and
Caffres.

To Mr. Fairbairn,* the able and intrepid editor of the
South African Commercial Advertiser, a debt of grati-

* On the 1st January, 1835, there appeared an advertisement
in the Graham's Town Journal, signed by some hundred persons,
charging the South African Commercial Advertiser with " misre-
presentation, falsehood, and treason," and concluding with these
words : " We consider it our duty to call upon all well-wishers to
this country, to implore all who would not wilfully be made in-
strumental in stifling the cries of the widow and the fatherless for
protection, to use their best endeavours to suppress the circulation
of the South African Advertiser, during the continuance of the
present awful crisis."

One of the ringleaders of these " implorers," was the notorious
Wesleyan missionary, W. J. Shrewsbury, the author of the six
articles, to be found in the Parliamentary Paper, C. W. p. 44.

Mr. Fairbairn took no notice of this outrageous attack for some
weeks, but when it might have been surmised that the passion of
his enemies had somewhat subsided, he addressed a polite letter
to Mr. Shrewsbury, amongst others, requesting him, as a conspicuous " implorer," to substantiate his charges, and particularly, that

tude is owing, which it would be difficult to estimate too highly, for if it be a thankless and unprofitable task even in this country to advocate unremittingly the cause of the oppressed, what must it not be in the colony of the Cape of Good Hope, where the great mass of society is thoroughly imbued with the doctrines of injustice, where the most reckless principles of tyranny are openly avowed, and where the frowns or smiles of authority can scare the timid into a cautious neutrality, or encourage the violent into a more rabid profession of ultra-despotism?

To add Dr. Philip's name to the catalogue of benefactors would be superfluous; his praise is recorded in the revivescence of an almost exterminated nation, and in their protection when the chains of slavery had again been forged for their destruction: but if philan-

---

very grave one, in which Mr. Fairbairn's visit to the frontier is declared to have been "a chief cause of the confederacy of the Caffre chiefs, which threatened the total destruction of the colony." To this letter, in which there was not one expression that could possibly give offence, thus did that vulgar methodist think proper to reply, writing his answer *on the back of Mr. Fairbairn's returned letter*, which he sent through the post-office:—" Mr. Shrewsbury returns Mr. Fairbairn's letter, and requests that Mr. Fairbairn will have the honesty to pay the postage of his future letters to the Wesleyan missionaries, otherwise they will be invariably returned." (See South African Advertiser, Feb. 13th, 1836.)

The deeds of such a person would, indeed, be beneath the notice of history, if the miserable state of society in the colony had not raised him into the friendship of the Governor, who condescended to mention his methodist friend with high eulogiums, in a despatch to the home government.

thropy should be mute in his praise, then let us hear
it amidst the execrations of disappointed slave-drivers,
the rage of baffled tyrants, and the outcries of discomfited intriguers, who feel that he has hopelessly
perplexed their projects.

Lord Glenelg is the first minister of the British
nation who has dared to check the misrule of South
Africa, and he has done it so effectually in his golden
despatch to Sir Benjamin D'Urban, that it will not be
easy for the violent party to reconstruct the old system.
It now stands on record, that the home government
has thoroughly examined, and entirely condemned the
aggressive policy; and the labours of the committee of
the House of Commons have produced a mass of evidence, which not only abundantly justifies all the
positions of Lord Glenelg's despatch, but overwhelms
the old system with a weight of condemnation, from
which it will never entirely recover.

To the British public, therefore, I offer the following
narrative as a preface to Lord Glenelg's despatch; and
if our colonial policy shall henceforward be remodelled
according to the views of that invaluable document,
we may then roll from us that reproach which the
poet Dante, in chastising Florence, may be thought
to have designed for England in the prophetic strain:

> Godi, Firenze, poi che se' sì grande,
> Che per mare e per terra batti l'ali,
> E per lo 'nferno i tuo nome si spande.

CONTENTS.

Explanation of the abbreviated References to Authorities in the course of this Narrative.

Ab.—Minutes of Evidence before the Select Committee of the House of Commons, on the *Aborigines* in the British settlements. (538.)

C.W.—Caffre War and Death of Hintza, a Parliamentary Paper. Cape of Good Hope. 279.

P.P.—Parliamentary Papers, Cape of Good Hope, No. i. 50.—No. ii. 252.—No. i. refers to Hottentots, Bosjesmen, Caffres, Griquas.—No. ii. the same subject continued.

P.P. 371.—Further Papers, Cape of Good Hope, May, 1827. 371.

The reports of the Commissioners of Inquiry (Parliamentary Paper, Cape of Good Hope, 282) are also referred to. No. i. is on " the Administration of the Cape of Good Hope."—No. ii. on " the Finances of the Cape of Good Hope."—Another is headed " Hottentot Population, Cape of Good Hope," July, 1830. 584.

THE CAFFRES.

CHAPTER I.

Early History of the Colony of the Cape of Good Hope.—Extirpation of the Aboriginal Tribes.

THE southern part of Africa was discovered by the Portuguese. The great promontory of the African Continent, conspicuous by a range of mountains they called the Cape of Good Hope, to designate the *good hope* they entertained that the discovery of this Cape would open a way for navigation to the East Indies. In 1497, they equipped a small squadron with this object, doubled the promontory, and safely arrived at the Malabar coast. Vasco de Gama was the commander of that expedition.

The way being thus opened, vessels of the Portuguese, English, and Dutch nations touched at the Cape of Good Hope on their voyage to India, but no attempt was made at appropriating the soil till the year 1620, when the Crown of England endeavoured to make a lodgement in the country. In the year 1652, the Dutch took possession of the Cape, but not without a

B

previous struggle with the inhabitants, who resisted the Batavian settlement, as they had formerly Francisco de Almeida, the first Viceroy of the Portuguese in India, whom they slew with his party, in a fierce conflict at the Salt River, near the spot where Cape Town now stands. This battle took place in the year 1510, so that the aborigines seem to have resisted the dominion of foreign intruders for nearly half a century.

The portion of territory of which the Dutch took possession, was ultimately ceded by treaty, the Hottentots being in those days a numerous and unconquered nation, with whom it was requisite to observe the national decencies of treaties in war or peace, till it afterwards became more convenient and less troublesome to hunt them down like wild beasts.

The Quaiquæ, called by the Europeans Hottentots, were, unless exasperated, an eminently peaceful people. They lived in villages, had their hereditary chiefs, were in possession of large flocks and herds, and, like their descendants, were able and determined huntsmen. The necessity of defending their cattle from the beasts of prey, compelled them to cultivate the arts of the chase, and by stratagem as well as by open attack to contend with the lion, hyæna, and the wolf, for the dominion of the desert. They had their occasional quarrels also with the neighbouring tribes, and these quarrels sometimes called them forth to the fight, but their wars were conducted with far less animosity, and led to far less bloodshed than is recorded in the history of any other savage nation. At first the Dutch do not seem to have felt themselves in a condition to plunder, enslave, or massacre the Hottentots, and as their intercourse with them was by barter and treaty, oppression had not yet developed the vindictive retaliation of the oppressed. In

those days, therefore, the Dutch colonists bore testimony
to the virtues of the surrounding Hottentot tribes, whom
they honoured with the distinguishing appellation of
" the good men." These " good men," however, possessed very valuable and attractive cattle,* which it
was far more convenient to take by force than to pay
for by barter. The flocks and herds therefore, they
gradually took away by violence, and then as their
stock was thus augmented, other fields and pasture
lands, other fountains and streams of water were requisite to support their newly-acquired cattle. This
led to seizure of lands, and forcible ejectment of the
lawful proprietors, who were either expelled by the

---

* In the journal of Van Riebeck, the Governor, we see the
morals of the colony displayed, without any attempt at concealment. The journal is dated Dec. 1652 : " To-day the Hottentots
came with thousands of cattle and sheep close to our fort, but
we could not succeed in traffic with them; we feel vexed to see
so many fine herds of cattle, and not to be able to buy to any considerable extent. If it had been, indeed, allowed, we had opportunity enough to deprive them to-day of ten thousand head ; which,
however, if we obtain orders to that effect, can be done at any
time, and even more conveniently, because they will, by that time,
have greater confidence in us. With one hundred and fifty
men, 11,000 head of black cattle might be obtained without
danger of losing one man, and many savages might be taken without resistance, in order to be sent as slaves to India, as they will
always come to us unarmed :—if no further trade is to be expected
with them, what should it matter much to take, at once, six or
eight thousand beasts from them ? There is opportunity enough
for it, as they are not strong in number, and very timid ; and
since not more than two or three men often graze a thousand
cattle, close to our cannons, who might easily be cut off," &c. &c.
Much more to the same effect does his excellency, Van Riebeck,
record of his private sentiments, frankly confessing that which
English governors have cloaked in the disguise of " a just and
necessary war."

armed colonists, or shot in their kraals; e
those instances where a want of agricultural
or herdsmen, saved some from death, and
them for the more hideous mercy of slave
" good men," who escaped from their oppress
now driven into the bush, they roamed a
mountains, or wandered in the wilderness
home, houses, or lands; many perished of fan
many, driven to despair, returned by stealth
oppressors, and drove away into the wildern
small portion of their own cattle. The "
were pursued, and if overtaken, were either r
or kept as slaves; and thus began that frigh
tory of plunder, bloodshed, bondage, and un
cruelty, which is scarcely terminated at this
hour. It were long to tell the story of this
and oppressed nation, and as it is only intr
to the history of the Caffres, we must here
ourselves with taking a hasty glance at this me
subject. So great was the cruelty exercised
Hottentot tribes by the Dutch colonists,
aborigines speedily wasted away, leaving
deserted solitude of territory to their merciless
or pining away in bondage, sunk under the
intolerable ill treatment. The rapid dimini
their numbers attests the extremity of their su
and there can be no doubt that if the y
not been somewhat lightened within the last
years, the Hottentots would certainly have l
terminated, and have been recorded only amo
tinct nations.

In the year 1774, the whole race of Busl
wandering Hottentots, not yet reduced to s
was ordered by the Dutch government to be s

extirpated; an order which the Dutch Boors or farmers were not slow to execute. The privilege of slavery was reserved for the women or children, the men were to be put to death.

The mode of executing this order was through "commandos," a word of bloody import in our South African colony. A "commando," is an arming of the Boors of the district, sometimes, and of late, generally, assisted by the troops of the line, which under the order of the provincial magistrates whose jurisdiction is near the scene of action, goes forth to scour the country, "to murder, to steal, and to destroy." The commandos sent out against the Bushmen, were generally conducted with as much secrecy as the undertaking would allow. It was the object of the Boors and soldiers to take the Bushmen by surprise, to come upon them at night, or by early dawn of day, and to begin the work of slaughter before their destined victims had time to arm themselves or to make their escape. In too many instances, they were successful, and the stories that are told of these terrible commandos, stories authenticated by living witnesses, may rival the worst narratives of sanguinary wickedness.

In September 1774, a commando, under Van Wyk, in the space of eight days succeeded in shooting ninety-six Bushmen, the women and children were taken prisoners, and distributed amongst the Boors for slavery. Another commando under Vander Meiroe, murdered one hundred and forty-two Bushmen: on another occasion they took captive one hundred and eighteen women, putting to death of course all the males.

In the year 1787, two field-cornets having reported

that they had killed sixty-seven Bushmen, declared
that they were unable to do greater execution, for *want
of powder and lead*. " The Bushmen," they declared
to government, " live in the mountains like baboons;
we may fire fifty or a hundred times before we kill
them : we therefore most humbly apply to you to send
us six hundred pounds of gunpowder, and twelve hundred pounds of lead."

" At that time," says Dr. Philip, " the condition
of the aborigines formed a strong contrast with that
peaceful and independent state in which they had
been found by the Dutch.   In the course of about a
century and a half, the Hottentots had been despoiled
of their lands, robbed or cajoled out of their flocks
and herds, and with a few exceptions reduced to personal servitude, under circumstances which rendered
them more wretched and more helpless than the slaves
with whom they were associated.   The numerous free
villages with which the country had abounded, had
almost entirely disappeared, and the few paltry and
miserable hordes who had established themselves in
some of the districts, had no longer the power of
choosing their chiefs."

A Bosjesman, a son of one of the aboriginal chiefs,
whose tribe had fled from the colonists beyond the
snow-mountains of the Pampus, having become a convert to Christianity, told the missionaries " that they
never suffered any stranger to come to them, and if
any of their people go away and become Christians,
they dare not return, or they would be murdered.
They live chiefly by plunder.   Formerly they, as well
as the other Hottentot tribes, were a quiet and well-
disposed people, but being deprived of their land and

ing up the number of Bushmen shot by himself and his associates. He says, however, that he never "captured any," meaning clearly that no quarter was given, the commandos indiscriminately massacred men, women, and children.

Another letter, dated 1822, from G. D. Joubert, field-cornet, states that " a small shooting party having received information that some Bushmen were in the neighbouring mountains, went in pursuit of them, and chased them amongst the rocks; a skirmish ensued : how many were killed he is not able to say, but they took away seven sleeping babes of the Bushmen, and two of their elder children." The poor creatures who had thus lost their children, and who had been wantonly shot at by a hunting party, would of course be ready for any mischief, and hence we read in these bloody chronicles, that the Bushmen not only drove off the sheep, horses, and cattle of the barbarous Boors, but frequently stabbed them in the fold-yard, or houghed them in the fields. Rendered desperate with inexpressible cruelties, they cared not for the consequences, and though the cup of revenge were poisoned even to their own injury, it was sweet to them if it had any chance of punishing their oppressors. The Boors themselves, or their slaves, were sometimes transfixed with poisoned arrows, when the hunted Bushmen could find an opportunity, from behind some projecting rock, or through the scanty opening of the tangled thicket, to send the well-aimed message of revenge into the heart of the exterminator.

The evidence of two captured Bushmen, taken before the landdrost of Beaufort is authentic, and painfully interesting :—

" Do you know who committed the murder a short time ago, at the place of the Burghe Jordaan, of the Talbaach district ?"

" Yes, we do; the party of Bushmen under their Captain Platje."

" How do you know that Platje's people or party committed the murder on the boy belonging to Jordaan ?"

" They related it to us themselves, that it was their intention to murder the master, who was not to be found : they killed one of his horses.   On their return, came the second party to pursue the master, when finding the boy at the Klip fountain, they murdered him, and took away the sheep."

"What object have the Bushmen in view in murdering the Christians ?"

" *To obtain their cattle, having no means of subsistence.*"[*]

In this way have the miserable aborigines been extirpated by foreign intruders, and like wild-beasts, have been hunted down in a country, which from time immemorial belonged to their peaceful and harmless ancestors; driven from one mountain to another, from one stream to another, farther and farther into the desert, and living in daily dread lest a commando, or a " hunting party," should find them out in their last retreat—without any certain dwelling place, or rather living in the certainty, that if they build any habitation visible to their merciless enemies, they should be discovered and shot; knowing that the cruel hunter was always on their track, and thus not daring to cultivate the ground, or to rear any cattle, they were driven to

* P. P. i. 79.

the most woeful means of subsistence, to rifle the ant-
hill, to devour the maggot and worm, to catch the vermin, or to grub up the wretched roots of the wilderness;
unless, when pinched by the last pangs of hunger, they
ventured in the shades of night, to steal a sheep from
the fold, or a horse from the field, and prolong their
wretched existence till overtaken, sooner or later, by
their murderers. In their highest prosperity, then, and
when food was most abundant for them, they were
living the lives of hungry wolves, and were but on an
equality with the brutes of the desert. Man, however,
is not meant by his Creator, to live the life of a beast;
his moral as well as his physical constitution are in-
surmountable obstacles to the continuance of such a
destiny, and though adversity may for a time drive him
into this horrid degradation, it cannot be sustained:
his heart pines under affliction, in which there is no
ray of hope, and his body wastes away under the unmitigated pressure of famine, watchfulness, fatigue,
and terror. The poor Bushmen have, consequently,
been extirpated, not only in separate families here and
there, but by whole tribes; extensive districts, once
peopled with a numerous and happy pastoral race, are
now left without inhabitants, except where the white
intruder is occasionally to be found, occupying farms
of ten thousand acres, and enjoying the grim tranquillity of undisputed rapine. "If a traveller who had
visited South Africa, twenty-five years ago, were to
take his stand on the banks of the Sunday River,
and ask what had become of the natives whom he saw
there in his former visit; if he were to take his stand
again on the Fish River, and thus extend his views to
Caffraria, he might ask the same question; and were
he to take his stand upon the snow-mountain, behind

Graaf-Reynet, (he would have before him a country containing 40,000 square miles), and ask where were the various tribes that he saw there twenty-five years ago, *no man could tell him where they were !*"*

It would be awful indeed to open the great volume of blood against 'the Boors and settlers in the colony, and to set in open day the names of those whose hands have been steeped in aboriginal carnage. "There is a spot upon their hands, that would the multitudinous seas incarnadine, and make the green one red." Enough of this might easily be published to fix the guilt of murder, on many, very many families, and on some too that have enjoyed the smiles, and have been enriched by the patronage of the colonial government; these things are well known at the Cape, and the records of guilt are too authentic and notorious to be

* Dr. Philip's speech at the London Missionary meeting, August 10, 1836.

The same witness, in a document addressed to the governor of the Cape, dated March, 1834, says, "A few years ago we had one thousand eight hundred Bushmen belonging to two Missionary institutions among that people, between the Snewbergen and the Orange river, a country comprehending 42,000 square miles, and had we been able to treble the number of our missionary stations over that district, we might have had five thousand of that people under instruction. In 1832, I spent seventeen days in that country, travelling over it in different directions; I then found the country occupied by the Boors, and the Bushmen population had disappeared with the exception of those that had been brought up from infancy in the service of the Boors. In the whole of my journey, during seventeen days I was in the country, I met with two men and one woman only of the free inhabitants who had escaped the commando system. Their tale was a lamentable one : their children had been taken from them by the Boors, and they were wandering about in this manner from place to place in the hope of getting a sight of them." Ab. 694.

contradicted. But, as our object here would not be advanced by such a publication, this chapter may be concluded by some additional evidence, confirming the facts already mentioned.

A letter dated July, 1823 :—" You are desirous of being made acquainted with the state of the Bushmen, and informed of any particulars that I might pick up relative to these unhappy creatures. It is with pain that I have to observe that the commando system is still carried on to a great extent, and to the destruction annually of a great many of our fellow-creatures. It seems to me, as if the Boors considered it meritorious to destroy them like wild beasts of the desert. No doubt the Boors are at this moment much plagued by the Bushmen; but who were the first aggressors? who robbed them of their country? who drove them from their native haunts? the very people who now continue to extirpate the race.

" I understand that upwards of one hundred Bushmen were destroyed last year by these commandos in the district of Cradock alone; this fact is stated to me by Mr. ——, a person in the government employ, and who, of course, does not wish his name to be mentioned. On my passing Beaufort, I learnt that a commando had lately returned, and those Boors who brought me across the Gamka told me they had been on this commando, and that there were shot seventy-six men, two women, and two children. By such measures the race is fast approaching annihilation; these miserable creatures now fly to the secret recesses of the mountains or thickets, from whence they only emerge to the calls of hunger."*

* Philip's Researches, ii. 40.

"In November, 1829, a commando went out against a horde of Bushmen, near the Sack River, who were reported to have been guilty of some depredations. The party, however, did not find the horde they were in search of; but in returning, they came upon another horde who were at that time living in peace with the colonists, and who were not accused, or even suspected, of any offence. This kraal they thought fit to surprise, and shot seven of the unsuspecting and unresisting people in cold blood. As the party returned from this doughty exploit, a Bushwoman was observed lying near the path, wrapped up in her caross apparently asleep. The commander, without uttering a word, or asking a question, levelled his musket and fired. The kaross heaved up, and an aged female in the agonies of death, rolled out, and the party rolled on without considering the matter worthy of a passing remark. The facts of this murder have been substantiated by the oaths of several persons present, and the evidence sent to the Attorney-General at Cape Town, but there the matter rested."*

* Pringle, 242.

CHAPTER II.

A sketch of the Oppression of the Hottentots.

BEFORE we proceed with the great object of this narrative—the wrongs of the Caffre nation—it will be expedient to dedicate one chapter more to the continuation of that subject, of which we have taken a hasty glance. A few pages have been given to the history of the destruction of the aboriginal race; we must now turn our eyes to the wretched condition of the Hottentots in their state of bondage, till the emancipating ordinance of 1829 gave them a precarious*, but we must hope, not a fallacious liberty.

It will be requisite to have an insight into this subject, as explanatory of some historical events hereafter to be recorded, and as illustrating the general tone of tyranny which has more or less prevailed in all the public acts of the colony. When we find a population habitually and generally indulging in domestic cruelty of the worst sort, and when we discover that the government has fostered and protected that cruelty, we shall be at no loss to comprehend the want of

---

* For the meaning of this epithet, see the last chapter but one of this narrative.

principle exhibited by such a people and such a government, in all their relations with their neighbours : they that are systematically wicked at home can never be expected to be very virtuous abroad.

The progress of aggression having taken away every acre of soil from the Hottentots, there did but remain one more possible manifestation of injustice towards the ousted proprietors, the seizing of their persons, and condemning them to hopeless slavery. In the *legal* sense of the words, the Hottentots were not slaves to the colonists, for the colonial laws did not allow them to be bought and sold; but with the exception of that one item in slavery, which, if it had been the lot of the Hottentots, would perhaps* have been to their advantage, they were indeed slaves; they did not enjoy the protection of the laws, they had no legal tenure in the land, nor could have any; they had no property of their own; they were assigned to forced tasks under the Boors, and had no right to the free disposal of their

---

* "Until the Hottentots were placed, in 1828, on the same footing with the rest of his Majesty's *free* subjects in the colony, they were decidedly in a more degraded condition than the slaves in every respect, except that they were not saleable, and this very distinction was itself one cause of their greater degradation. They were employed in every species of occupation in which slaves are employed, and were subject to the same sort of coercion and punishment; they were not so well fed as the slaves, and seldom clad by the master. There was not the interest to render them comfortable which operated with the master. The dangers and privations to which the slave-owner would never think of exposing his purchased bondman, were forced upon the Hottentot without scruple or hesitation. In places infested with lions, Hottentots were almost always sent to attend the cattle, the lives of the slaves being considered too valuable to be risked, while a Hottentot could be replaced with little trouble and at no expense."—*Correspondent in Pringle*, p. 261.

own labour; they could not claim, or if they did claim, they had no hopes of receiving any just wages; they could turn to no one for protection or commisseration, and therefore were, in every sense of the word, condemned to the worst species of bondage. But, for particulars of their woeful state, we will now apply to the evidence of eye-witnesses:—" At that time," says Mr. Barrow, speaking of the year 1800-2, " the Hottentots were a miserable abject race of people, generally living in the service of the Boors, who had so many of them that they were thought of little value as servants, and were treated more like brute beasts than human beings; indeed, the colonists scarcely considered them human. They were mostly naked, seldom was one of them to be seen with any other clothing than the sheep-skin kaross, together with a piece of jackal's skin for the men, and a wretched sort of leathern apron for the women, attached to a girdle of raw hide, which encircled their loins. Their food was the flesh of old ewes, or any animal the Boors expected to die from age. If he was short of' that, he shot a few quaggas (wild asses) or other game for them. Their wages were generally a few strings of glass beads in the year; or, when the Boor returned from a journey to Cape Town, a tinder-box and a knife were considered a reward for faithful services. Perhaps a very obedient Hottentot, and more than commonly industrious, got a heifer or a couple of ewes in the year; and if by accident any of these poor people happened to possess a few cattle, there was often some means fallen upon by the Boor to get rid of him, and thus his cattle became his master's. When a Hottentot offended a Boor or Booress, he was immediately tied up to the waggon wheel, and flogged in the most barbarous manner. Or, if the master took

a serious dislike to any of these unhappy creatures, it
was no uncommon practice to send out the Hottentot,
on some pretended message, and then to follow and
shoot him on the road; and when thus put out of the
way, his relations durst not make inquiries about him,
else they also were severely punished.". . . . . " There is
scarcely an instance of cruelty said to have been committed against the slaves in the West Indian islands,
that could not find a parallel from the Dutch farmers
of the colony towards the Hottentots in their service.
Beating and cutting with thongs of the hide of the hippo-
potamus or rhinoceros, are only gentle punishments;
though these sort of whips, which they call *sjambocs*, are
most horrid instruments, being tough, pliant, and heavy
almost as lead. Firing small shot into the legs and
thighs of a Hottentot, is a punishment not unknown to
some of the masters who inhabit the neighbourhood of
Camtoos River." This account relates to the year
1800, but twenty-five years afterwards it was in no
degree ameliorated, for I find that Dr. Philip, in a
memorial presented to the Colonial Government against
a projected vagrant law, aimed against the Hottentots,
thus states what he saw:—" Your memorialist, in the
year 1825, visited a great portion of the districts of
Graaf-Reynet, and Beaufort, and in these two districts
he found the Hottentots, Bushmen, and other people of
colour, in the service of the former, under the system
of forced labour, in the most deplorable condition in
which it is possible to imagine any class of labourers
to exist; they were for the most part without any
clothing but the filthy sheep-skin kaross; in their
appearance indecent, in their habits filthy in the extreme, often without any food but the offal of sheep
killed for the families of their masters, with no stimulus

to labour but forced coercion, their countenance exhibiting every mark of the deepest dejection and wretchedness."*

Mr. Read, before the committee of the House of Commons, says :—" When I arrived in the colony, the Hottentots were in a most wretched condition; they had lost their country, except a few kraals in the Zwellendan district. As to property, some had cattle and sheep with the Boors, *but could not get them ;* the greater part were in the service of the Boors, kept by compulsion, and treated worse than slaves, being without any clothing, without proper lodging, and without medicine when sick. The whole nation of the Hottentots was without clothing, with few exceptions, from one end to the other ; without the knowledge of God, and unable either to read or write. On the arrival of the Dutch, Dr. Vanderkemp commenced a correspondence with General Jansen, (the governor,) and at his request, on the subject of the sufferings and general state of the Hottentots, and continued his representations till they displeased the governor, who called him and myself to Cape Town, and refused to let us return to Bethelsdorf, (the Missionary institution). We then determined to leave the colony, and were looking for a ship to take us to Madagascar, when the English expedition of 1806 arrived, and gave us our liberty. General Baird kindly allowed us to return, and gave us every aid we needed. The Hottentots breathed for a while, but oppression and cruel barbarity continued. In 1810, I wrote to a friend in England, stating two or three cases of murder and maltreatment, which were published in an English periodical. The home govern-

---

* Ab. 729.

ment took notice of them, and ordered Lord Caledon, the governor, to investigate the grievances of the Hottentots. Dr. Vanderkemp and I were called to Cape Town, *and gave in upwards of one hundred murders*, with very many cases of maltreatment, and instances of cattle and wages withheld from the Hottentots. The most of the murders had taken place under the former English government, or under the Batavian government, and, therefore, it was said, could not be punished."

As an instance of one of those wicked deeds, two Boors were returning in the evening from a shooting expedition; they passed in the neighbourhood of a missionary institution, and met an old Hottentot returning home from his day's labour. They began chasing him; those who were in his company fled, and told the missionaries they were afraid the Boors were murdering " old Joe." Early in the morning the missionary went forth with the Hottentots to look for the old man, and found his corpse lying across an ant-hill, with the throat cut. They had killed him as they would a sheep; and crimes like these could not be punished!

Dr. Vanderkemp, in one of the letters which he addressed to General Jansens, says :—" You acknowledge the great wrong that the colonists, *perhaps here and there*, do to the Hottentots. This expression, governor, shows that you are still uninformed of the true situation of things in this country, or, at least, in the Uitenhage district. Not *perhaps*, and *here and there*, but very certainly, and pretty nearly, in all parts does this oppression prevail. The Landdrost Alberti has thought fit to oblige Hottentots, who were free and settled here with their wives and children, to hire themselves to the inhabitants, and with the violence of corporal punishment, by armed inhabitants, to take away out of their

houses, at Bethelsdorp, others to the service of the army
—Hottentots, who, according to your own words, are
free-born, and on the ground originally belonging to
them, should be able to find freedom, security, and the
means of subsistence."*

The evidence of Andrew Stoffels, himself a Hottentot
and, by experience, well fitted to describe the afflictions
of his nation, was thus examined on the subject by the
committee of the House of Commons :—

Q. "Where did you spend your early years ?—We lived
in the mountains, till the missionaries, Dr. Vanderkemp
and Mr. Read came amongst us, then I came amongst
human beings."

" You knew Dr. Vanderkemp?—Yes."

" Was he a good man ?—Yes."

" Did he labour hard for the benefit of the Hottentots ?
—Yes. It was after Dr. Vanderkemp and Mr. Read
came among us that we put off our skins and put on
clothes."

" Have the other Europeans, except the missionaries,
done much to improve the aborigines of South Africa?—
Not the least."

" If they have done them no good, have they done
them harm ?—They have done them evil, but have not
done them the least good."

" What evil have they done ?—They have beaten
them to death, and otherwise ill-treated them."

........" You spoke of the Hottentot nation having
been reduced considerably in numbers. Were they not
reduced in consequence of the war with the Caffres ?"—
No, it is not in consequence of that."

" Never ?—No, we were destroyed day after day, till
there was no deliverance."

* Philip's Researches, ii. 445.

" By whom ?—By the white man."

" Beaten to death ?—Tied with a reem, or cord, and shot."

" Will you state to the committee some of the examples of the sort you have mentioned ?—If one of the gentlemen in this room could accompany me back, *I would bring him on the spot where I saw a great many of those people killed.*"

" Where was the spot ? It was on the Bruntjeshoogt, at a place called Luiskraal, on the Braak river. This was done by the commandant, Runsberg."

" What was the reason that the Hottentots were treated in that cruel way ?—I do not know ; the white people must know. I do not know that we ever gave them any cause to treat us thus."

" In what way do the English now oppress the Hottentots ?—They oppress them in their wages—in short, they oppress them every way. I have been asked, ' what is this pressure ?' I say, ' The Hottentot has no water ; he has no blade of grass ; he has no lands ; he has no wood ; he has no place where he can sleep ; all that he now has is the missionary and the Bible. And now that we have been taught to read, the Bible is taken away from us, and they want to remove the missionaries from us. And there is another law, the vagrant law, that they want to oppress us with ; a law that presses down the Hottentots.' "—Ab. 588.

The Parliamentary evidence furnishes us with a very striking instance of the injustice and cruelty under which the Hottentots have groaned. It is the evidence of Mr. Parker, a gentleman who went to settle in the colony in the year 1820, and received a grant of land then possessed and cultivated by a Hottentot family, whose claims and rights were as little esteemed by the colonial government, as if they had been baboons or quaggas. "On the 22d of June, 1820," says Mr. Parker, "the Deputy Landdrost of Clanwilliam, Mr. Berg, wrote me a letter desiring me to take possession of the lands of Varhen's Fontein, in the district of Clanwilliam, of which I could get possession at once. Fortunately, a Moravian missionary was at the house of Mr. Berg, a Mr. Marquard, and he said to me, ' Mr. Parker, the government here are acting on principles totally subversive of Christianity. I place implicit confidence in your honour and protection of me, for the information which I am now going to give you respecting the unfortunate natives of this colony,' alluding to the coloured race. He said, ' If you will go and see the lands of the Hottentots at Varhen's Fontein, you will be astonished at the industry which they have practised there, the beauty of the cultivation, and the comforts which they enjoy.' I went to view this place accordingly, and there was not a more beautifully cultivated place in the colony. On my arrival there, the senior Hottentot received me at his house, and he said, ' You have instructions to take possession of these lands and houses, which I have long improved, and in which I have made myself happy and comfortable, and I am desired by the government to give you possession of them all. Of course,' he added, ' I am bound by the precepts of Christianity to obey the powers that be.'—*

* Thus did they treat the christian natives in 1820, having dismally retrograded since the year 1680; for, in that year, the Council resolved, "that a slave girl, who had been christened, should be emancipated, on account of her professing the christian faith."—Borchard's Notes. P. i. 15. Indeed, in those days they seemed to have entertained feelings of humanity, which have been long unknown in the colony; for instance, Sept. 1686, " Resolved,

They were Christian Hottentots. I said, 'If you obey the powers that be, and give me possession of your lands and houses, (there were about fourteen, built comfortably in the English style), what will become of you in case I take possession of the land?' He replied, 'I shall retire towards the northern regions, and avoid all intercourse with Europeans, for after having been here fifty years, and endeavouring, through the instruction of the missionaries, to cultivate these lands and improve them, and now to be deprived of them in my old age, I can have no further confidence in the truths of professing Christians, or their conduct.' He had a large Bible on the table, and he turned to the 13th chapter of Romans, and he then said, 'Pursuant to these instructions, which I consider divine, I will yield to the powers that be, and I beseech you to take my lands. I am told you are a Christian; you may be of service hereafter to me' in the wilderness. I am now past seventy years of age; my children, grand-children, and great-grand-children, are all Christians—IT IS A HARD CASE.' Several of the settlers that accompanied me in this visit were *extremely anxious to get possession of these lands*, which in beauty of cultivation exceeded any thing I had seen in the colony. I told Abraham Lwortz, the old Hottentot, and head of the family :—'I have not come here to be an instrument of mischief to

---

a slave having complained that his master had ill-treated him, and killed a fellow-slave, but which was not proved, the council ordered that the slave should be publicly sold, *so that he might not be exposed to the revenge of his master.* Dec. 1687. To encourage slaves and other children to exert themselves in school, an examination was ordered by the council to take place every Christmas day: silver tokens, and cakes were to be distributed, *and to slave children in particular 'sweet cakes.'* " Id.

any human being, and I will not allow any of my settlers
to disturb you.   On the contrary, I shall write to the
governor, pointing out to his excellency the injustice
that is attempted to be practised on you, and requesting that you should be confirmed in those lands by some
legal title, to preserve you from these disturbances.'   I
having thus refused to disturb the Hottentot, the deputy-
landdrost sent an account of the circumstance to the
governor, when a communication was received by the
deputy-landdrost, with very strong expressions of indignation against myself."—(Ab. 40.)

What a story of enormous wickedness is this !   Were
not the dogs ready to lick the blood of the governor in
the vineyard of Abraham Lwortz ?

But we are in possession now of facts sufficient to
understand the position of the Hottentots in the colony.

CHAPTER III.

First Aggressions of the Colony on Caffreland.

THE British colony of the Cape of Good Hope extends from east to west about 700 miles, and from north to south about 300 miles in the broadest part.

Dividing the colony into east and west, according to the late arrangements of the Home Government, there are in the western division, the districts of Clan William, Beaufort, the Cape District, Stellenbosch, Worcester, Swertlendam, and George: in the eastern division, Graaff-Reynet, Uitenhage, Somerset, Albany. To these last was added, for a short time, the province of Queen Adelaide, a name conferred on that territory which the late war had wrested from the Caffres. That province, however, had only an ephemeral existence, for the Home Government had renounced the unrighteous conquest, and given it back to its lawful owners.

To give some idea of the size of these districts, it may be noticed that Uitenhage has 14,928 acres in cultivation, and 1,477,690 acres in pasturage; Albany contains 3,072,000 English acres; Graaff-Reynet and its sub-division, Beaufort, contains 32,000,000 acres,— nearly twice the size of Ireland. In all this vast colony there are only 150,000 inhabitants.

The chief town and seat of Government is Cape Town, on the extreme western promontory, distant from the new eastern capital, Graham's Town, by the government road, 600 miles.

The rivers to be mentioned in the following narrative we take from the west, and so proceed eastward into Caffreland. The first which is of importance in this history is the Gamtoos river, entering into the sea a little to the west of Algoa Bay and the town of Uitenhage, and about 250 miles east of Cape Town. Proceeding eastwards, the next historical stream is the Sunday river, about 40 miles distant from the Gamtoos; then about 70 miles farther to the east, the Fish river; beyond which, at the distance of 30 miles, is the Keiskamma.

To understand, therefore, the history of Caffreland, the reader must consider the Gamtoos river as the ancient division between the Hottentots and the Caffres : he must suppose all the country west of that stream to have been gradually wrested from the Hottentots, who with their territory had also lost their personal liberty, and had been reduced to a state of pitiable bondage, leaving the Dutch or the English colonists to contend with the Caffres, a warlike and powerful nation, bounding the colony to the east, whom it was requisite to dispossess, if the cupidity of conquest could not rest satisfied with its western acquisitions.

The Batavian Government, in the middle of the last century, issued many orders to the eastern settlers of the colony, regulating their conduct and dealing towards the Caffres, sometimes prohibiting the Boors from entering into Caffreland for the purpose of hunting the elephant, and sometimes permitting them. They were, however, determined that there should be no regular

trade opened with the Caffres, which they frequently
prohibited * under severe penalties. The attention of
the government was also turned to the eastern boundary of the colony, not apparently so much with a view
to restrain the Caffres, as to prevent their own people
from wandering beyond the reach of the colonial tax-
gatherer. Thus, in the year 1770, they passed the
following resolution in council :—"The commission
appointed to fix the boundary of Stellenbosch and
Zwellendan districts, having found, *between the Gamtoos and Fish rivers*, several families with large flocks
of cattle, wandering from one spot to another, at a great
distance from their own farms, and thereby defrauding
the revenue, and carrying on an illicit trade with the
Caffres, with whom they have opened a direct communication, the Council orders the landdrost to oblige
every person beyond the Gamtoos river to decamp,
and that every one should graze his cattle on his own
place, on pain of confiscation."† In this order it is
clear that they consider the Gamtoos (more than a hundred miles west of the Fish river) the boundary of the
colony ; and indeed in various proclamations, dated
1739, 1770, 1744, and 1788, the Gamtoos is recognised
as the boundary between Caffreland and the colony.‡

The lawless Boors were not, however, to be restrained
by orders of Council, and in spite of reiterated prohibi-
tions, persisted in passing the prescribed boundaries,
not only for the purpose of grazing their cattle, but to
fix themselves in new habitations and estates of their
own choosing. It was impossible that such intruders
should approach Caffreland without provoking the in-

* They passed a resolution to that effect as early as the year
1732.

† P. P. i. 19.   ‡ Ab. p. 676.

habitants, and hence there soon arose an ill feeling between the Boors and the Caffres, the one plundering, and the other avenging themselves on the intruders. In the meanwhile the government seems to have taken no effectual steps to prevent the eastern aggressions of the colonists, and to have tacitly allowed the extension of the boundary. The result of these proceedings we find in the following entries :—" July 1780. Two inhabitants named Joshua Joubert and Petrus Hendrik Feneira, together with a number of others, having thought proper to form a large commando without authority, and having killed a great number of Caffres, and carried off their cattle and divided the same without permission of the authorities, the landdrosts of Stellenbosch and Zwellendan are ordered to make a strict inquiry into the circumstances, and if they should find the parties without urgent cause had committed any culpable act, to proceed against them before the court of justice."

" Oct. 1780. The Caffres having committed hostilities at De Burgers Hoogte, the landdrost proposed to send a great commando against them." This was approved of.

Here then the system began. The colonists arm themselves to plunder the Caffres of their cattle ; the Caffres retaliate by seizures of colonial cattle, which the colonists avenge by a commando and a far greater booty, to pay themselves for their trouble, and to punish " the savages ;" but finding this method very inefficient for the security of the eastern settlers, they see no way to terminate the difficulties which their own violence has created, but by extending the colonial boundary to a vast distance, and by prohibiting " the savages" from passing the line which it may please their enemies to name. With this feeling the colonial go-

vernment, so early as 1780, endeavoured to make the
Caffres consider the Fish river as the limit between Caffreland, and the colony, though for their own arrangements, and for the government of their own people, they
had no idea at that time, of extending the settlement thus
far.   In 1778, the governor, Van Plettenberg, having,
in the course of an extensive tour which he made
into the interior, visited Bruintjeshoogté, and finding a
considerable number of colonists occupying tracts beyond the frontier, instead of calling them beyond the
legal limits, he extended the boundary by a stroke of
his pen, adding about 30,000 square miles to the colonial territory.   It was at this period that the Great Fish
river was first declared the colonial boundary on the
east; the rights of the Ghonaquas, and other independent Hottentot tribes within the extensive region thus
acquired, do not appear to have occupied a single
thought; the Boors were left to deal with them as they
had dealt with their extinct brethren. *   With the more
formidable Caffres the form of an agreement was observed, and according to Colonel Collins' account, a
few of the chiefs agreed with the governor that the
Great Fish river should be the boundary between the
two countries. This, however, seems an apocryphal
story, for nothing is known of this treaty in Caffreland,
nor were any of the great chiefs a party to it. The
governor probably procured the assent of some petty
chieftain, with the people of his kraal, but so little is
known of this treaty, even in the colony, that it seems
to be some mistake on the part of Colonel Collins, and
it certainly does not agree with the authentic acts of
the colonial government, or with subsequent proclamations.

* Pringle, 285.

Jalumba, a chief of the Amadanka clan, then residing in Bruintjes-Hoogté, was by no means willing to
comply with the terms of this imaginary treaty or decree of the governor, and was consequently the victim
of the Boors, who in a large commando attacked his
clan, killed the chief, and many of his tribe, and took
a plunder of 5200 head of cattle. This took place in
the year 1781. Dlodlo, the son of Jalumba, was slain
the next year in endeavouring to resist the intruders.

Some five or six years after this aggression, there
was war between Slambi and the chief Zaka, the Boors
entered into confederacy with Slambi, and drove out
Zaka from the Zureveld, now Albany. But Congo,
Maloo, and Toli, sons of Zaka, with other chiefs, re-
established themselves by force in the Zureveld, and in
their turn seized the cattle of the colonists.

The following entries may suffice as an epitome of
the doings of that period. "June 1793, the Caffres
again committed various hostilities, and ammunition
was granted to the colonists.—October, 1793. The hope
of plunder and the love of gain, joined to the cruel
treatment on the part of the colonists induced the
Caffres, Hottentots, and other native tribes to avenge
themselves on the inhabitants. They committed the
greatest depredations, and defensive operations were in
consequence unavoidable.

The Parliamentary Papers supply us with some
valuable materials in this part of our inquiry. H.
Maynier, landdrost of Graaf-Reynet in 1792, says,
" I accompanied the commando which entered Caffraria in 1793, and that for the following reasons :
Years before I was appointed landdrost, I had made
several journeys to the eastern and northern limits, and
from what fell under my observation then, and after-

wards during the time I had been landdrost, I was
convinced that the complaints of the Boors about the
Caffre depredations were *altogether unfounded*, and
always exaggerated; originating from a design to
enrich themselves with the cattle they were in the habit
of taking from the Caffres in the commandos which
they were allowed to conduct, under no other control
than that of officers appointed from their number, and
consequently having the same object in view. I recollect particularly to have witnessed on one of those
journeys, the distribution of the cattle taken from the
Caffres by a commando, under the orders of a certain
field-commandant, Daniel Kuhn, when the number of
the cattle taken from the Caffres was computed to be
thirty thousand head."*

 Mr. Maynier was an eye-witness, and a landdrost;
personally and officially he knew the colonists
thoroughly, he had seen their transactions, and came
to that conclusion which every spectator, not under
the influence of colonial feeling, must adopt; that the
commandos were appointed not to punish but to commit robberies, and that the plea of Caffre depredations
was set up, to conceal the cupidity and rapine of the
colonists. He describes indeed transactions in the
close of the last century, but it will presently be seen
that his description is good, for transactions of the
present century up to the autumn of 1835.

Thieving and lying have been the two great charac-
teristics of the conduct of the colonists towards their
neighbours for the last thirty-five years.

* Papers, i. p. 27.

CHAPTER IV.

The Expulsion of the Caffres over the Great Fish River in 1811.

WE have already seen a specimen of the wavering and uncertain policy of the colonial government relating to the proper boundary of the colony. We shall now see how the Caffre nation has suffered by the caprice or cupidity of their unprincipled neighbours. And here then first we must notice a proclamation issued by the governor, Lord Macartney, in 1798.

" Whereas *no exact limits have hitherto been marked out* respecting the proper boundaries between this colony, the Caffres and the Bosjesmen; and in consequence of such limits not being regularly ascertained, several of the inhabitants in the more distant parts of this settlement *have united in injuring the peaceful possessors of those countries,* and under pretence of bartering cattle with them, reduced the wretched natives to misery and want, which at length compels them to the cruel necessity of having recourse to robbery and various other irregularities in order to support life....
I do therefore declare the Great Fish River to be the proper boundary between this colony and the Caffres."

Lord Macartney acknowledges that no precise limits had hitherto been fixed between the colony and Caffre-

land—that the colonists had driven the Caffres and
Bosjesmen to deeds of robbery and other irregularities
to support life:" and on these acknowledgments, and
in order to remedy these disorders, enacts that the
Fish River should henceforward be the acknowledged
boundary.

The preamble is good, the enactment following the
preamble vicious in the extreme; for his lordship
knew that if his proclamation had then been carried
into effect, a large population of " the peaceful possessors of the country," between the Sunday and the
Fish rivers, must have been ejected, without consult-
ing their wishes, or even acknowledging their existence
as rational creatures. The object of the proclamation
seems therefore to have been to give so ample a territory
to the vagrant Boors, as would fully satisfy their
largest designs of vagrancy, and at the same time to
let them know that the colony had *some* fixed boundary.
The interests of the lawful possessors living west of the
Fish River, do not receive a moment's consideration in
this arbitrary decree. Fourteen years afterwards, the
decree was put in execution, and the Caffres were
driven by force out of their territory.

In this style, however, has the colony continually
extended its limits : the claims of the lawful possessors
have never been taken into calculation ; no hesitation
has been felt in driving out the aboriginal proprietors ;
no thought of a treaty or purchase ever for a moment
entertained : their sole idea has been this : " we have a
desire for so many thousand square miles which we do
not now possess; we are stronger than those who are
now in possession, and therefore, we will take what we
want." A military man has generally determined
these matters; he has gone with engineers and land-

drosts to view the desirable country, and making his observations with a military eye, has come to the decision that from the general outlines of the country, "nature has evidently determined," that this or that river or mountain should be the boundary, and that all lands between that mountain or river and the colony, should by a stroke of the pen be added to the colonial possessions, in order to make the map look comely, and to satisfy military men in their ideas of territorial defence. Thus in the year 1821, Captain Stockenstrom, with Lieutenants Bonamy and Setch, pursuant to instructions from the colonial government, made a survey of the northern and north-eastern boundary, and laid out a plan for extending the line so as to include 48,750 square miles, or 325 miles of mean length, and 150 miles of mean breadth,* a plan which was as a matter of course adopted without hesitation: five years afterwards the commissioners of inquiry state "that all the kraals of the Bushmen have been removed within those tracts, and the whole of their children are now in the service of the Boors:" and, continue the commissioners, "we have no difficulty in stating that the redemption of these unfortunate people from the state of misery and servile dependance to which they are now reduced, and their settlement in kraals or villages in favourable situations, will be a measure of justice that we shall be prepared to recommend to his majesty's government."

A recommendation that up to this day has never been attended to.

It is instructive to hear the language of Captain Stockenstrom on this occasion, when he was thus ex-

* P. P. i. 125. Commissioners' Report.

tending the limits of the colony with gigantic measurement. " Nature, has, as it were, there placed a mark, which it is surprising escaped those who were sent to fix the boundary before. The Swarte river, to its junction with the Sea-cow river, can never be mistaken," &c.[*]

The secret reasons for this sort of logic are to be found in a letter of General Bourke, then acting governor : " I am of opinion that it would be an ineffectual attempt to bring back the Boors of Graaff-Reynet within the line proposed by Lord Macartney, in 1798. To do it by force would be impossible, nor do I believe that the most liberal offers of land in the interior, if such could be found, would tempt them to quit their present seats. You must therefore either agree to the extension of the colony beyond their abodes, or consider them as removed beyond our dominion and government."[†]

This is the secret history of all our frightful injustice towards the natives of South Africa ; we allow a lawless race of violent and unprincipled men, for such the Boors are, to set at defiance all the regulations of the colony—we connive at their breaking the line and carrying forth destruction and rapine into the interior —and then a few years afterwards we say there is no remedy for the disorders, which our own feebleness or collusion has created, but to extend the limits of the colony beyond the march of the Boors. This has been done without restraint, till Lord Glenelg's despatch, for the first time checked the progress of aggression in the East ; but even now the Boors are breaking boundary toward the North, unrestrained by the authorities of this ill-governed colony.

[*] P. P. i. 120.   [†] P. P. i. 124.

With this short preface we shall now be able to comprehend more exactly the expulsion of the Caffres over the Fish River, in the year 1812. The preparatory notes of the coming storm were audible some time before it burst forth. In the year 1809, Colonel Collins, in a document addressed to the governor, calmly discusses the expulsion of the Caffres from their country: and in the usual manner he compares the nature of the existing limits, with those which he proposes to fix further to the east, and after duly weighing the advantages of such a measure to the colony, without any scruple decides that it ought to be forthwith executed: "The country situated between Agter Bruintjes-Hoogte and the Konaba River, abounds in excellent fountains. The soil is good, and the timber growing on the mountains is superior to any in the colony. The acquisition of this tract would strengthen the frontier, not only by the great number of inhabitants that would be brought together, in consequence of the land being granted in small portions, but also by affording the advantage of a shorter line of defence, and the consequent greater facility of communication and support. The loss of this part of *their territory* would occasion no inconvenience to the Caffres, for they have not a single hut on its whole extent; and they have always been averse to inhabiting it, on account of its being an open country, [what! with all these fountains and woods?] I do not think that much objection would be made by that people to its occupancy, but they would at all events be easily induced to transfer their right to it for an adequate payment of cattle. The greatest obstacle towards effecting these arrangements, would, I think, arise from the difficulty of acquiring the increased number of inhabitants necessary to fill up the

frontier; supposing the tract near the mouth of the
great Fish River, and that proposed to be annexed to
the colony, to be altogether 1200 square miles, it
would require about 6000 settlers to people it; to look
for all these people within the colony were useless."
This is certainly undisguised language; but in the same
document, the colonel throws off even the slight appearance of decency which he has preserved in men-
tioning a treaty of purchase, by the following notable
words: "Before hostilities are commenced, measures
should be taken to fill up the country *from which the
Caffres are to be driven*, as soon as it is evacuated."*

Another letter of a colonist will shew the colonial
appetency for Caffreland; it is from Mr. George Young
to Mr. Maynier, dated at the Cape, 1800 :—" When
I have spoken of the Fish River as a boundary, I have
alluded to it as being only a natural limit, and for that
reason better than any that would be uncertain; but I
beg you not to take my observation as a positive instruction, because I go still farther, and could not be prepared
to say, even now, that if the time and circumstances
were such, that the practicability of establishing the
boundary of the river were clearly indicated, that it
would be advisable to effect it; but all these sort of
things depend upon the time and even the hour, and it
is probable that many years may elapse before it can
be thought of. *It is never, however, wrong to foresee
what is likely to happen.* I will only at present say,
that the Fish River is at present a limit that it will be
desirable to establish, *when practicable;* but to effect
it we should never make war, nor embroil ourselves, if
it could at any time be accomplished by means of good

* P. P. i. 46, 47.

offices or by conciliation. If by means of good offices
or by gifts, the measure may hereafter be made agreeable to both parties, it will be very desirable."*

The time, alas! did arrive, twelve years after the
date of this letter, when the colonists considered it
" practicable," to drive the Caffres over the Fish River,
but it was not by "good offices," or by "gifts:" this
great stroke of rapine was effected in the year 1812,
at the point of the bayonet; and about 10,000 square
miles of territory were violently added to the colony,
to acquire what is called ' a natural boundary.'

Some few persons there were, nevertheless, to be
found in this land of outrage, who could disapprove
the projected expulsion, which had for many years been
a favourite plan with the colonists. Mr. Maynier, the
landdrost of Graaf-Reynet, saw both the impolicy and
the injustice of the measure. " The plan," says that
gentleman, " of driving the Caffres and Hottentots beyond the Great Fish River, so much favored by some,
I have always disapproved, and maintain that whoever
knows the state of that part of the country where they
live, and the immense woods and dens which offer a
safe retreat to them, will look upon such a measure as
unwise, because greatly difficult to be accomplished,
and still more so to confine them there, and cruel on
account of the hardships which they must consequently
suffer. And I feel the most perfect conviction, that
peace may be preserved with these creatures, by fair
means, and with little trouble."†

Captain Alberti, the landdrost of Uitenhage, in an
official report dated June 1st, 1805, exculpated the
Caffres from those charges of wholesale robbery with

* P. P. i. 34.   † P. P. i. 44.

which the Boors have constantly been in the habit of loading the Caffres, to conceal their own crimes.

"A report having been spread that the inhabitants of the Zwaartkops River, and the environs, had quitted their farms, for fear of another Caffre revolt, he considered himself bound, for the public satisfaction, to declare that no farm had been left; and the Caffre chiefs had acted with so much propriety, that there was no reason whatever to doubt the continuance of peace with them. Probably a few thefts committed by single Caffres have given rise to this false report; but in those instances the owners have already recovered the greatest part of the stolen cattle. There is, in reality, the best proof that we have nothing to fear from the bulk of the Caffre nation, the chiefs, and well disposed part thereof, having strongly condemned the few plunderers, and assisted zealously to punish them, and recover what was stolen.

(Signed) ALBERTI."

But as the hunger for Caffre-land increased, and as the means of making the seizure now seemed ' practicable,' and as the colonists felt themselves fully able to drive out the lawful proprietors, they employed another sort of language shortly before they made the attack. In the latter part of 1811, a proclamation appeared, declaring the Caffres to be "irreclaimable, barbarous, and perpetual enemies," whilst the conduct of the colonists was set forth as most unoffending towards "those faithless and unrelenting disturbers of peace,"* and orders were issued for the utter expulsion of every Caffre who might be found west of the Fish River.

* Kay, 253.

At the time the commando assembled to accomplish this object, it was in the summer, when their crops of vegetables were fit for using. It is a curious fact, that the Caffres had purchased* the territory between the Fish and Sunday River of the Gonaquas, so that these "irreclaimable, barbarous" savages, had set an example of honesty, which their Christain oppressors were little disposed to follow; they had occupied the land the greater part of a century, and were living mixed with the Gonaquas, for the territory was still large enough for the two tribes, so that the Gonaquas had sold a right of entry to the Caffres, but had not themselves removed to make way for the new comers. But Gonaquas and Caffres were both now to retire before the civilized and Christian foe; and to the amount of 20,000 souls were forcibly driven out of the country, leaving much of their cattle behind them, and all their huts and villages in flames, in which incendiary work, as well as in trampling down the fields of corn, and other crops of native culture, the troops were employed for several weeks† together. It is not, however, to be supposed that all this havoc was committed without bloodshed; the Caffres were shot indiscriminately, men as well as women,‡ wherever they were found lingering in the country, unwilling to leave their homes, and to obey the

---

* Kay, 254. and 108. This purchase took place in the reign of the chieftain Togue, about the year 1670, or not long after. The Gonaquas sold the territory along the coast between the Sunday and Fish rivers, and moved further northwards to the parts about the Bruintjes Hoogté. The colonists however, ere long drove them away, with great cruelty, and infringed on the rights of the Caffres also.

† Pringle, 293. Kay, 254.

‡ Journal of Lieutenant Hart, quoted by Pringle, 291.

commands of their cruel enemy. Urgently did the Caffre chiefs plead the hardship of abandoning their crops of maize and millet, which were at that time nearly ripe, and the loss of which would subject them to a year of famine. Not a day's delay was allowed them, the enemy was a stranger to pity, and was in haste to take possession.

The following entry, from Mr. Hart's journal, will shew the barbarity of this warfare:—" Sunday, Jan. 12, 1812, at noon, Commandant Stolly went out with two companies to look for the chief Slambi, but saw nothing of him; they met only with a few Caffres, men and women, whom they shot. About sunset five Caffres were seen at a distance, one of whom came to the camp with a message from Slambi's son (Dushani), requesting permission to remain until the harvest was over, and that then he, if his father would not, would go over the Fish River quietly. The messenger knew nothing about Slambi, or would say nothing of him. *However, after having been put in irons, and fastened on a wheel, with a leather thong about his neck,* he said that if the commando went with him before day-light, he would bring them upon two hundred Caffres asleep." It would appear incredible, and almost impossible, that they should thus have seized and put on the rack the envoy of a native prince, if similar atrocities had not subsequently been enacted by the colonists; proving too certainly that any crime may have been committed by these oppressors of " irreclaimable savages." The party that thus maltreated the envoy of Dushani, was under the command of Captain Fraser, and set out next morning with their captive bound, to find " the Caffres asleep; " but the poor fellow was faithful to his country, and so misled the commando, about four hundred and sixty strong, that they never found a single Caffre under his guidance. Nothing is said of his fate, but we can hardly suppose that he was not put to death, and if without torture we may be thankful.*

The principal chiefs that suffered by this expulsion were Slambi and Congo. Congo, who was dying of a mortal disease, and unable to rise from his mat, was butchered by a party of Boors, under circumstances of great barbarity. Slambi lost his territory, and lived to a great age to experience repeatedly the further aggressions and outrages of his Christian neighbours.

There are, however, other circumstances attending this tragedy, which make it peculiarly painful. The military system of the frontier having as yet not been established, there had been nothing hitherto to prevent the Boors passing into Caffreland beyond the Sunday River, excepting the edicts of the colonial government, which they had never regarded. Consequently, several Boors had fixed themselves here and there in this

---

* Some other extracts from Hart's Journal, may serve to shew the barbarian character of this campaign.

"Friday 17th, two parties of one hundred men each were sent to destroy the gardens, and burn the villages: the gardens here are very large and numerous; and here also are the best garden pumpkins, and the largest Indian corn I have ever seen: some of the pumpkins are 5½ feet round, and the corn 10 feet high.

"Saturday 18th, three hundred men went early to destroy gardens and huts, taking with them six hundred oxen to trample down the corn and vegetables in the gardens.

"Sunday 19th, three hundred men went by day-light to destroy gardens and burn huts. About 2 o'clock P. M. a detachment returned having fallen in with a kraal of Caffres, they shot three dead on the spot, and wounded several: three women and four children they brought prisoners away."

terrritory, wherever they found room sufficient for their herds, and as they could make their lodgments without curtailing their neighbour's pasture land, they had lived amongst the Caffres and Gonaquas in a sort of friendly relation, which seems wonderful when compared with the murderous hatred that prevailed ever afterwards. But, in fact, till the second possession of the colony by the English, the Boors never seem to have considered themselves able to overpower the Caffres, and indeed, in the year 1798, in an attempt to try their strength in a commando, they were thoroughly defeated, and driven back into the colony with shame. Their captain, Van der Welt,* was killed on that occasion. But, now that they were backed by a more vigorous and military government, they disdained to live any longer in partnership of the land with the Caffres, and would be contented with nothing short of a total expulsion of their neighbours. As this expulsion was to be effected with such severity that not a single native was to be left behind, it of necessity broke up many a friendly connexion existing between the colonists and the Caffres, for it was impossible that the two nations should have lived for many years intermixed, without having given rise to some intimacy, and

---

* The weakness of the government in those days may be seen in the fact, that General Dundas, "as the only means of restoring even temporary tranquillity to the colony, directed a commission to conclude a peace with the Hottentots and Caffres: this was done upon no other condition than that each party should retain possession of the cattle that had fallen into their hands, and this treaty was afterwards confirmed by a similar deputation *sent to the Sunday river* by the Batavian government in 1803." (P. P. i. 44.)

In 1803, therefore, the Batavian government considered the Sunday river the boundary of Caffreland.

without drawing into some friendly connexion the
colonists and the coloured race. In what way these
friendships were thus violently terminated, we may see
by the following pathetic extracts:—

" It is something difficult," says Mr. Moodie*, " to
account for the cruel measure of driving out so many
of those unfortunate people, who had lived for many
years with the inhabitants, who had forgot their savage
habits, and even their language, who had acquired
habits which made them dependent upon the colony.
The most heart-rending scenes occurred upon this expulsion, and the simple but emphatic argument of these
half-reclaimed savages, just about to be replunged
into barbarism, and turned into our bitterest and most
dangerous enemies, may at once shew us something of
their native state, and yield us an instructive lesson
for the future. The old men said—' we have been
with you fifteen or twenty years, we are your friends,
we have watched your cattle, when they were taken
away by our countrymen we have followed them, reclaimed them from the captors and brought them back;
our wives have cultivated your gardens; our children
and yours speak the same language; if the chiefs
receive us, it will only be till we have a number of
cattle, when they will kill us and take them to themselves.' The young men prayed at least to remain
until they could earn cattle enough to purchase them
wives, and asked where now they could procure
their tobacco, their iron, their beads, or a bit of
bread. These are not fictitious pleas put into their
mouths for effect, they are the expressions of these
poor people, which have been a hundred times re-

* P. P, i. 176.

peated to me. I will venture to relate a single instance:—In 1812, when the commando was sweeping
the country, a Boor of the name of De Witt told his
Caffre servant, ' I have an order from the field-cornet
to send you to your country.' 'To my country? *this
is my country.* I have been fourteen years in your
service, you are my father; your wife is my mother; I
have never been in Caffreland except to bring back
your cattle, *I will have no other country.*' The order
was repeated without effect, by the field-cornet himself.
' No! you may shoot me upon the spot, for I will not
leave it.' The field-cornet, laying aside his gun, and
taking his samboch, beat the poor wretch until he went
off into the woods, whence his master heard him *howl-
ing,* as he expressed it, for the remainder of the day.
For some time, in defiance of the barbarian order
which subjected him to death, he returned every night
to his master to beg a little food; but finding no
chance of relaxation of his sentence, he adopted the
last advice of his master to return to his former country,
' and never cross the Fish River whilst an Englishman
is in the land.' I know not where, in the annals of
tyranny, one could meet with an anecdote more
affecting than this,—a faithful servant loving his master
and mistress, looking up to them as his parents, and
enjoying their esteem and good will, is by dint of
scourging driven out of the country, and permanently
separated from his friends, merely because he is of the
Caffre nation, not one of which it suited the conscience
of the oppressors to see within the newly acquired
territory."

Mrs. Gardener, a resident in the Uitenhage district,
from the year 1793, to the year 1825, has given ample
testimony to the fidelity of the Caffres, and their use-

fulness as servants before this expulsion. "I recollect," says she, "the expulsion of the Caffres and Ghonas, and particularly remember that my brother-in-law, Dupré, lost on that occasion the services of a very faithful family of Ghonas, who had long resided with him, and who were very desirous of remaining, but were driven with others into Caffraria. The Caffre tribes of Slambi, Congo, Toli, and Jaloosi, were settled in Zureveldt, (Albany), and some of the farmers occupied lands between their kraals; amongst others, my father remained at his place, Cormie, and was surrounded by nine different kraals. During this period the farmers were in the habit, if they lost cattle, to apply to the chief of the kraal to which the depredators were traced, and when the cattle were discovered they were restored by the chief, and the depredators were sometimes beaten by order of the chief. If the cattle had been killed, there was an equivalent given, either from the stock of the depredator or his family. Cattle which had been stolen were sometimes traced by the Caffres, who were in the service of the Boors. They generally engaged in service for a year, but frequently remained much longer, and after revisiting the country they often returned to the service of the same master.

"Their men were the best herdsmen to be obtained, and the women were disposed to work very hard, from being accustomed to it."[*]

After the expulsion of 1812, began, what is called "the military system," that is, the new boundary was guarded by military posts, and orders were given to shoot every Caffre to the west of the Fish River. "It was or-

* P. P. i. 174.

dered," says Captain Dundas, " that the Caffres who were on the right bank of the Fish River, should be followed up and shot, *and many, I have reason to believe, were shot.*"—(Ab. p. 133.)

Colonel Graham commanded the expedition, by which the Caffres were expelled from their country; Lieutenant-Colonel Arbuthnot, Lieutenant-Colonel Lyster, and Major Cuyler were also employed in this service.

CHAPTER V.

Some Account of the Caffres, their Customs, &c.

THE progress of this narrative will now render acceptable a short sketch of the manners and customs of the
Caffre nation.

The Amakosæ Caffres occupy that country which
forms the eastern boundary of the colony, extending,
before the expulsion of 1812, from the Sunday river to
the river Bashee*, and it is with them that we are concerned in this inquiry. The Umkumkani, or Sovereign
of this nation was Hintza.

Beyond the Bashee river, the eastern limit of Hintza's
kingdom, are the Amaponda Caffres, commonly called
the Mambookies, their territory extending to the river
Umsikalia, about thirty miles beyond the St. John or
Umzivoobo river. The sovereign of this nation is Fako.

To the north of the Amakosæ, and at the sources of
the river Bashee, are the Amamtembu Caffres, commonly called the Tambookies. Vadanna is the supreme
chief of this nation, which, by contiguity and consan-
guinity is closely united with the Amakosæ. The Amakosæ frequently seek their wives amongst the Tambookies.

* The Bashee is about 160 miles east of the Fish River.

D

The fourth great division of the Caffres is the Ama-
zoolu, or Zoolu, or Vatvahs, inhabiting a vast country
to the north and east of the Mamlookies. The king of
this nation is Dingarn, brother and successor of Chaka,
whom he murdered. This tyrant has established a stern
monarchy, assuming to himself a despotic power, unknown in the other Caffre nations. His designs of conquest seem unbounded ; he has spread desolation and
destruction amongst his neighbours, and with his army
of fifty thousand warriors will probably be all his life-
time a scourge to the interior of Southern Africa.

The ancient government of the Caffre tribes is feudal ;
an aristocracy of chiefs, acknowledging the supremacy
of the sovereign or paramount chief, but, excepting on
extraordinary occasions, acting independently of his
power. The population of each Caffre tribe is divided
into kraals or hamlets, containing from a dozen to about
a score families. There is generally a petty chief,
called the Unnumxana, who rules over these kraals with
a patriarchal authority; but he is subordinate to a great
chief, who is prince of a whole district, and is almost
always one of the ancient royal lineage. Thus, Gaika
and Slambi were rulers of large districts, having under-
neath them numerous petty chiefs ; but the sovereign of
Gaika and Slambi was Hintza. This sovereign is the
head of the nation, the chief of chiefs, the ἄναξ ἀνδρῶν
Αγαμεμνων, who, in a council of chiefs, is very powerful, and is looked upon by all the nobles and the people 'with unbounded respect. In national emergencies
" he sends his word" by messengers to the high chiefs,
and this word, of course, carries great weight with
those to whom it is addressed.

The chiefs, especially those of the royal lineage, are
invested with much authority, but it is an authority

founded on habitual reverence for high rank, rather
than on the coercion of arbitrary power. They live
amongst the people as friends and fellow-labourers, and
have never adopted that haughty exclusion and parade
with which the noble caste is invested in other countries. The people respect the lineage of their rulers,
and being guided by traditional habits, handed down
from their forefathers, shew an attachment and reverence to the high chiefs, such as, perhaps, once existed
in Europe in the feudal days of the middle ages.

The Caffres take a lively interest in the marriages of
their princes; they consider them national contracts, in
which the people are not less concerned than the chiefs
themselves, and hence they determine these matters,
not without many councils and long debates. The
councillors of the chiefs, the Amapakatæ, arrange the
marriages of their prince with scrupulous attention, and
take special care that the son of the most noble mother
shall succeed to the authority of the father. Sometimes
they are not satisfied with the marriages already con-
tracted by their chief: they do not think he has sufficiently consulted the dignity of his house, and the
honour of the tribe, and they then find him another
wife, whom they will not allow him to reject without
paying a heavy fine of cattle to the clan.

Their ideas of high birth being more sensitive than
ours, they consider the mother's pedigree full as much
as the father's, so that the child born of the daughter
of some foreign prince, though the youngest of all the
chief's sons, and born too, perhaps, in his old age, is preferred by them to all the older sons. Hence it sometimes
happens that a brother forty years old or upwards, is
acting as regent for a little boy, left as the acknowledged chief of the clan on the death of the father.

In this way Macomo* is regent of the western Amokosæ, in the name and on the behalf of his younger brother Sandili, who, when he becomes of age, will, without doubt, be acknowledged as ruling chief by his elder brothers as well as by the people.

When one of the royal chiefs has become the father of several sons, and when the people and the Amapa-katæ think it time to fix the succession, they send an embassy to the king, or supreme chief, with a state-ment of the pedigree of the young princes, requesting him to acknowledge the proper successor. He duly considers the matter amongst his counsellors, and then sends back by the embassy a present of cattle to the most noble mother of the chief's sons. This present from the king is the seal of the succession ; the son of the mother who has been so honoured becomes the heir apparent to the chieftainship.

The Amakosæ generally select wives for their chiefs from their kindred nation the Tambookies : the mothers of the high chiefs by whom the royal lineage is per-petuated are of that stock.

The evils of polygamy are very conspicuous amongst the Caffres, for as their wives are not shut up in a harem, but unrestrainedly mix in society, and as cus-tom forbids the husband to visit his wife till the last-born child has been weaned, which is delayed some-

* Macomo has, in the case of his own children, succeeded in changing Caffre law : struck with the injustice of superseding the offspring of the first wife, he declared that his eldest son Cona should be his successor, and that he should not be set aside by any son of a more noble marriage. Macomo's great influence in his nation, and the assent of his father Gaika, have therefore fixed the succession on Cona, though this young prince has more noble brothers than himself.

times to the third or fourth year, the crime of adultery
is far from uncommon in the nation. Each wife lives
in a separate kraal, and is occasionally visited by her
husband, but it is considered irregular for a husband
to show a marked preference to any one of his wives,
or to make one of them his especial favourite. Adultery is punished by a fine, but the jealousy of the orien-
tals never torments the bosoms of the Caffre chiefs,
who by no means consider adultery an unpardonable
offence.

The polygamy of the nation has, however, mainly
contributed to perpetuate the lineage of the chiefs, as
will be apparent by considering the pedigree of the
royal house at the end of this chapter. We there find
Gaika and Slambi, of a lineage recorded for several
centuries, leaving a numerous offspring of sons, besides
their still more numerous daughters not there mentioned. That two princes of the same house should be
the fathers of *more* than twelve sons, (for the pedigree is
by no means complete, and does not record *all* the male
posterity), is a proof that polygamy contributes to the
perpetuity of a family; and that if this were the only
object to aim at in framing the conjugal law, it would
be preferable to monogamy; but it is indeed a poor
recompense for all the domestic evils created by a plu-
rality of wives.

The Caffre chief is with the advice and consent of
his council a puissant ruler,* for custom, more powerful

* The great chiefs of the royal lineage consider the people
whom they govern, their subjects and property, and the people
equally consider themselves the property of their chiefs, for a
custom prevails amongst them on the death of one of the tribe
that the family of the deceased should present an ox to the chief,
by way of consoling him for the loss he has sustained through the
death of one of his subjects.

than law, compels the chief to take the advice of his
counsellors, amongst whom his opinions and wishes are
of course very influential. The popular feeling is
nevertheless sometimes too strong for the wishes of the
prince, and the clamour of the council occasionally
overpowers the better judgment of their president.
The last Caffre war was decreed by the people, the
chiefs after vainly endeavouring to resist the torrent of
popular feeling, were at last carried away by the stream,
even though King Hintza had sent "his word" forbidding them to fight. On some occasions, too, a chief
acting in his judicial character, has been compelled to
pass a more severe sentence on a culprit than was
consistent with his ideas of justice and mercy.

The personal character of the chief will, of course,
more or less contribute to his authority. Macomo was
elected regent in the minority of his brother Sandili,
by a decree of a national council, which selected him
as a person whose abilities and integrity gave a pre-
eminence over the other brothers.

The Caffres are a pastoral people; their flocks and
herds constitute their chief riches : they *love* their cattle
with all the simplicity of a purely nomade affection.
They study the habits and properties of their beasts
with great care, single out their favourites, and boast
of their promising qualities. The young herdsmen
amuse themselves with twisting the nascent horns of
the cattle into fantastic shapes, which give them a
strange appearance when they grow old. They ride
races also on the fleetest of their herd, and the
victor beast is extolled to the skies with a thousand eulogies. Of late years horses have been introduced
amongst them, and some English gentlemen have kindly
endeavoured to improve their breed by presents of va-

luable brood mares and stallions. Horses have become, as was likely, amongst such people, surpassing
favourites; and it is probable that the bullock-race will
be forgotten in the superior attraction of the horse-
race. They have large flocks of sheep and goats, but
do not as yet pay sufficient attention to the cultivation
of the ground, for though they grow Indian corn, millet, and other cereals, it is only for immediate use—
the pastoral cares entirely preponderate.

The Caffres are in personal appearance a remarkably
fine race of men; their noble figures and power of
limb, their lofty stature and graceful deportment, have
drawn the attention and excited the admiration of
many travellers; probably no people could any where
be found, surpassing them in manly strength and
comely proportions. Their colour is a dark brown,
mixed with a warmer tint of yellow; their hair is black
and woolly, but their faces approach to the European
model, and far surpass, in our ideas of beauty, the
Hottentot's or the Negro's. They have no clothing but
a cloak of skin, and this chiefly for ornament, as in
other respects the men are quite naked.

In dispositions they are cheerful, frank, and good
natured, very intelligent, great talkers, and like the
Athenians, in one respect at least, always ready " either
to tell or to hear something new." They are much
alive to the national honour, and deeply feel an injury
to the tribe or an insult to their chiefs, and yet they
are withal eminently placable when compared with the
vindictive barbarians of other nations. This appears
to me the fairest part of their character, for surely it is
no small merit to overlook offences such as civilized
nations never forgive, and to pass over grievous provocations as soon as a wish for conciliation is manifested.

Some perhaps would attribute this more to indifference and to a careless spirit, than to any nobler trait in their character, but I believe it may with justice be traced to their good natured dispositions, and to a natural cheerfulness incompatible with long resentment and deep-brooding revenge.

The Caffres have not any national religion; they have superstitious feelings, or a few unmeaning rites which may be considered the ruins of some forgotten creed. They practise circumcision, abhor swine's flesh and fish, and have a reverential fear for the great serpents, which indicate, in my opinion, an acquaintance of their progenitors with the old Egyptian religion of Isis and Osiris. On some occasions, though very rarely, they make oblations and offer sacrifices, but having long ago either lost or rejected their priests, they retain nothing of their pristine faith but a few isolated superstitions, of which they know neither the history nor the meaning.

A belief in witchcraft is the pest and burthen of the nation; so deplorably does this superstitious dread of the sorcerer's art prevail amongst them, that they never attribute the death of their people to natural causes; if a Caffre should chance to die, even of extreme old age, and of the visible decay of nature, they would nevertheless consider him the victim of poison or witchcraft. The Amaqira, or wizard *, generally a

---

* For a short time after the last Caffre war, a large province of Caffreland was annexed to the colony, and was to be governed by English law. Witchcraft was in consequence prohibited, and the chiefs were enjoined to punish all witches and their abettors. The following record of the trial of a witch, before Queen Sutu and Macomo, on the 26th of November, 1835, will illustrate the popular superstition :—" That on or about the 22d of November,

woman, is therefore in great request, who, after sundry incantations and rites of imposture, of which a mystical dance usually forms a part, declares that the deceased died by the black arts of some poor innocent person in the tribe; the accusation of the witch is synonymous with a condemnation, and thereon there immediately follows the havoc of vengeance, the destruction of the kraal, the seizure of cattle, and frequently the torture and death of the individual whom the cruel impostor has pointed out for vengeance. The extent of suffering and iniquity which this deadly superstition has fostered, it would not be easy to calculate, but the vehement protestations of the missionaries have made the Caffres somewhat ashamed of their superstition, perhaps have shaken their faith in the real power of the witch, or at any rate have driven the actors in their tragedies of magic to conceal their cruelties from the observation of Europeans. It is probable that the chiefs may have secretly countenanced the Amaqiræ, as

1835, several Caffres did wilfully and maliciously with intent to kill, inflict on the body of the woman Cassi, various wounds with assegais, on the charge that a child of Anti, had been bewitched by the said Cassi. The prisoner pleaded *guilty*, and stated to the court, that a beast something in resemblance to a man, having two legs, and which hovered about the Keiskamma river, had appeared to her in a dream, and did then and there reveal to the prisoner Nodousa, that Cassi by enchantments did vex and torment the body of Anti's infant child, by which means it became deadly sick; and as a fit punishment for such wickedness, she had in ignorance of English law, charged Cassi with witchcraft, and condemned her to death. The prisoner appealed to the magistrate-chiefs in support of the lawfulness of her proceedings, according to Caffre usage. Macomo, the magistrate, said, ' You ought to know the English law by this time—you are no child, and therefore you, Nodousa, are fined ten head of cattle for the benefit of the plaintiff Cassi.' "

a sort of state inquisitors, by whose collusion a trouble-
some subject might occasionally be ruined or got out
of the way, without embroiling the rulers with the
people; and it is certain, that the witch has always ·
directed the oracle in such a manner as not to offend
or injure the prince. It should be noticed also, that
the property of the individual who is condemned by
the witch, is confiscated to the feudal chief, who
therefore, to say the least, can have no direct interest
in suppressing the superstition. On the death of a
great chief there has too often followed some scene of
violence, through the lying response of the witch, and
the blind credulity of those who consulted her.

Another class of sorcerers, the Abanisi-bamvula, or
rain-maker, is upheld by the national superstitions.
The Caffres believe that these rain-makers have power
to draw down rain from the heavens by their incantations in seasons of drought. But the rain-makers take
good care not to prepare themselves to confer the required blessing till they have been first encouraged with
a handsome fee. Sometimes, by careful observation of
the atmospheric appearances, these rogues contrive to
promise rain with success; their successful prophecies
are highly extolled, but if the drought is obstinate, and
if after many days of prayers and fees, the faith and
patience of the people begin to flag, the disappointed
sorcerer decamps in the night-time to another district,
to find a new opening for his too successful imposture.

The colonists, on the principle apparently, that if
we wish to hang a dog, we ought first to give him a
bad name, are accustomed to charge the Caffres with
an incurable propensity to thieving; and indeed, one
gentleman has assured the Committee of the House of
Commons, that they are " natural-born thieves," even

as a bee is a natural born thief of honey, or a wolf of sheep; but whether there be any truth in these accusations, or in the theological ideas of the " original sin" of Caffreland, as propounded by that gentleman, remains to be seen in the following narrative. Neither should we pay too much attention to the official dogma of Sir Benjamin D'Urban, that the Caffres are " treacherous and irreclaimable savages," for certainly neither Sir Benjamin D'Urban, nor any of his predecessors, have ever taken one single step towards reclaiming these " savages," but have done all in their power to prevent their possibility of emerging from the savage state; and if we must inquire into the article of " treachery," it will perhaps turn out that it belongs entirely to the other side.

In an external view, the Caffres may be called savages, for they go nearly naked, live in very rude huts, have no written laws, nor indeed any letters, and are of course totally uninstructed and ignorant; but if we look a little deeper, and examine their manners and customs, their intellectual grade, their polity, and their patriarchal life—if we take the trouble to notice the grace and dignified deportment of the princes, their consciousness of superiority, and the courtesy established between those of equal rank; if we consider the open and manly bearing of the whole people, their unrestrained and easy gait totally devoid of awkwardness and *mauvaise honte*, the traits of generosity and kind feeling which they frequently exhibit, their good-natured attentions to strangers and visiters, their quick and grateful perception of friendly feeling; and especially their placable dispositions, which, by extreme and long-continued injustice has never yet been stimulated into more than temporary revenge—we must hesitate before we term them " savages." It appears to me, that setting aside the externals of clothing, and conveniences of civilized life, and viewing the savage mind in a moral and philosophical light, the lower orders of the English nation are in many places far more *savage* than the Caffres—more savage in coarseness of mind and manners, more desperate, unrestraineu, and uncivilized, and in one word, very far below the Amakosæ in the scale of recovered humanity.

But it is time to confirm this opinion, according to the general plan of the narrative, by reference to the Parliamentary Evidence.

Captain Stockenstrom says, " The Caffres are barbarians but *not* savages; *it is a mistake to call them savages,* as much as to call them gentle and inoffen-'sive; they are just as people in their circumstances may be expected to be : they cultivate land to an enormous amount, and the commando with which I went into the Zuurveld against them, in 1812, (the expulsion over the Fish River) were many weeks in destroying their corn; they are, therefore, an agricultural people, and they have extensive flocks.   There are plunderers amongst them, but I cannot call them ' a nation of thieves,' and *I believe there are civilized nations in which the proportion of thieves is greater.*"[*]   Mr. Shaw, the Wesleyan missionary, says, " I did not find the Caffres at all insensible to acts of kindness, so much the contrary, that they having some notion that I had promoted their interests, with reference to the correspondence with government, about the neutral territory, and other affairs, I had acquired almost unbounded influence over them.'[†] The same witness informs us, that when he took up his residence amongst the Caffres as a mis-

* Ab. p. 91.   † Id. 56.

sionary, they were fully sensible of his friendly intention, and gave him a kind and cordial reception: they received him with loud huzzas, as if he had been making a triumphal entry.

Saxe Bannister, Esq., says, "I think they are capable of any degree of civilization which any nation may obtain; and I think I saw enough of them to justify this opinion as to their general capacity. I think their state of society approaches much nearer to the barbarian than to the savage." (Id. 175.)

Dr. Philip says, "The Caffres have very regular tribunals. I have seen an instance of a man who was accused of assisting in robbing the cattle that were stolen from the different kraals, and he had of course a great number of accusers; but Gaika's brother, who attended as a judge, took compassion on him. He took the part of the prisoner, and very much wished to have spared him, and that he should not be so severely punished, as his accusers claimed, for they make the offending party restore eight or ten for every one stolen: The chief in this instance appealed to their passions, he said, ' You will ruin him, if you insist on his paying this heavy fine.' The answer was, that he had given them much trouble, that he denied having taken them, and that he had produced the skins disguised, and that if he had not acted in that improper way, they would not have claimed the full penalty. At last the chief said, ' I can do no good for him: I must, therefore, decide that he be fined the full number of cattle claimed.'" *

Thomas Philips, Esq. narrates a circumstance illustrative of their manners. "A few years back a circumstance occurred, of which, at the time, I published a

* Id. 35.

concise account, and as it refers to what I consider a
great act of justice and propriety on the part of the
Caffres, I will, if the committee allow me, read part of
it; but I must premise, that on the traders being allowed to go into Caffreland, first of all, they were not
well provided with waggons to bring out the produce
which they purchased, and they were in the habit of
hiring waggons for the purpose. A trader, hired of
my son in law, more waggons, oxen, and servants to
conduct the waggons; this man, by accident, it is
hoped, shot a Caffre; he declared he did not know
the gun was loaded, but became so alarmed that he
fled out of Caffreland, and my son-in-law's servants,
fled likewise. They did not apply to Colonel Somerset
for military assistance, but simply for an interpreter,
and it was granted. The Caffre killed was a subject of
Boochoo, brother of the great chief Hintza, and whenever a Caffre is killed, it is the power of the chief to
demand the property of the slayer, as a kind of deo-
dand, in the same way as we do. The conduct of Boochoo, after the loss of his subject, was truly laudable,
and worthy of remark, as it exhibited traits that ought
to have been encouraged. He no sooner heard that
the trader had absconded, than he despatched messengers to the mission village of Butterworth, recommending some trust-worthy person being immediately
put in charge of the property, three waggons, oxen,
and a quantity of merchandise, which he had left behind; the oxen and waggons belonged to a person
near Graham's Town, who, accompanied by a friend,
hastened to the spot to claim them. After being informed that they were in no way connected with the
delinquent, excepting in having let their waggons to
him, the chief received them with great kindness, and

ordered a council to be held on the subject the following day. Accordingly two hundred armed warriors
attended the next day, and the whole day was spent in
debate, with a view, apparently, of securing the forfeiture of property; great acuteness was evinced by
some of the council, in endeavouring to prove a connexion with him, and 'You belong to him,' 'You are
his servants,' 'You are employed by him who·has
killed one of our people,' were frequently reiterated.
A division at length arose, which the interpreter feared
would not be confined to words; happily, however,
this passed off, and it was finally adjudged that the
property should be immediately restored to its rightful
owner." Id. 29.

Here we find a tribe, by the direction of its prince,
spending the whole day in solving a difficult question
in law, and deciding at last perhaps more on the lenient
side, than was consistent with the interests of their
feudal lord, for they might have decided thus:—" The
man·would have forfeited this property by our law, had
he been guilty of mere chance slaughter, but he has
fled, and by his flight seems to plead guilty to murder;
we shall, therefore, escheat his merchandise at any rate,
and shall detain your waggons till he returns to take
his trial, that we may pass a proper sentence on his
offence, and take also his evidence about the waggons.
If he is innocent no harm will come to him but a forfeiture of his merchandise; if he will not come he ought
to be punished, and you must apply to the colonial
authorities to make him come, that your property may
be restored."

Mr. Gisborne also tells an interesting story of a trial
before king Hintza, of one of his (Mr. Gisborne's) servants, for accidentally killing a Caffre, who was playing

with him. The king saved the lad's life; called a council, inquired the law in the colony on these occasions, and pronounced sentence of a fine of two hundred and forty buttons to the widow of the deceased." —Id. 366.

These anecdotes satisfactorily prove that the Caffres have substantial ideas of law and equity.

THE GENEALOGY OF THE CHIEFS.

N.B. These genealogies are to be taken as a mere sketch, but perhaps sufficient to assist the reader in some important parts of the narrative. No female is entered in the genealogy.

To catch the pronunciation of these names as near as may be, the reader should observe, that the vowels *a*, *e*, *i*, are to receive the Italian sound.

Some of the names it is impossible to write so as to give the proper sound: for instance, the son of Hintsa, is written Hhälli, the nearest approximation to the true Caffre pronunciation, which no letters could accurately represent.

On the death of Palo, (No. 10) the Amakosæ divided into two empires, Galeka remaining in the east, and his younger brother Cahabi removing a hundred miles further west. Cahabi was grandfather of Gaika.

(1) THLINGA, (about A. D. 1470—1500.)

(2) Goösh.

(3) Chawi.

(4) Kosiamtwana.

(5) Malangāna.

(6) Skomo.

(7) Togue.

(8) Gondé.

(9) Isheo.
|
(10) Palo.   Cahăbé, 2nd son of Palo. (10)
| |
(11) Galeka.   La-ow—Slambi.
| |
(12) Ca-oute—Wilhēla—Kăànzi. Gaika.
| |
(13) Hintza—Bookoo.   Macomo — Cheăli or
| Tyali--Xo-xo--Dundăs
(14) Hhăăli.   — Matwōa — Neelash
                         Xana--Gaicăno—San-
                         dĭli—Dingwīa—Tinta,
                         &c.

N. B.—The sons of Gaika are not placed according to their ages, which are unknown. Sandili is the filius princeps.

Cona is filius princeps of Macomo.

JAN. TZATZO AND SLAMBI.

Tindy, 2nd son of Togue. (7)
|
Hala.   Slambi, 2nd son of Cahăbi.
| |
Bangé.   Mfundis — Nomāla — Coosé — Umhāla —
| Kai—Kamba—Maiyé—Kalo—Copēso—
Kega.   Dushāni—Tsyăló—Zetu, &c.
| |
Tchatchoo.   Siwāna—Quasāna.
|
Jan: Tzatzoe—Morlo, &c.
|
Johannes Tzatzoe, &c.

Genealogy of the Caffre Chiefs—continued.

SEKO, 3rd son of Cahăbi.

Gu-āna.

Yalöosa, 4th son of Cahăbi.

Vivi.   Fishla.*

Neuka, 5th son of Cahăbi.

Gazelli.   Vitĕka.   Toogood.

———

BOTMAN. ENO.

CHEOU, 2nd son of Malangana. (5)

Medang.

Mahōti.   Langa, 3rd son of Palo. (10)

Jalăka.   Eno—Malow—Toli.

Maintla.   Stok—Golésh.

Botman.

Fandăla—Yonas.

* Fishla was killed in the late Caffre war.

———

The Plebeian Chiefs.

Quana.
|
Charka.
|
Conga.
|
Kama*—Pato—Cobus.

N. B.—Quana was a plebeian, but was raised to the chieftainship in consideration of his abilities in trouble-some times; his descendants, it is said, do not sustain their chieftainship, without dispute, in consequence of their defective genealogy.

The Fingoes are "refugees," remnants of tribes broken up by the attacks of the Zoolus, Ficani, and others, in the interior; they voluntarily placed themselves under Hintza's protection, and became his vassals. Their chiefs are :— 1. Umslambisa of the Slubi ; 2. Matomela of the Kelidwani ; 3. Jogweni of

---

* Kama is a Christian, the husband of one wife, he married Macomo's sister, daughter of Gaika; and though solicited by King Hintza, and others, to strengthen his house by contracting marriages with the first families, he has obeyed the Christian law of wedlock, and resisted these importunities.

Cobus married Slambi's daughter.

Pato married Eno's daughter.

All these chiefs, therefore, are by marriage now united to the royal chiefs.

Hintza the supreme chief of the Amakosæ, is succeeded by his son Hhääli—written sometimes Caly, or Creali.

Vadanna is supreme chief of the Amatembu or Tambookies.

Fada, of the Amapondæ, or Mambookies.

Umslambisa of the Fingoes.

Dingarn of the Zoolu Caffres.

the Lisi; 4. Umkenkwezi* of the Bili; 5. Uewana of the Gobizembi; 6. Uhliso† of the Sekuneni; 7. Umkwali of the Abaswawo; 8. Unom-tchatcho of Anotzaki; 9. Umkuzangwe of the Abayamini.

* Umkenkevezi, (4) has embraced Christianity.

† Uhliso, (6) is a professed rain-maker.

The Fingoes belonging to Hintza, were between 17,000 and 20,000 in number.

CHAPTER VI.

The first Treaty with Gaika.

THE great object at which the colonists had long been aiming was now achieved, and "the barbarous, irreclaimable, and perpetual enemies," the Caffres, were at last driven over the Fish River by main force. The officers of the expedition had been duly thanked and applauded, and the colony had received an enormous addition of territory, which, however, seemed more ornamental than useful, as the population was then wanting to occupy it.

In June, 1812, a proclamation was issued, inviting inhabitants from all parts of the colony to settle on the frontier. Not fewer than four families were to be located on one spot, and to each of them was to be granted, in perpetual quit-rent, a tract of land of four thousand acres. This same proclamation annulled the former "loan-places," in the Zuurveld, and thus several boors were induced, by these offers, to fix on particular spots, but soon withdrew into the interior, to escape the depredations of the late proprietors, who took care to help themselves to a forced rent from the intruders.

By a subsequent proclamation, the government again made offers of grants of land to the same extent, to any *single* boor that might choose to accept it, but neither would this lure avail,—the Caffres were too severe tax-gatherers for any farmer to face, and the Zuurveld had scarcely any occupants.

In 1814, another proclamation was issued, offering further favourable conditions, and to hasten its effects, confined the offers to the first fifty applicants. But the Boors were too wary, and objected to the smallness of the grant; four thousand acres did not come up to their ideas of elbow-room, and the Caffres were still on the look-out to exact a cattle-rent.

In 1817, Lord Charles Somerset made a fresh attempt to effect this object, and by advertisement confirmed the advantages offered in the preceding proclamations*, with other favourable conditions. To keep the Caffres in check, he also sent a commando against Slambi, and plundered him of two thousand head of cattle. But the remedy increased the disease, and the Caffres having lost more, were, of course, determined to recover more, so that the Boors were kept in constant "hot water," by a fire of their own lighting.

The government had, indeed, established military posts to guard the new territory, but an army forty thousand strong would not have been sufficient for the purpose. The boundary was too large, and the Caffres were too cunning for the military arrangements of the colonial government. In vain did the drums beat, and the soldiers march, for cattle still disappeared in spite of these elaborate and costly precautions. For five years this sort of neighbourhood existed—the colonists complaining of the savages, and the savages occasionally taxing the colonists. At length, in the year 1817, the

---

* Philip's Researches, i. 256.

governor, Lord Charles Somerset, visited Caffreland,
with a view to remedy these disorders, and contrive
some more efficient plan of protection for the Boors.
The consequences of this visit have been so disastrous,
that it will be important to describe it with minuteness,
which we are enabled to do by the evidence of two eye-
witnesses. Mr. Williams, a missionary of the London
Mission, had, in April, 1816, obtained permission of
the Caffre chiefs to take up his residence amongst them
as a Christian teacher. The chiefs, Slambi, Congo,
Tchatchou, and the prophet Makanna, received him
with great cordiality; and Gaika, the great chief of the
western Amakosæ, fixed a spot on the Kat river for
Mr. Williams's residence, near his own kraal. Mr.
Williams, therefore, was an eye-witness, and, indeed, a
sort of envoy of the colonial government, in the interview that took place between prince Gaika, and Lord
Charles Somerset, at the missionary institution on the
Kat river. On the 18th of April, 1817, Mr. Williams
went to see Gaika, with a message from the governor,—a
message the most singular with which a missionary
could be well entrusted. It purported that Lord Charles
Somerset conferred on Gaika the honour and title of
chief of his nation, and that his Lordship was anxious
to have an interview with prince Gaika on high matters
of state. Gaika, who, at that time, was suffering from
ophthalmia, returned this curious answer:—" He was
much obliged to his Lordship for conferring on him the
honour and title of chief of his nation, and begged *that
his Excellency would accept the same compliment from
himself*,"—words, which, though possibly meant to
convey the expression of mere ceremonious courtesy,
were, in fact, a severe derision of the governor and his
monstrous policy; for, to appreciate this message of

Lord C. Somerset, it should be understood, that, in
order to have short dealings with the Caffres, he was
determined to select one chief, to make him King, and
to consider him alone responsible for the conduct of the
whole nation, totally disregarding the power and privileges of the chieftain peers, and the established customs
of the tribes.   In fact, Lord C. Somerset had as little
right or power to declare Gaika " chief of the Caffre
nation," as Gaika had to declare Lord C. Somerset
" chief of the English nation."   Gaika declined the
interview.   A more pressing message was then sent
through Mr. Williams, intimating that his refusal to
meet the governor would be considered a mark of dis-
respect.   Still Gaika declined the proffered honour,
but the commands being urgent, Major Fraser begged
Mr. Williams to persuade Gaika, if possible, to come,
" pledging his honour and existence that no evil should
befal him through his meeting the governor."

On the 30th of April the missionary again saw Gaika,·
who called a council of his principal people, and sat in
debate with them a considerable time.   The council advised their chief to meet the governor, and he consented.   The following morning, Lord C. Somerset arrived
in great military parade at the Kat River, about three
miles distant from Gaika's residence.   The Caffre
prince, however, trembled as the interview drew near;
he dreaded some stroke of treachery or violence, and
with very great difficulty could be persuaded to meet
his armed friend and " brother king-maker."   Col.
Cuyler, Colonel Bird, and Major Fraser, with a party
of armed boors, went to escort Gaika to the interview,
who slowly and reluctantly, and with many long halts,
came to the Kat River; when he reached its banks, his
fears so much increased that he refused to advance any

farther. The officers being thus at a dead halt, sent
for the missionary, and thus partly by persuasion, and
partly by a gentle force, the officers taking Gaika by
the arm and leading him onwards, they brought the
Caffre prince into the presence of the governor.   Lord
Charles Somerset had drawn up the troops, about six
hundred strong, so as to form three sides of a square.
The vice-regal marquee stood in the centre, and two
cannons were stationed on the right and left.   Gaika
was led into the marquee, and placed in a chair at
his lordship's right hand.   Slambi, Gaika's uncle, was
present, and he, with Gaika's suite, stood round the
honoured chief.   According to Mr. Williams's account,
who was present and heard all that Lord C. Somerset
said, the topics discussed, through interpreters, were
the depredations committed on the colony, and the
remedies for these disorders.   Gaika agreed, that
if colonial cattle could be traced to a kraal, that kraal
should be considered responsible for them, and should
replace the number stolen ; the governor asked him to
collect and send out the cattle, horses, and remaining
slaves which were then in his country ; Gaika replied,
he would collect all among his own people, but there
were other independent chiefs who must be consulted
in Caffreland on this subject.   The governor would not
acknowledge any other chief but Gaika.   They then
agreed on a bartering commerce between the colony
and Caffreland, to be opened by two fairs on the boundary twice every year ; but that no Caffre was to come
to the fairs without a pass from Gaika.

Jan Tzatzoe, a Caffre chief of the royal lineage, was
present at this famous interview ; this is his account of
it.[*]   " The governor came to Kat River, to Mr. Wil-

* Aborigines, p. 569.

E

liams's station, and he then appointed Gaika as head
over all the chiefs in Caffreland. Gaika said to the
governor, ' We do not do things as you do them; you
have but one chief, but with us it is not so; but although I am a great man, and king of the other Caffres,
still every chief rules and governs his own people.'
Gaika said to the Governor ' *There is my uncle Slambi,
and there are the other chiefs.*' The governor then
said, " No ; *you* must be responsible for all the cattle
and the horses stolen.' The other chiefs then said to
Gaika, ' Say yes, that you will be responsible, *for we
see the man is getting angry ;*' for we had the cannon
and artillerymen, and soldiers, and boors with loaded
muskets standing about us. Gaika then complied.
He said he would be responsible for all the cattle and
horses stolen from the colony. The governor said
moreover, that the Caffres were not to pass the Fish
River; that the English were to drink on the other* side
of the river, and the Caffres were to drink on this side
of the river; that the middle of the river was the
boundary line. The governor said also, ' If the Caffres
pass the river I will shoot them; if my people pass the
river into your country, you are at liberty to kill
them.' "

These matters having thus been dispatched, Gaika
put a few theological questions to his lordship, who was
relieved from the perplexity in which they placed him
by his aides-de-camp; they contrived to satisfy the
curiosity of the Chief by general answers, such as soldiers
might be expected to give to such queries.

---

* Tzatzoe speaks here as a Caffre, the "other side" of the
river, would with him be the west side.

Then came the ceremony of presents, after which Gaika thinking himself now at liberty, took to his heels and ran away, so eager was he to escape from the alarming friendship of his brother king-maker.

The effects of Lord Charles Somerset's king-making will presently be seen.

CHAPTER VII.

-

LORD Charles Somerset's newly made king of Caffraria,
though exceedingly terrified with the alarming ceremony of his inauguration, seems to have thought himself afterwards a greater man than he really was.
' Some persons are born to greatness, and some have
greatness thrust upon them.' Gaika was indeed born
a prince, but a crown was now thrust upon his head,
and it seems to have turned it. His hereditary honours
he bore pretty well, but his supplementary honours
were his ruin. Reckoning on the alliance and support of the English, he began now to irritate his
neighbour chiefs with various acts of tyranny and
insult. Slambi (Gaika's uncle, and who during the
minority had, in his nephew's name, been the regent of
the western Amakosæ), was indignant to find himself
set aside by Lord Charles Somerset, and still more indignant to find his nephew acquiescing in this arrangement. The other chiefs participated in his feelings;
they saw that the customs of Caffreland were invaded,
and that the parity of their order was in danger; but
when Gaika, in the pride of power, forcibly seized
Tata the wife of one of Slambi's principal counsellors,
all Caffreland was in commotion, and a formidable

confederacy of the great princes, Hintza, the two brothers Slambi and Jaluhsa, Dushani, Habanna, Congo,
and the prophet Makanna, congregated against the
phantom king, to strip him of his imaginary power.
A battle was fought between the Buffalo River and the
Debe, and Gaika was totally routed with a great slaughter of all his chief counsellors and captains.   He fled to
the Koonap river, and the victors " divided the spoil ;"
they drove away the flocks and herds of the routed
" king."   This battle took place in the summer of
1818, within a twelvemonth after the mock treaty between Gaika and Lord C. Somerset ; so soon was this
new made empire overthrown.   Gaika, after his defeat,
lost no time in making his case known to the colonial
government, and by his express desire* an army
marched into Caffreland to punish the confederate
princes.   Surely nothing could be more imprudent and
impolitic than such a measure on the part of the colonial government, for if it was foolish at the first to attempt to force a king upon the throne against the established customs of the nation, far more foolish was it to
persist in this insane and puerile policy when the
experiment had eventually failed.   Towards the close
of the year 1818, Colonel Brereton marched with
a large force into Caffreland.   Slambi and the confederate chiefs protested against the invasion : " The
quarrel was between Gaika and themselves ; it was an
internal war of the nation, with which the colony had
been in no wise concerned.   They had not passed the
colonial boundary ; Gaika had been routed in Caffre-

* " Was the invasion of the Caffre territory in the first instance at the request of Gaika or not? Yes ; decidedly.'
Stockenstrom's Evidence.   Ab. p. 48.

land; they wished to be at peace with the colony, but
they would not submit to Gaika's yoke." All their protestations were in vain. The inhabitants of the villages were either slaughtered or driven into the woods,
and their cattle were plundered by Gaika's allies. In
this expedition the colonial forces took 23,000 head
of cattle, under the pretence of indemnifying Gaika for
the loss he had sustained, but more it would seem with
a view to enrich the ever-hungry and rapacious colony.
To use the laconic words of a Caffre chief, " They took
a great many cattle from Slambi's tribe, and shot a
great many people. Gaika only got a few old cows,
and the government took all the fat cows and the fat
oxen. Gaika brought all these troubles upon him for
having joined the English Government."*

We cannot, indeed, pity Gaika, for he had evidently
betrayed his country, and deserved all his misfortunes
by listening to the temptations of the colonial government; but it is piteous to think that all this bloodshed,
outrage, and rapine should have been brought upon an
unoffending nation to gratify the folly and the headstrong
violence of Lord C. Somerset, whose deeds of misgo-
vernment have laid a train of misfortunes and oppressions which are working to this hour with undiminished
severity. We shall follow the path of his mischief step
by step.

Before Gaika's overthrow by the confederate chiefs,
he had tasted the sweets of his alliance in an affair
of minor importance, to which we may now turn our
attention; it is an interlude fully characteristic of the
colonial government.

Shortly after the interview between Gaika and Lord

---

* Tzatzoe's Evidence. Ab. p. 570.

C. Somerset, at the Kat River, the new "king" sent
men into Caffreland, to see if they could find any
colonial cattle or horses. Two Boors came to make a
search at the same time, and were assisted by Kota,
Gaika's brother in law : they returned into the colony,
and reported that colonial cattle were amongst Slambi's
people. "We received a letter from Major Fraser,"
says the Caffre chief Tzatzoe, "stating that a commando was about to enter Slambi's country to recover
some cattle, but that the object of the commando was
not to attack either Gaika or his people, but was intended against Slambi. I took this letter to Gaika
by Mr. Williams (the missionary's) desire. Slambi
heard that a commando was coming, and he prepared
his people to fight. When Major Fraser came, he
found Slambi fully prepared to fight him. Slambi
divided his people into three divisions, and surrounded
the colonial troops, and then, when the Boors were
afraid, they said to Colonel Fraser, you should never
attack a bees' nest from behind but in front; it will
never do to fight the Caffres so far in their own country.
The commando then went back from Slambi's country,
passed Fort Wiltshire, and attacked Botman's people.
*The commando went on and attacked Gaika's people
on the Kat, Koonap, and Kovoem rivers.* We were
working the same day, cutting wood, and we heard the
commando firing on Gaika's people. Gaika then sent
a chief to say, ' How is it that you have treated me in
this way? You have betrayed me into the hands of these
people : you told me that the object of the commando
was not to fight against me, but against Slambi. *How is
it that I have been attacked and my people killed ?*' We
said to Gaika, 'We do not know, but we told you
what the letter said.' Mr. Williams then went home

and wrote a letter, and sent it to the commandant of the commando, but he received no answer. I went to Graham's Town and saw Major Fraser. I said to him, ' How is this, Major Fraser, that you have broken your word, and attacked Gaika ? It would have been much better, had you yourself gone to Gaika and told him this: you have ruined us : Gaika will never put any confidence in us.' Major Fraser asked ' Were those Gaika's people I attacked ?' I said, ' You know very well that these were Gaika's people : *you were present when the governor had a conference with Gaika on the Kat River:* if you had thought that those people belonged to Slambi, you would not have gone through Trumpeter's Drift, but you would have come by Brun's Drift. FRASER DID NOT SAY A WORD."[*]

This was the beginning of troubles to Gaika: first his dear allies come and shoot his people and attack his villages, merely, it would seem, because they could not find any other persons to shoot in their excursion : and this too, under the command of an officer who had been present at Gaika's inauguration, about six weeks before, and who had pledged honor and existence that no evil should befall him, through his meeting the governor. Then came his overthrow by the confederate chiefs ; then his " restoration" by his allies, which consisted in a present of a few lean and scrubby cows ; after which, as we shall see, followed a long train of tragical events, ending at last in Lord Charles Somerset endeavouring to kidnap the king whom he himself had made, with the intention, it may be surmised, of either hanging him or keeping him in prison for life. These were the fruits of colonial friendship!

* Ab. 569.

Extract from Lord Glenelg's despatch to Sir Benjamin D'Urban :—

"The Caffres had to resent, and endeavoured, justly, though impotently, to avenge a series of encroachments upon them, which had terminated in the assumption by Great Britain, first, of the dominion, and then of the exclusive possession of all the country between the Great Fish River and the Keishkamma. To effect this object, we commenced by ascribing to the chieftain Gaika, an authority which he did not possess, and then proceeded to punish him and his tribes, because he failed to exercise that imaginary power for our benefit. We held him responsible for the acts of his and our common enemy, and exacted from him and his people a forfeiture of their lands, as a penalty for the retaliation made by the chief Slambi, after the invasion of his country by Gaika and ourselves. We forced on our ally a treaty, which according to the usages of the Caffre nation, he had no authority to conclude, and proceeding on that treaty, we ejected the other Caffre chiefs, which were no parties to it, from their country." (p. 61.)

CHAPTER VIII.

Attack on Graham's Town in 1819.

THE immediate effect of Colonel Brereton's expedition into Caffreland, and the abduction of the immense booty mentioned in the last chapter, was an invasion of the colony by the irritated Caffres. They were instigated to this war by the exertions of Makanna, the celebrated prophet of the Amakosæ. This extraordinary man, a plebeian by birth, had by the energy of his character, the force of his talents, and the powers of his eloquence, raised himself to something more than an equality with the high hereditary chiefs of his nation. There was much enthusiasm in his disposition, mixed with some imposture; and with all the fervour of a high-spirited patriot, indignant under the degradation and oppressions of his country, he seems to have entertained the idea of raising himself to the priesthood and sovereignty of his nation. His orations to the people, produced all the effects that might be expected from impetuous and tragical eloquence, uttered in the striking idiom of his country, and appealing to all the lofty passions of the human heart. He took the tone of a religious reformer, as well as of a patriot and a warrior; and interwove some of the most solemn parts of the scripture history, with the gloomy superstitions of his tribe. Sometimes he inculcated a stricter morality, boldly upbraiding the most powerful chiefs with their vices, and sometimes he called in to his aid the arts of mystery, giving out that he was some great one, and had power with the universal Spirit. By degrees he gained a complete control over all the high chiefs, with the exception of Gaika, who, though he seems to have believed in his divine mission, feared and hated his political progress.

Makanna was the soul of the confederacy against Gaika, and under his directions also, the Caffres armed themselves for vengeance on the colony. Early in the year 1819, the prophet brought into the field ten thousand warriors, commanded by Dushâni, the eldest son of Slambi, the principal sufferer by Gaika's treaty with the colony, and if Makanna had trusted less to his power of working miracles, and studied more the prudential arts of war, by making the attack at night-time*, there is every reason to believe that not only would Graham's Town have fallen into his hands, but that all the colony would have been ravaged from one end to the other. A bloody battle was fought, but the Caffres could not resist the English artillery, and having left fourteen hundred of the warriors dead on the field, a general route ensued in spite of the exertions of their prophet to rally his dis-spirited countrymen.

The routed army retreated over the Fish River, and the colonial government breathing from, its late alarm, proposed a great expedition, to visit Caffreland with a severe punishment. The burgher militia and

* Having first sent a chivalrous message to the governor, " that they would breakfast next morning with Colonel Colston," the Caffres made a vigorous attack on Graham's Town,

the troops of the line collected from the various districts, entered the enemy's country in the month of
July, and spent the whole summer ravaging the terri-.
tory of the hostile tribes.   Slambi's followers retreated
to the Kie River, and though closely pursued by the
cavalry, completely succeeded in escaping from their
pursuers : the English troops could never come up with
the main body of the natives. · All the villages of the
Caffres were burnt, and the women and children who
could not escape, were cruelly shot* by the invading
troops.   The booty taken into the colony on this occasion amounted to thirty thousand head of cattle, which,
added to the plunder of the preceding year, made a
total of fifty-three thousand head taken from the Caffres
within a twelvemonth.

A price was set on the head of the prophet Makanna,
who, understanding that he was sought out, above all
others, to satiate the colonial vengeance, with great
magnanimity voluntarily gave himself up into the hands
of the English, stipulating only that his life should be
safe.   As he came into the camp he uttered these words:
"People say that I have occasioned this war: let me
see whether my delivering myself up to the conquerors
will restore peace to my country."   He then delivered
an oration to the British officers, of such force and
eloquence, that it drew even tears from some of his
auditors.   He had fallen, however, into the hands of a
base and treacherous enemy, for orders came from the
colonial government to remove him to Cape Town,
where he was confined in irons as a felon in the common gaol, and ultimately condemned to banishment for

* Kay, 266.

life to Robben Island,* the Botany Bay of the colony, where convicted felons work in chains in the slate quarries. The prophet, however, about a year afterwards, effected his escape in a boat, with some other of his fellow-prisoners, but the overloaded boat upset, and he was drowned before he could effect a landing.

The treatment of this extraordinary man was to the last degree infamous; a shame and a disgrace to the British nation. The magnanimity and high spirit of an enthusiastic patriot could not be otherwise than an object of loathing and a mark for persecution, to such a governor as then ruled the Colony.

In October of the year 1819, poor Gaika was once more dragged into the terrible embraces of his great friend, and once more was he compelled to bring mischief on his nation. These two brother " kingmakers" met, but in what place I cannot exactly find, probably somewhere near the Kat River. The following is Captain Stockenstrom's account of the meeting:—" Lord Charles Somerset, in 1819, again visited the frontier; the Caffre chiefs were assembled on a prominent hill, and there was much discussion with them, which passed through me as interpreter of the Dutch language, minuted down by the colonial secretary, then Col. Bird, who also understood the Dutch language, and afterwards inserted it in the Government Gazette. The result of this discussion was, that the

---

* In the government expenses of this year, under the article " provisioning criminal and civil prisoners," there is noted an increase of 1,995 rix-dollars; with this explanation " owing to a number of Caffres having been sent from the interior, who are detained as prisoners of war at Robben Island."—P. P. 371. p. 61.

boundary line was taken from a high peak situate at the sources of the Chumie and Keiskamma Rivers, taking a bend eastwards between those two rivers, along a ridge running into the Keiskamma, and from thence to the sea; the Keiskamma was to be the boundary. Gaika objected to this, saying, that he wished to retain possession of the basin or amphitheatre, formed at the various sources of the Chumie River, which by the first arrangement was included in the ceded territory, using these metaphorical words: ' I have been born and bred up there, and wish to die there.' His Lordship ultimately agreed that the line should run from that high peak, not eastward, so as to embrace the sources of the Chumie River, but westward, so as to run upon the ridge between the Kat River sources and the Chumie River sources." (Ab. p. 45.)

This is the famous treaty of the " neutral territory," called afterwards, when we had changed its *neutrality* into *partiality** , " the ceded territory." But, according to this arrangement, the colonial government said

---

* " It was called in the first instance the Neutral Colony : did it ever acquire the name of ceded territory ?"

" I have heard it frequently termed a ceded territory, but I do not exactly recollect the time at which it got the name. *I know it has latterly been termed ceded territory.*"

" Do you recollect its being occupied after the treaty was made, by the Boors in any numbers ?"

" The northern part of it was."

" At that time (i. e. soon after the treaty) were any of the burghers permitted to enter the neutral territory ?"

" For some time afterwards, not."

" Were they at any subsequent period allowed ?"

" Yes."

Captain Aitchison's Evidence.   Ab. p. 3.

that Gaika consented to give up this valuable district, about thirty miles broad and seventy long, that it was henceforward to be occupied by neither Caffres nor Englishmen, but to stand a solitude between the colony and Caffreland, for the express object of keeping the two neighbours wide apart. This treaty must be examined in a separate chapter.

CHAPTER IX.

Examination of the Treaty of 1819.

By far the most important witness that we have of the pretended treaty of 1819, is Captain Stockenstrom, who not only was an eye witness, and an interpreter in the transaction, but who, with considerable warmth, advocates its validity, for a very intelligible reason, as we shall presently discover. Here then, in endeavouring to elucidate this subject, we will examine—

1st, The manner and method of making the treaty.

It was not in writing; to this point Captain Stockenstrom is quite clear, as also is Captain Aitchison,*

---

* Captain Aitchison, a thorough disciple of the Colonial School, gives a characteristic opinion on this point.

"Are you aware whether the circumstance of that treaty not having been a written one, has been the cause of constant irritation from that period? *There has been a great deal of bad feeling caused by it.* The Caffre does not care one farthing for any agreement; he has no principle about him. I believe there would have been the same quibbles if there had been a written agreement." (Ab. p. 3.)

We might ask the gallant captain how he knows that the Caffres do not care one farthing for any written agreement when we

another eye-witness, who says it was "altogether verbal." The treaty was verbal on the side of the Caffres, but as soon as Lord C. Somerset returned to the seat of government, the Cape Gazette came forth, containing a very precise and formal document, which gave, in technical language, this "treaty" with Gaika. The Gazette, containing the "treaty," was never sent to Gaika to be explained by interpreters, nor was he ever informed, to his dying day, the exact nature of the treaty which was attributed to him.

The verbal treaty was by *double* interpretation. "Much discussion passed through me," says Captain Stockenstrom, "as interpreter in the Dutch language." Now, as Gaika and the chiefs could not speak the Dutch language, but only the Caffre tongue, the meaning of this is, that some interpreter who understood the Caffre tongue and the Dutch, but not the English, translated the "discussion" into Dutch, and that Captain Stockenstrom translated what the interpreter said out of Dutch into English. Here was plenty of opportunity for mistakes and mis-statements; and Gaika, when he was afterwards told of the cession treaty, protested he knew nothing about it, and that it was all a mistake of the interpreters. A "mistake" was perhaps a gentle word to represent the fact.

never yet have tried them that way? How, moreover, does he know that they would have made "*the same quibbles?*" what quibbles have they made on the subject? They totally deny the existence as well as the validity of this pretended treaty; they declare that the territory never was ceded by Gaika, and they also declare that he had no power to cede it had he wished it.

But the Caffres "have no principle *about* them:" when they see such a total want of principle all *about* them, when they contemplate the villany, violence, and fraud of the colony, it is not very wonderful that they should have no principle *about* them.

2d, The illegality of the treaty.

Gaika had no power to make the treaty; he was giving away that which did not belong to him, and his word was of no sort of avail, without the consent of the other chiefs. It was a thing quite unknown in Caffre law and custom, that one chief should cede any part of Caffreland without the full consent and approbation of all the chiefs who had a right to sit in council; but here we have Lord Charles Somerset's new king again.

The following is the evidence to this point—the first is by Captain Aitchison:—" The territory between the Great Fish River and the Keiskamma, ceded to the British Government, did not belong to Gaika?—Certainly not.

" You are not aware that the other chiefs, who had a joint interest with him in the land, were consenting parties to the treaty.—*Slambi positively refused.*"

. Captain Stockenstrom's evidence.

" Had Gaika authority to represent the other chiefs in possession, so as to surrender their territory? *The government had constituted him the supreme authority there.*" A very important answer this from Captain Stockenstrom, as it is evidently an evasion of the question, by stating what the government did *de facto*, and avoiding the inquiry *de jure*.

. " Is it your impression that Gaika was not in such a degree the sovereign of that district, as to be empowered to surrender it, save and except by the authority conferred on him by the British Government? *No, certainly:* he was not the chief of all the tribes. There was a tribe known under the name of Pato, which never was subject to his control, and that country, also towards the coast, I do not think was ever properly under Gaika's dominion.

" Then you do believe that Gaika, being constituted by our government the sovereign of the country, did surrender that, which, according to Caffre usages, he had no control over? The Caffre chiefs certainly did not *think* him authorized in doing so.

" But those chiefs who were present at the time of that interview with Lord Charles Somerset, were consenting parties, were they not? Lord Charles Somerset only consulted Gaika, and only considered *him* responsible, and only communicated with *him*. The discussions among the chiefs took place between themselves, *and no one knows* what their objections or what their acquiescence was at that time.

" But as they made no objection, might it be taken for granted they were consenting parties? It is very difficult to say whether they consented or not in the discussions with him; *but we being the stronger party did not give that latitude to objections on the part of the native tribes, which may be allowed on other occasions;* a discussion with the Caffres was not treated with so much formality as at present.

" Then these are the facts of the case, that we interfered with the quarrel between Gaika and the other Caffre tribes; that we made an inroad into the Caffre territory, in consequence of which we took from them a considerable quantity of cattle; that that led to an incursion on their part into the colony, and that then having chosen to consider Gaika as the only responsible chief, we obtained his unwilling and reluctant consent to the sacrifice of this rich district of land? *Yes, decidedly.*

" So that in the first instance, in consequence of our

interference, we obtained a considerable quantity of the personal property of these natives; and in the second place we obtained a considerable space of territory? *Yes.*

" Do you know all these facts of your own knowledge? *Yes, decidedly.*"

Now, this being the evidence of an unwilling witness, and that witness no less a person than a governor of the eastern parts of the colony, it is unnecessary to add to its force by similar evidence from the colonial party, as might be done abundantly from the Parliamentary papers. It remains only to see what the Caffres say on this subject.

Tzatzoe, the Caffre chief's evidence.

" Had the ground been given by the Caffres to the English ?—No.

" Had the ground been taken away from the Caffres by the English?—Yes, the Caffres never gave the ground to the English, but the English took the ground.

" Did the English consider that the ground belonged to them ?—If the Caffres had given the ground away to the English, they should have called them all together, and the chiefs should have said, ' We give this ground to the English,' or the English should have said, ' We take this ground from you to-day."*—(Ab. p. 568.)

---

* So also Mr. Shaw, the Wesleyan missionary, says that Pato and the other chiefs, living at the southern part of the neutral territory, "especially urged that Gaika with whom Lord Charles Somerset made the treaty, by which they were expelled the country, had no right whatever over those lands, and that they ought to have been consulted previously to the alienation of their lands; in short, that they ought to have been parties consulted on that treaty. (Ab. 52.)

3d. The pretended treaty was with an ally, a chief whom we had made king of the country at a great cost, and whom we were determined to uphold at any rate; nevertheless, this treaty was forced upon him by intimidation, and by intimidation we took from him a most valuable portion of his territory.

Captain Stockenstrom's evidence.

" Is the committee to understand that the English government first went and took cattle from Slambi, and then took territory from Gaika, *their ally* ?—The territory was taken from Gaika, *because we refused to negotiate with any body but Gaika.*

" Are you aware that Gaika has since remonstrated strongly, and said, that in consequence of his having united with us in that expedition against the Caffre tribes, he, *our ally*, had been dispossessed of his territory ?—No, I have not heard Gaika say so, but I have heard his sons, Macomo and Tyali say so, *as a sort of reproach.*"—Ab. 48.

" Was this boundary assented to by Gaika ?—Certainly assented to, but unwillingly.

" Then do you consider that Gaika acquiesced from an apprehension of the superior force of the British troops ?—I am decidedly of opinion that Gaika would not have parted with that country if it had not been under such an apprehension *that he could not avoid it.*"—Ab. 46.

. Here then we have materials enough from which to form a judgment on this mockery of a treaty, a treaty with a friendly ally, whom we thus contrived to cheat out of his territory, and to make him an unwilling instrument of the ruin of his nation. It might be supposed that it was impossible to add to the dark features

of this swindling transaction, but we shall soon see
that the governors of the colony have been adepts in the
science of political dishonesty, beyond the reach of
ordinary diplomatists. In the meantime, it will be
instructing and amusing to contemplate the secrets of
the colonial cabinet, laid open, as they have been, by
the imprudence of Colonel Wade, in his voluntary testimony before the Parliamentary committee. That
officer, a most ardent partizan of strong measures, has,
in his evidence, published the private instructions of
Lord Charles Somerset, relating to the invasion of Caffreland, and the subsequent treaty. Thus speaks his
Lordship, immediately *before* the expedition:—" It will
be your object to protect and strengthen Gaika, by
concerting with him, and establishing his own immediate residence so near to a strong post of ours, ade-
quately secured, (for, in intercourse with savages, it is
always essential to exert the greatest vigilance), to be
chosen by you, as shall protect him from personal
danger, and, at the same time, admit of his gradually
exerting himself to regain the ground he has lost.
Whatever, therefore, he may want, and we can conveniently supply him with, should be given to him; and
the chiefs who are in his interest, or who can be brought
over to it, should be, as far as possible, *by promises and
conciliatory presents*, induced to give him their support."

His Lordship then desires that Mr. Brownlee, the
missionary, should be located near Gaika, as a sort of
envoy, chaplain, and spy, or, as his Lordship most
delicately terms it, " a confidential person ;" and, further, intimates his wish to have Gaika's sons educated
in the colony.—(Ab. p. 401.)

But thus writes his Lordship *after* the expedition :—

" By the occupation of strong permanent posts in the ceded territory, *containing each a force sufficient for aggression*, it is not to be doubted but that Gaika and his subordinate chiefs*may be* controlled. It has been agreed, that as soon as the next full moon arrives, Gaika and his people shall remove from the Kakaberg, behind the Chumie. It will be essential, previous to your withdrawing the troops, that you seek an interview with Gaika, and inform him, that, as he is now the recognized chief of all the country, between the colonial boundary and Hintza's territories, it is from him the colonial government will exact satisfaction, if depredations are committed on the colony ; and that a force sufficient for the object, will be constantly at hand to enforce my orders on this head ; *that, therefore, it will not avail him to say that his inferior chiefs do not attend to his injunctions ;* he must control them, and point out the depredators, who will be punished with exemplary severity."—(Ab. 404.)

Alas ! King Gaika ! in so short a space of time as from February to October, does all the colonial friendship terminate with this grim message ; the chaplain, the presents, the conciliatory soothing, and the education of the young princes, all forgotten ; and now, he is told that he is to be responsible for all the depredations of all the Çaffre nation ; that he is not to pretend that he *cannot* restrain his chiefs, for *he must ;* so that our dear ally and chosen king, is truly in as perilous and unpleasant a situation, (besides the loss of two-thirds of his territory), as ever an ally and king was placed by unkind fortune.

CHAPTER X.

The Results of the Treaty with Gaika.

THE history of the " neutral territory" may as well be here continued; though, in so doing, we shall anticipate some events in the chronological arrangement of this narrative.

The first point on which there can be no dispute, is the fact, that, by this treaty, such as Lord Charles Somerset chose to represent it, (and he had the representation of it all in his own hands), no colonists, Dutch or English, were, on any account, to settle in it; the Caffres were to leave it, and no other persons were to take possession of it. The Fish River was to continue, as heretofore, the eastern boundary of the colony, and the neutral territory was a *tertium quid* between the colony and Caffraria—a waste land without occupants. " The colonial government seeks no enlargement of its territory," says Lord C. Somerset, in his private instructions; "the known boundary of its settlement, the Great Fish River, it does not desire to pass; on the contrary, it rigidly prohibits its subjects from crossing the line of demarcation."—Ab. 398. This also was the language of the Gazette announcing the pretended treaty.

No one, however, who was the least acquainted with the morality of the colonial government, could, for a moment suppose, that 3,000 square miles of the richest country, abounding with wood and water, would be allowed to stand thus unoccupied, enjoying the sanctity of holy ground, even though guarded by a thousand oaths, and a thousand treaties; and hence we shall find, that before a twelvemonth had elapsed, the sanctity was violated, and the treaty disregarded. This is Captain Stockenstrom's account of our next step in aggression and robbery.

"After the *surrender* of that land by Gaika, a question originated as to the occupation of that territory on the spot before we parted; and it was understood between him and the colonial government then, that it was to be neutral territory. In order to explain that correctly, as interpreter, and in order to convey it to the chiefs' mind, I used these words: "That the waters of the River Gonappe, Karoomo, and the Kat River, were to run in future undisturbed into the sea; *that neither Caffres nor whites were to inhabit the territory*." Lord C. Somerset returned to the Cape, and shortly afterwards the intelligence arrived from this country that the House of Commons had voted a certain sum for emigration, and that a great number of settlers would be poured into that colony. A difference of opinion then originated between the governor and the colonial secretary, as to the right of occupation, *as his Lordship was anxious to avail himself of that territory for the location of the settlers*. His Lordship was then on the point of returning to England, and Sir Rufane Donkin was to take charge of the colony in his absence. *His Lordship considered that the acting governor, in his absence, would be perfectly justified in locating settlers on the territory*, which Colonel Bird denied, and the question being referred to me, I repeated the words of

F

the so-called treaty—(so-called!)   That was in the
discussion between Colonel Bird and the governor,
before I had any intercourse with the acting governor.
Sir Rufane Donkin came to the frontier soon after, in
1820, taking upon himself the charge of the government, and told me that he had scruples himself on the
subject, and wished to know my sentiments, telling me
what Colonel Bird, the colonial secretary, had said on
the subject.   I repeated the words of the treaty, and
the acting governor said, " Then I shall proceed no
farther without first seeing Gaika."   Gaika was accordingly sent for.   (Poor *king* Gaika!)   The acting governor had then a long discussion with me as to the best
mode of securing the frontier.   He said, that though it
was extremely desirable, in order to obtain an efficient
population for defence on the frontier, that this territory should be occupied, he would not allow it to be
done if it was a breach of treaty, and that he could
determine nothing before he had seen Gaika....His
excellency waited some time, and Gaika was very long
in coming, but just as he was preparing to depart,
Gaika did arrive, and his departure was postponed in
order that the discussion might take place; *and then it
was agreed that the government should have the right
of locating people in the territory*.   I was immediately
sent to view the lands at the sources of the Kat River,
surveyed for this Scotch party, which was done.   The
Scotch party, however, did not come. ....
Towards the end of 1820, Lord Charles Somerset returned, and put a stop to a settlement on the Beka, so
that the whole of the *ceded* territory then became
vacant, and gradually a number of people from the
frontier districts emigrated into it with their flocks. * *
Sir Rufane Donkin told me at the time :—"As Captain

Grant is, I daresay, an educated man, and a man who will be very efficient, from having been a military man, just to meet the objects I had in view, he may have a magisterial authority if he is fit for it; and, at any rate, he will be able to keep these people, (the Scotch settlers, and others in the *neutral* territory), in such a sort of military discipline, *as to be able to act against the Caffres in defence of the frontiers.*"

The committee of the House of Commons ask some very pertinent questions of Captain Stockenstrom, which it is requisite to exhibit, with his strange answers. " Did Gaika give a willing consent to Sir Rufane Donkin, at their interview, to the occupation of the ceded territory ?—I think from first to last the cession was an unwilling one. There was no force used of any kind, *but the Caffres never would give up such a territory willingly*; therefore, if they had understood that they could have resisted and re-occupied the ceded territory, even at the period of the discussion with Sir Rufane Donkin, I think the Caffres would have done so. They would have wished to recover the country back there is no doubt, *but having lost the territory,* and after having been dispossessed of it so long (less than a twelvemonth) the Caffres became more reconciled to it; and certainly there were no objections stated to Sir Rufane Donkin, but I think that they were not at all more willing to give it up.

" Then is the Committee to understand, that though the Caffres still retained their objection to being dispossessed of the territory, yet, as they were dispossessed of it, it was a matter of little moment to them whether the territory was or was not occupied? Yes; *that is exactly what I wanted to convey*, because it must be understood that in one instance the treaty contained-the exclusion of the Caffres from the territory; and at the time of the second, the question between Sir Rufane Donkin and Gaika was merely whether it should be occupied on our part, the Caffres being then already excluded.

Were any other chiefs consulted with respect to these arrangements? *No; he only came with two or three of his interpreters.*" (49 Ab.)

What a mass of villany is here before us for examination! 1st, Lord Charles Somerset having, in the most solemn manner, by his own letters, by his own words, by his own proclamations, declared that the territory was to be strictly neutral, before a twelvemonth had elapsed " thinks that he should be perfectly justified in locating settlers in the territory." 2d, His successor and *alter ego*, having doubts on the subject, has a second interview with Gaika to ascertain the strict meaning of this pretended treaty. 3d, Gaika is *sent for*, a king in his own country is sent for, and after much hesitation, arrives;—he has no chiefs with him, no counsellors, all his peers absent, and he with only two or three interpreters is swindled out of the neutrality of his territory, by such interpretation as his enemies choose to put on their own words or his. 4th, It is all a verbal " treaty," a discussion by double interpretation ; no writing, no parchment, no formal treaty, no record of any sort or description, about a territory which was of immense value to the ceding party. 5th, One reason for wishing to possess the " neutral" territory was to place there a population " under military discipline, so as to be able to act against the Caffres." The gift was to be turned into a farther means of aggression, rapine, and tyranny. 6th, It was " from first to last an unwilling consent;" but, nevertheless, Captain Stockenstrom thinks that Gaika and his nation did not care about the occupation of the neutral territory by their enemies, for as they had been driven out of it themselves, as they had been ejected about nine months, "they had became reconciled to their loss," and considered it "a matter of little moment whether it was occupied or not," and yet, concludes Captain Stockenstrom, "they were not at all willing to give it up"! ! !

This then was the history of the " neutral," now transformed into "ceded" territory. * The Caffres were all violently driven out of their lands, the chiefs Slambi and Dushani, Eno, Habanna, Congo, Kama, and Pato, Botman, and many others, were hunted over the Kei River at the point of the bayonet, stripped of all their worldly possessions, with their houses reduced to ashes, and all their standing crops utterly ruined; and thus were they cast on the mercy and pity of the kindred tribes into whose territory they were now thrust as unwelcome visitants.

When this work was fully accomplished, and when Sir Rufane Donkin had gone through the farce of an interview with Gaika, as already described, he issued a proclamation, in which he called the neutral ground "newly acquired territory," and annexed it to the province of Albany.*, This was preparatory to the loca- .

* Dr. Philip's Evidence.

" It had been utterly denied that any treaty of the kind ever took place. I recollect perfectly well when Sir Rufane Donkin returned from the frontier, he mentioned to me that he had made a treaty with the Caffres, but at the moment he mentioned that, I had a letter from Mr. Brownlie, a missionary, in which he stated

tion of some English settlers in the " newly acquired territory," half-pay officers and others, whom he wished to serve ; but anon Lord C. Somerset retired from England to his government, and having a pique with his deputy, resumed his grants, and called back the settlers within the boundary of the colony. The commissioners of inquiry inform us, " that the occupation of this land was regarded by his excellency as a departure from the policy that had induced him to interpose a neutral space between the colonists and the Caffres ;" but, nevertheless, his lordship soon appropriated part of the neutral ground himself, and by large donations of vast farms to his favourites, soon manifested that he reverenced the sanctity of the " neutral" ground as little as his deputy had done.

Thus by degrees the neutral territory was stolen by the colonial government ; the poor Caffres, not daring to thrust out the thieves who, in disregard of their own mock treaties and engagements, were undisputedly removing their neighbours' landmarks. Then came, after several prefatory acts of plunder, the expulsion of the Prince Macomo in the year 1829 from the Kat River, a most valuable part of the neutral territory, which he held as eldest son of Gaika, the ally of the English, and which they allowed him to hold, owing to the irresistible force of his claims, which even the colonial government could not deny. This is the blackest part of the tragedy, and will be separately and minutely examined.

Hitherto, as far as we know, the colonial government

___

that Gaika did not understand that there was any treaty of the kind, and that he had it from Gaika himself, and *Gaika declared to his dying day to the missionaries, that he never entered into any treaty.*" Ab. 619.

had been acting on its own responsibility, had been exhibiting its own morals, but in the year 1831, Lord
Goderich, in a despatch to Sir G. L. Cole, thus authenticated the breach of treaty, and thus consummated our national disgrace.

"The consideration of this subject," says his Lordship, " has led me to think that the lands of the ceded
territory might henceforth be appropriated to general
purposes of settlement. I collect from the accounts
which have reached my office, that all the lands within
the ancient limits of the colony, which are considered
adapted to the purposes of agriculture, have already
been disposed of, and this is a fact so well known, *that
it has deterred many respectable persons from emi-
grating from this country to the colony.* It is also
presumed, that there are many colonists who would
be glad to transfer their industry and their capital
to lands *capable of yielding more profitable returns.*
For these reasons, I am of opinion that it will be proper
to make arrangements for locating respectable settlers
in the ceded territory."*

The cool intrepidity and gravity of language in which
this act of spoliation and infraction of treaty is recommended, could hardly be equalled in the annals of
political immorality.

This chapter may be concluded with some important
evidence from unexpected sources.†

Major-General Bourke, Lieut.-governor of the Cape,
in a letter to the commissioners, dated 3d July, 1826,
says, " That boundary would assuredly be the most advantageous for the colony. I cannot, indeed, admit,
from all I have been able to learn of the parole treaty

* P. P. part ii. p. 57.   † Kay, 495.

of 1819, that we are in any way entitled to it, but if by any further arrangement or treaty we could acquire *a just title* to the possession of this tract of country, it would be of the greatest importance to the colony."

Sir Rufane Donkin informed the committee of the House of Commons that Colonel Bird, the colonial secretary, twice or thrice said to him, in the year 1820:—" I hope you will not allow any representations which may be made to you to make you believe that Gaika has ceded the territory to the colony : he has done no such thing, for I was present during the whole of the conference last year. If, therefore, you want the territory, and find it for the benefit of the colony *that you should get possession of it,* it can only be by following up the treaty of last year, and by inducing Gaika by fair means, and by his own consent to abandon the land to you."

CHAPTER XI.

Attempted Seizure of Gaika's Person by the Colonial
Government.

GAIKA had now gained sufficient experience to comprehend the full extent of the emoluments and dignities conferred on him by his great western ally. Looking round him, he saw the mountains on the north by which he was cooped up; looking to the south, he saw the whole of the territory from his own circumscribed estates down to the ocean, a distance of sixty miles, entirely depopulated, excepting where a few military stations and newly erected barracks, occupied by the soldiers of his ally, gave him to understand that he was but a tolerated and suspected prisoner in his own dominions.

His sons, young men of high spirit, and fully alive to their hereditary expectations, both in power and possessions, were driven out of their lands with the other chiefs; and he had to bear the loud complaints and remonstrances both of his own family, and of all the princes of the Amakosæ. But this was not all, his tyrannical allies evidently made a puppet of him, sent for him when they wanted him, as if he were their servant, and insisted upon his going through the ceremony of assenting to pretended treaties which he did not understand, and which he had no power to ratify : with all this accumulated disgrace and tribulation, he had, moreover, to bear the burthensome and perilous office of chief-constable or thief-taker of all Caffreland, under the colonial government : to him his allies looked for restitution of all colonial property lost, or said to be lost by the depredators of his nation, and gave him to understand, that if he did not find out the thieves and punish them, they would punish him, and indemnify themselves by seizing his cattle. It was no wonder, therefore, that Gaika at last aroused himself to adopt a more patriotic policy ; what he had hitherto done had been the result of timidity or low cunning, hoping probably that he might find some opportunity for out-witting his enemy, whom he dared not meet in the field, and with whom he thought it safer to simulate friend-ship, than to go to war. The great extent of his ca-lamities, and the rapidity with which they had come upon him, shewed him the necessity of backing out of the colonial friendship without delay, and hence he very soon joined himself with his natural friends, the chiefs and princes of his nation. Had he possessed the integrity and moral fortitude of his eldest son Macomo, or the patriotism and indomitable spirit of the prophet Makanna, he never would have fallen so low, nor found himself entangled in these inextricable difficulties ; for it is hard to suppose that even Lord Charles Somerset would have dared by personal violence to push his villanous " treaties," if Gaika had firmly and respectfully declined to meet his lordship, or to accept his proffered friendship.

A letter of Major James, dated Graham's Town, Oct.

13th, 1821, elucidates this part of our history—it is directed to Colonel Scott.

"SIR,—I beg to acquaint you, for the information of his excellency, that about a month ago forty-eight head of cattle together with an English boy who herded them, were missing from Mr. Smith's location, about twelve or fourteen miles from this place; I could discover no traces of them for some time. On the 4th instant, I received a letter from Mr. Brownlie, the missionary at the Chumie, (to whom I had sent a description of them) stating that the cattle were stolen by Slambi's Caffres. The thieves were intercepted, and the cattle taken from them by a son of the above-mentioned chief, who lives between the Kieskamma and Buffalo Rivers. Gaika had heard this from Slambi's Caffres.

" On the 5th, I saw Mr. Brownlie at Wiltshire barracks, who told me that Gaika, who had given the information as *positive*, now wished it to be understood merely as *a report*. I rode over to Gaika's kraal, and though I urged him to give me what information he could on the subject, yet he evaded it, and declined giving me guides to the kraals where the cattle were supposed to be; but offered to send a messenger to Slambi, to beg him to give up the cattle and the boy. I was unwilling such a communication should be made to Slambi, as it would put him on his guard, but as many thought the boy might be still alive, and that there was a greater chance by sending such a messenger to recover him, I consented to it, and desired an answer might be sent to Fort Wiltshire.

"Slasla, a brother of Slambi, then visiting Gaika, at last gave me the desired information; he told me the cattle were taken by Nambrielie's people, one of Slambi's councillors, and that Dushani had taken from the thieves part of the cattle for himself.

"I apprehend Gaika sent a messenger not to Slambi, but to Nambrealie's people, to give them timely warning; we pushed on with our cavalry, but arrived at Nambreelie's kraal too late—the people were off with the cattle, and it was useless, fatigued as we' were, to pursue them.

"This was owing to Gaika ;—very little reliance can be placed on that chief, who from all accounts *appears to be now on good terms with Slambi*, or at least very much in awe of him," &c.

At the close of the year 1821, Lord Charles Somerset resumed his government of the colony, and probably was not a little disappointed to find that *his* king of Caffreland had so soon turned restive, and shewn himself thus ungrateful for all the eminent royalties and benefits conferred upon him. His lordship, however, was one who delighted in violent counsels, and on this occasion he seems to have indulged his propensities to the extreme. He gave orders in the month of March 1822, to seize Gaika at his own residence, and to bring him captive into the colony! Colonel Scott was the officer entrusted with the execution of this monstrous outrage, but owing to the extraordinary watchfulness of the Caffres when the interests of their chiefs are concerned, the plot failed. Gaika received intimation of his intended capture, and only escaped by disguising himself as one of his wives, and pretending to be engaged in some female occupation. When this perfidious plot was divulged, it of course excited the utmost indignation in Caffreland ; and indeed the iniquity of such a treatment of a prince, who was *par excellence* the ally of the colonial government, roused even the servile spirit of the colonists to protest against a policy which was as dangerous as it was unprincipled. There can be no doubt that another Caffre war would have been the result of this stroke of treachery if it had succeeded, and such was the apprehension of the colonists, who ventured to protest against the madness of their autocrat.

We can only conjecture what the object of Lord Charles Somerset could be, in thus attempting to kidnap the Caffre prince; judging, however, from the tender mercies of the governor's disposition, and his treatment of the voluntary prisoner, prophet, and patriot, Makaana, we may surmise that Gaika probably escaped a catastrophe, which would, in one view, at least, have placed him on an equality with Napoleon's royal prisoner of Vincennes.

The characteristic termination of this affair, I give in Mr. Pringle's words :—" Lord Charles, when called upon by his Majesty's commissioners to reply to the complaints of the Albany settlers to Earl Bathurst, upon this, among many other injurious acts, peremptorily denied all knowledge of the transaction. ' The seizing of Gaika,' he says, ' I never heard of, until I read it in this tissue of falsehood.' But what shall be said of this *assertion* of his Lordship's, when I add, that when the commissioners afterwards discovered the letter in his own hand-writing, at Graham's Town, directing this attack upon Gaika, he boldly defended the measure, and only expressed his regret that it had not succeeded. 'Colonel Bird* has, in his pamphlet,

* Colonel Bird quarrelled with Lord C. Somerset, as most of the employés at the Cape did sooner or later: the result of this

published extracts from other letters of his Lordship,
proving that the plan was his."—(Pringle, pp. 310.)

The passage in which Lord Charles Somerset *acknowledges* the plot, (having, at first, flatly denied it), is in
these words : — " With regard to the attack upon
Gaika, *it is to be regretted* that it was not so judiciously
planned by Lieut.-Col. Scott, as to ensure the success
of the object in making it. The orders given Lieut.-
Col. Scott tended at all times to conciliate the Caffres,
but when it was necessary to punish them, to do so
effectually, and to leave no chance of failure."—(P. P.
for 1827, No. 371, p. 43.)

This, then, makes the story of this alliance complete:
there did but want this crowning outrage to give it
a character of enormity, which, though it might be
equalled, could not be surpassed.

quarrel was the publication of a pamphlet revealing some of the
secrets of government: amongst these secrets were extracts of
letters to Colonel Bird, before and after the attempted seizure of
Gaika. The first extract is dated Wednesday, 13th March,
1822. "Roger's letters from the frontier have not yet been sent out,
but I enclose you a private one from Scott, which makes the next
post interesting. FOR I HOPE WE HAVE GAIKA IN OUR
TRAMMELS." The second extract is dated 21st March.
" The letters from the frontier are this moment arrived ; I have
just skimmed over a letter from Scott. *Gaika ran away and succeeded in escaping* : but I think the business was as well conducted
as possible (as far as I have yet read) and that the effect will be
very advantageous. Yours, &c. C. H. S." Again, Wednesday,
April 3d, 1822. "It is not characteristic of the Caffres to attempt hostilities when they have been greatly frightened, which
no doubt they were by Stuart's last visit: however Stuart has
done the wisest thing he could do, *only I wish he could keep
matters more secret* ; from what I heard, I have no doubt that the
brigade major was the propagator of the intended operations
against Gaika by the cavalry."

As Gaika does not hereafter appear prominently in the history of his country, we may state that he lived ingloriously till 1829, in which year he died, not of old age, for he was not above fifty-six years old, but a victim of intemperate habits, having latterly given way to intoxication, in which, like many other brokenhearted persons, he had in vain sought for a remedy of his afflictions. He was, however, fully sensible of the insufficiency of this wretched consolation, and in his last moments expressed unfeigned sorrow that he had paid so little attention to the Gospel, and earnestly conjured his sons, counsellors, and chiefs who surrounded his dying bed, to favour and encourage the missionaries, whom he acknowledged to be the best friends both of the chiefs and the people. He also desired that his youngest son, Dingweea, might be educated by Mr. Read, the esteemed missionary at the Kat River settlement. This boy was born not long before his father's death.

Gaika, the son of La-ou, was left by his father in a long minority. Slambi, his father's brother, was his tutor and guardian, and acted as regent in his name; and thus he was early initiated into scenes of violence, as Slambi was for many years engaged in active warfare with the eastern tribes, and particularly with a powerful chieftain, Langa, whom he conquered and took captive, offering to sell him to the colonists, to whom the captive had made himself obnoxious. When Gaika came to manhood, Slambi was indisposed to surrender his authority, and persisted in acting as regent beyond the time allowed by Caffre law. This led to a war between the nephew and the uncle. Gaika had considerable talent for war, and though totally devoid of moral courage, was brave in the field. He defeated his uncle, and drove him into his own country; but Slambi, unwilling still to resign the reins of authority, brought another army against his nephew, and was again defeated and taken prisoner. After this, Gaika was at war with Wilbela, the regent of Caffreland, in the minority of his nephew, king Hintza. A great battle took place, and victory declared in favour of Gaika, who pursued the fugitives with a great slaughter, and took the young king, Hintza, prisoner. It was probably in this decisive battle that Gaika slew Kaanzi, one of the uncles of king Hintza, with his own hand.

After this victory, Gaika became the most important and powerful chief of the Amakosæ; but when Hintza came of age, the unalterable customs of the nation prevailed, and Gaika, in spite of his superiority in arms, descended, as a matter of course, to the second rank. His connexion with the colony brought him down into deep humiliation and disgrace. His name can never be forgotten in the history of the colony.

CHAPTER XII.

Macomo, son of Gaika.

MACOMO, the eldest son of Gaika, the most interesting hero in Caffre history, was born about the year 1796. He was therefore in his twenty-fourth year when the colonial government tricked his father out of the neutral territory. It is probable that Macomo did not understand the manœuvre and fraud of his father's great ally, as the whole ceremony of the pretended " treaties" was an unintelligible farce, not only to the Caffre chiefs, but to Gaika himself: this dry fact, however, he could understand,—that the territory which he had expected quietly to inherit, and which had been the territory of his great-grandfather Khahabi, was no longer his, and that he must find lands beyond the Keiskamma, unless he were contented to be a lack-land prince. The location, however, which he took for his kraals and his cattle, was on the banks of Kat River, and its tributary the Mankansana, a favoured valley which has since become the settlement of the Hottentots, the first land of rest to that afflicted people. The Kat River valley is a little to the west of the line prescribed in the pretended treaty of 1817, just over the mountain ridge, which Lord Charles Somerset was

pleased to name as the boundary of Gaika's lands, and
of the neutral ground. Here then Macomo was in the
enemy's clutches, according to their own interpretation
of their own treaties, and we shall see, ere long, what
use they made of this circumstance.

It appears that the first attack made on Macomo by
the colony, was in the year 1823*, about a year after
they had attempted to kidnap his father. This attack
was made by Major Henry Somerset, the son of Lord
Charles Somerset, who having obtained the command
of the eastern frontier, was anxious to signalize himself

---

* We learn by the Report of the Commissioners, (dated 25th
May, 1825,) that in *April* of 1823, Major Henry Somerset had
another interview with Gaika, as I can find no record of this any
where but in the Report, I give it in the words of the commissioners. "It was the decided opinion of the commandant that
the depredations which were committed along the eastern frontier
during the year 1822, were in consequence of this interference,
(i. e. attempt to seize Gaika) and with a view *to regain the confidence* of Gaika (!) he with difficulty obtained an interview with
him in April 1823, at which the chief was induced to renew his
promise to check the depredations, and the commandant engaged
to promote an amicable intercourse with the Caffres by the establishment of a fair near the residence of Gaika. It is alleged by
the commandant that the depredations ceased from the period of
this conference, till the public tranquillity was again *disturbed by
the misconduct of the Boors* upon a part of the frontier at that time
beyond the limits of his command." (P. P. i. p. 198.)

This deserves attention, for we find by the Commissioners'
Report; 1 That the attempt to seize Gaika, had unsettled all
the hopes of peace with the Caffres, and caused a renewal of depredations. 2. That an interview with Gaika restored matters
till *the misconduct of the Boors* disturbed the public tranquillity:
and yet seven months afterwards, this very commandant who had
given this testimony in favour of the Caffres, goes and makes a
sanguinary attack upon the eldest son of the chief whose friendship he and his father had so sedulously cultivated!

as the Achilles of the Boors. This young gentleman,
the hero of all commandos, reaped his first laurels in a
campaign against Macomo, whom, unsuspecting, and
unprepared, he assailed with a large commando in the
Kat River valley, killed as many Caffres as he considered sufficient to establish the gallantry of the
campaign, and took off an enormous plunder of 7000
head of cattle. The Government Gazette of December
20, 1823, thus describes this brilliant business :—" At
day-break, on the 5th, Major Somerset having here
collected his force, passed with celerity along the ridge,
and at day-light *had the satisfaction* of pouring into
the centre of Macomo's kraal, with a rapidity that ·at
once astonished and completely overset the Caffres. A
few assegais were thrown, but the attack was made
with such vigour, that *little resistance could be made.*
As many Caffres having been destroyed as it was
thought *would evince our superiority and power*, Major
Somerset stopped the slaughter, and secured the cattle
to the amount of 7000 head, and had them driven to
Fort Beaufort, where kraals had been previously prepared for them." We need not comment on this affair,
it speaks for itself—it is like all the acts of the colonists
towards the aborigines, a mixture of treachery and inhuman cruelty painful to contemplate.

Similar attacks were about the same time made on
the other chiefs, and with similar success ; a large
booty of cattle was brought out of Caffreland, and distributed amongst the Boors, to indemnify them for
pretended losses of cattle, and for the trouble of the campaign, losses such as they themselves chose to represent, and which, on all these occasions, have uniformly
been received as true and authentic, without any inquiry or examination. The delighted Boors extolled

the name of the young commander to the skies, and Major Henry Somerset became the darling of the frontier.

The plea of losses of colonial cattle which has been repeated times innumerable, to justify aggressions on the Caffres, will be examined in a separate chapter, but at present we will continue our narrative.

Eleven months after this first outrage on Macomo, that is to say, in November 1824, the colony sent another commando against him. It appears that one of the eastern Boors, named Louw, or Lodewyk, Bothma, a friend and political partizan of Lord Charles Somerset, had lost nine calves, which had either strayed, or been killed by the wild beasts, or, according to the more profitable phraseology of the Boors, been " stolen by the Caffres;" for as the Caffres were at hand, and still possessed flocks and herds in spite of the immense plunder they had sustained, it was more politic to lay the blame of real or imaginary loss of cattle to their door, then to charge the wild Bushmen with the theft, who was too poor to repay the trouble of a commando, or the lordly lion who could take care of himself. Without any inquiry then, or any proof demanded, " the commandant," that is to say, Major H. Somerset, despatched the Honorable Captain Massey, with a strong force, to plunder once more the kraal of Macomo. They could not trace the calves to the kraal, nor was there any evidence of their having been received by any of Macomo's clan;* but a commando

---

* The missionaries resident in the vicinity inquired into the matter, and were satisfied of the innocence of Macomo's people on this occasion.

never yet went out *for nothing,* and these brave warriors marched off with four hundred and eleven head of cattle, which was something more than compound interest for eleven calves.

Macomo, who not only is innocent of cattle-stealing, but has moral feeling and honour enough to be much pained with the calumnious accusation, bore this second attack on his property and character, with surprising command of temper; for two days afterwards he sent three of his people to the residence of the Field-cornet Vandernest, at Glen-Linden, bringing with them two oxen and a slave woman. These envoys of the chief came with a message of peace, " they had by Macomo's orders brought these oxen, belonging to the colony, which his people had captured from some Bushmen in the neighbourhood, and with them the slave woman, who had run away from the Boors; this he had done to prove his desire to live at peace with the colony— but he besought the field-cornet in return to exert his influence with the ' commandant,' that the cattle which had been unjustly taken away from him, might be restored."

The barbarous reception of this embassy is almost incredible, but thus it is recorded: " Vandernest had at that time a patrol party of twelve armed Boors, stationed under his orders; they were now standing around him, and he hastily ordered them to bring out their guns. The Caffres hearing this, and judging from other indications that their message had given offence, became alarmed for their safety, and ran off with precipitation to the forest. Vandernest called upon them to stop, but they were frightened and continued their flight. He then ordered his men to fire. One of

the Caffres was shot on the spot; another mortally*
wounded, crawled into the thicket and was there left
to perish! the third only escaped to tell the bloody
story to his chief.   The effect that this truly detestable
murder produced in Caffreland was a feeling of the
deepest indignation and abhorrence."

The Parliamentary Papers furnish us with some additional evidence on this subject well worthy attention.

1st. We have the murderers' own account.

" Sir.—I have to inform you that yesterday evening
at sun-set, three Caffres came here with two oxen which
they had stolen on the 2d January, 1822; one from my
brother Hendrek, and the other from my brother-in-law
Coenraad B. Klopper. A female slave named Rachel
accompanied the Caffres. She stated that she had
been upwards of a year in Caffreland. *The Caffres
were exceedingly impudent,* and as they approached
me with arms in their hands, I desired four men to
arm and take them prisoners, *for I considered them
spies.* When the Caffres perceived the armed men
they took to flight. I pursued them with the remainder
of my men, and called upon them upwards of ten times
to stand, stating *that I would do them no harm,* (only
take them prisoners as spies) it being only my wish to
speak to them; but as they would not surrender, I
ordered the four armed men to fire upon them, in consequence of which one was killed. The female slave
informed me that the Caffre who was shot, is the one
who *intended* to have stolen my oxen. She says that

---

* It is not certain whether the second wounded Caffre died, or
recovered from his wounds.

the Caffre now killed, with two others, brought the oxen to Captain Macomo's kraal. The oxen belonging to me and my brother are still in Macomo's kraal, as the female slave told me.

I am,

Bavian's River,   C. J. Vandernest, Field-cornet.
14th Nov. 1824."

Captain Stockenstrom, the landdrost of the district, viewed the matter in its proper light, as a most unjustifiable murder ;* but the other dignitaries of the colony cast their mantle over the murderer. Mr. Mackay,† the deputy landdrost of Cradock, writes—"I beg in justice to the field-cornet, to say that he had been for a considerable time previous to the occurrence, greatly irritated by Caffre depredations, and, *harassed in his person,* and injured by them in his property, and *that he had reason at the time to expect an attack from them,* though at the same time I must admit, that nothing contained in the information given to me, could in my opinion, justify the field-cornet in the *rash and inconsiderate* act committed by him."

It seems then that "the expectation of an attack" from some unknown persons in a nation, would justify us in shooting the envoys of that nation, coming to us with a friendly and peaceful message ; or that at the worst, it would be only a "rash and inconsiderate" act so to kill the envoys!!!

---

* See his letter. P. P. part i. p. 180.

† Mr. Mackay, the landdrost of Somerset, was one of Lord Charles Somerset's "loyal" men, a promoter of loyal addresses to his lordship, and a buttress of his tottering government, which, about this time, began to betray marks of caducity.

The letter of the Commandant Henry Somerset, is truly remarkable: it is addressed to the commissioners.

"GENTLEMEN.—I have the honour to acknowledge the receipt of your communication of the 23d, inquiring into the circumstance of some Caffres being shot at the place of Field-cornet Vandernest. *From information I have received, it did not appear to me that any culpability could be attached to Vandernest;* this I explained to the Caffre chief Macomo, and no doubt remained on my mind, that the arrival of the Caffres on the spot, and the story they pretended to relate, was a *ruse de guerre*, to enable them to plunder with more certainty of success.

" I have now, however, called on Captain Massey to send me a minute and circumstantial detail of this affair, which I shall have the honour to forward," &c.

The eagerness of exculpation manifested in this extraordinary epistle of the commandant is too glaring to escape observation. He gives a very decided opinion in favour of the guilty party, even when, by his own showing, he had not yet obtained " the minute and circumstantial details" requisite for him to form an opinion on a matter of such serious import. What Macomo thought of his " explanations" we are not informed, but we may conjecture that he little agreed with the officious commandant in the view that he took of the murder of his envoys.

The letter of the governor, through his secretary, to Captain Stockenstrom, completes this story, making the end of it exactly correspond with the beginning:—

" SIR,—I have submitted to his Excellency your

letters relating to the Caffres shot by the Field-cornet
Vandernest. In reply I am directed to acquaint you
that although the existing regulations with regard to
the relations between the Caffres and the colony, order
that *all male Caffres found within the boundary of*
the colony shall be shot, his Excellency cannot learn
but with deep regret that the Field-cornet Vandernest should have been *so hasty* on the present occasion. In making this observation upon the Field-
cornet's conduct, his Excellency has fully considered the
hostile disposition and practices of the Caffres in that
quarter, and *probable hostility* of the individuals in
question, from being armed ; and although his Excellency is willing to acknowledge the *zeal and activity*
of the Field-cornet in question, and the imperative necessity of the continuance of that zeal and activity, he
desires that his anxious wishes in all cases not to risk
the sacrifice of a human being may *be impressed* on him,
and all inhabitants of the border, except in cases of
positive self-defence, or *when the public service shall*
render it indispensable.

" RICHARD PLASKET, Secretary."*

His Excellency suggests, as a help to the Field-cornet,
the order that all male Caffres found within the colony
are to be shot—(an order of truly savage cruelty)—but
forgets three important points, 1st, That Macomo's
envoys came in the sacred character of ambassadors,
with a peaceful message, and undeniable proofs of
friendly intentions ; 2d, That Macomo was eldest son
of Gaika, the friend and ally of the colony, the king of
the governor's making ; 3d, That it was absolutely

* See P. P. part i. p. 178—183.

G

imperative on Gaika, and part of the treaty forced on
him, to restore cattle and colonial property, so that
Macomo was in fact fulfilling the most important part
of his father's engagements. The other suggestions of
his Excellency—"the hostile disposition of the Caffres
generally, and the *probable* hostility of the individuals
in question," are, indeed, wretched excuses.

"The hostility of disposition". was, under existing
circumstances, not very marvellous, though unquestionably aggression was all on the side of the colony ;
and it should be remembered, that Vandernest had,
two days before the murder, been with the commando
plundering Macomo's kraal.   But, if *probable* hostilities could justify such an atrocious deed, who can be
safe as long as suspicion, or fear, or hatred, are passions
of the human breast ?

His Excellency in order to shield Vandernest does
not forget that the envoys were " armed ;" that is, that
they carried assegais, each man having his spear : but
to this we answer, that they were guarding a run-a-way
slave, that they had also oxen to take care of, and
that, in passing over a wild country with such a
charge, few persons would have gone without arms.
Moreover, it is the custom of the Caffres to carry the
assegai whenever they leave their kraals ; and as the
country abounds in wild beasts, it could not have been
prudent to drive cattle without some weapons of defence.   But, indeed, such a paltry excuse as this it is
scarcely requisite to notice, for what would these poor
Caffres have done with their assegais, or what did they
attempt to do, against a large party of Boors armed
with loaded muskets ? or was it for a moment to be
supposed that Macomo's envoys, coming with a peaceful message from their prince, and soliciting an inter-

change of friendly offices, would dare to attack the
Field-cornet on his own grounds?

This iniquitous affair then will, in all its details
from first to last, thoroughly elucidate the sort of justice
which prevails in the colony whenever the Aborigines
are concerned : and in conclusion we have only to state,
that after this mild rebuke from his Excellency, Vandernest was not put on his trial for a capital felony,
but was allowed to retain the office of Field-cornet,
and, together with the rest of the party who had thus
imbrued their hands in innocent blood, was enriched
with large grants of land in the " neutral territory,"
from which Macomo himself was afterwards violently
and iniquitously expelled.

CHAPTER XIII.

Macomo's Expulsion from the Kat River, in 1829.

THE colonial government has never paused long in its progress of aggression ; and has, with a steady pace continually marched onwards against the house of Gaika. We have seen the acts of robbery by commandos against Macomo, in the last chapter, which were but preparatory to a grander stroke of injustice, the expulsion of the chief and all his numerous tribe from the Kat River. This expulsion took place in May 1829. It was entirely by force, and was accompanied with acts of cruelty that must leave indelible disgrace on the character of the British nation.

We will, however, here examine, 1st, The plea for this act of violence put up by the colonial party ; 2d, The mode of the expulsion.

Although the colonial government, in its conduct towards the aborigines has never taken the trouble to assume even the conventional decencies of the law of nations, but has, with open violence, trampled upon their weaker neighbours, as if they were irrational animals ; yet, in the matter of Macomo's expulsion, they have been compelled by subsequent events, and especially by the parliamentary inquiry, to find some

justification for this outrage, and much have they said
in order to give some colour of justice to the deed. It
will, however, be manifest that their excuses are in fact
a confession of guilt, and that chiefly by the confusion,
contradiction, and multiplicity of their pleas. They
urge, 1. That Macomo had in a pitched battle routed
the Tambookies, a neighbouring nation, and taken from
them much spoil in cattle, an act of violence which it
was their duty to punish. 2. That Macomo had committed many depredations on the colony. 3. That
Macomo occupied the territory only by sufferance, and
that the treaty with Gaika had ceded the country to
the colony. It is remarkable that none of the colonial
advocates agree in their reasons; some say one thing,
and some another; and it is our duty now to examine
their special pleading.

Captain Stockenstrom* takes a very conspicuous part
in this affair; indeed it is perfectly well understood that
Macomo's expulsion was his idea, and in his evidence
before the committee he speaks at length on the subject, and with an eagerness that brings to light some
important facts. " A field-cornet of the district," says
this gentleman, " reported to me, in the year 1822, that

* In a document which he drew up to explain his views of the
colonial policy, dated Dec. 1833, thus does Captain Stockenstrom
express himself,—" I have no hesitation in saying that I would
not scruple to recommend the expulsion from the ceded territory
of every kraal of Caffres, which could be clearly proved guilty,
as a body, of carrying on depredations, either against the colony
or others of their neighbours; and I am equally positive in the
opinion, that the murders perpetrated by Macomo's people on the
Bavians river *subsequent to the said expulsion*, ought to have been
visited with the severest punishment, *even if it had involved the
destruction of the whole kraal*, or its expulsion from Caffreland
itself." (Ab. 100.)

the Caffres had come back to, and were residing in the
ceded territory. This report went amongst others in
the usual course to the colonial office, and it was referred to the commandant of the frontier, and I received
a letter telling me that there was no such thing, that
the Caffres were not within the ceded territory. I then
considered it my duty to inquire, and found that they
were, and consequently my report to the government
was to that effect. A few weeks afterwards I was ordered to proceed and show the authorities in the engi-
neer department the frontier as I understood it to exist. The report was made accordingly to the government. A few weeks after that again, I received a communication from the colonial office, telling me that as
the military commandant (Major H. Somerset) had
permitted the Caffres to come to the territory, *they
should be allowed to remain as long as they. behaved
themselves quietly*. I had nothing more to say, *but
felt extremely sorry*, considering this (though it might
have proceeded from the most humane motives) a most
injurious measure; and I believe *any military* man
will say with me*, that the sources of the Kat and Go-

* Other "military men" do say precisely the same thing. In
the minutes of evidence taken before the Committee of the House
of Commons, thus teacheth Major William B. Dundas,—" It
would have been much more humane to take possession of the
neutral territory at first, for the allowing of it to remain unoccupied was one of the great causes of depredation. It was a
bone of contention, being unoccupied between us and the Caffres,
and it was perfectly impossible to watch it narrowly.

" Do you think that if we have an inconvenient military frontier,
that we have a right, for the purpose of improving that, in a military point of view, to make any encroachment whatever on the
property of the natives ?

" I would answer that, by telling you to look back to the history

nappe rivers constitute the strongest hold in the whole
of the frontier line from the Orange River down to the
sea, and therefore allowing a people which was often
called "an enemy" to gain a footing there, so as to
break entirely in on the best line of the frontier defence
we could find, if ever we should attempt to make an
effective one, was impolitic.

Every word of this is important towards Macomo's
rights. Captain Stockenstrom tells us that "the colonial office ordered that the Caffres should stay in the
neutral territory, as long as they behaved quietly," *i.e.*
did not harass or go to war with the colony : that he
was "extremely sorry" on receiving this order, for he
would fain have driven out Macomo even then : that
the Kat River territory was important for a frontier
defence in a military point of view : that to give it up
was impolitic.

Here then is clearly proved an *animus* even so far
back as 1822 to seize this territory : and this being
proved, we may be sure that such longings would sooner
or later be satisfied.

Captain Stockenstrom proceeds : "I went to the
frontier in 1828, with a view of inquiring into some
points connected with the frontier; I met Lieut.-
colonel Somerset, who was then the commandant on
the Gonappe post, where a great assemblage of
farmers had come to complain of the constant depredations of the Caffres, (they wanted another com-

of the world ; *where have you found that when people have power they
have not used that power ?*" (Ab. 136.)

Here the gallant Major and ex-landdrost speaks, indeed, to the
point ; he discloses the penetralia of the colonial temple of justice,
which other witnesses have endeavoured to shroud with the veil
of cant and hypocrisy.

mando to seize the cattle of the Caffres) but Colonel
Somerset said, " that of late, MACOMO AND HIS PEOPLE
HAD BEEN VERY QUIET, AND THAT HE HAD RECEIVED
GREAT ASSISTANCE FROM HIM IN PREVENTING DEPRE-
DATIONS. I myself had a conversation with Macomo,
and received his solemn assurance that he would continue to behave as Colonel Somerset said he had lately
done, and I warned him of the consequence of his
doing otherwise." This is a full exculpation of any
charge of depredations against Macomo. It informs
us that this commandant Somerset, a very sharp and
severe neighbour to the Caffre chief, (as Macomo
knew to his cost,) who had been closely watching him
for some time, freely acknowledged not only that
Macomo and his people had been very quiet of late,
but that they rendered material assistance in preventing depredations. After such testimony as this, all
accusation of " stealing cattle," is a manifest falsehood and calumny: Macomo is exculpated by his
bitterest enemies, his innocence is proved by his opponents and oppressors.

. Captain Stockenstrom now gives *his* version of the
expulsion.

" A few months afterwards, Macomo, with his
Caffres, had made an attack upon the Tambooki
kraals, then living peaceably on the borders of the
Tamba district: he had deprived them of their cattle,
and murdered a great number of them, and even those
that fled in the colony were pursued and massacred in
the very midst of *our* population.....A difference of
opinion existed between the civil commissioner, Captain Campbell and the commandant of the frontier,
who represented that Macomo had acted as an aux-
iliary to some Tambooki chief, and at the request of
that chief; but the government *concluded* that there

was no foundation for that excuse of Macomo. *The government then consulted me*, (poor Macomo!) and I gave it as my opinion that the Caffres being there entirely conditionally, that they having repeatedly broken their engagements, *that they being in possession of a position very injurious to our frontier*, if we should have any disturbance with Caffreland, THEY SHOULD BE REMOVED. The goverament determined upon clearing that part of the country of the Caffres altogether, and I was sent up to co-operate with the civil commissioner and the commandant in carrying this into effect."*

This affair of the Tambookies, was indeed a windfall to the colonial government, though it is not to be doubted that without it they would have ousted Macomo: but it is observable that when they were debating the propriety of laying hold of this plea of violence on their ally, misgivings did arise in the minds of some, and that even Colonel Somerset defended Macomo on the true and just grounds; his defence was however overruled, and Captain Stockenstrom, who, as far back as the year 1822, had been "extremely sorry" to find the Caffres on the Kat River, now had the satisfaction of driving out Macomo at the point of the bayonet. The proper boundary in a military point of view was secured, "military men" were set at ease, and the colony was safe!!! Captain Stockenstrom never seemed, at that time, to have heard or known that justice is a stronger wall for a frontier than mountains and valleys gained by rapine, and that national integrity is worth a thousand cannons, and a hundred thousand soldiers.†

* Ab. 82.

† It gives me real pain to be compelled, in the impartial progress of history, thus to unveil the aberrations of mind, of one who,

It is not however to be supposed that the committee of the House of Commons, would let this excuse of the Tambookie war pass without examination; their questions and Captain Stockenstrom's answers must not be omitted.

" Were the Tambookies under our protection ?"

" They were living on our border, and had been living peaceably, and the government was always in the habit of threatening any tribe that disturbed them."

" Did the government consider themselves bound to afford them protection ?"

" Yes; because whenever they were plundered, and their cattle taken away, they had no alternative but to rush into the colony and plunder us."

" It appears then it was not a matter of treaty but a matter of expediency which induced us to afford them protection ?"

" CERTAINLY THERE WAS NO TREATY WHATEVER."

" Were the Caffres aware that when they plundered or murdered, or ill-treated the Tambookies, they would give us offence ?"

" They were aware they would give us offence by plundering the Tambookies, and they must have been

---

notwithstanding the affair of Macomo's expulsion, is now, at least, the friend of the oppressed; who, in his private life, has exhibited some bright instances of humanity, and who is looked up to by the few philanthropists in the colony as their chief hope and support. We need only peruse Captain Stockenstrom's evidence to see how impossible it is for an upright mind to support a bad cause with any effort of reasoning; and after the perusal, we may safely come to the conclusion, that military habits of acting and thinking are not only inconsistent with the development of justice, but can so confuse the understanding as to make the noblest dispositions assent to the propositions of tyranny, as if they were wise and virtuous maxims.

aware that we would not allow them to pursue them
into the colony. *I have no other clue to suppose that
they would have thought we should take the side of
the Tambookies.*" (Ab. 81, 82.)

We then are to gather that though there was no
treaty between the colony and the Tambookies, yet
that from our abstract love of peace and inherent
tendency to humanity, we should be sure to punish
the Caffres, an independent nation, for fighting
another nation with whom we had no connection in
any way!

But hear now the true statement of this affair: I
give it in Dr. Philip's words, as fully entering into all
the points of this question. "The Caffres and Tambookies were independent of the colonial government,
and we had no right to interfere in their quarrels,—
could we have established such a right, the impolicy
was obvious enough, as it would keep the colony constantly involved in all the petty quarrels of the frontier tribes. The defence of our conduct on the ground
that Chiala was our ally, is untenable, as Bowana
whom Chiala had robbed, was also our ally; and if it
was our duty to protect one ally against another, we
should have punished Chiala for his attack on
Bowana, and that would have prevented the necessity of Macomo's interference. The favourable
character given of Chiala, by the accusers of Macomo,
is not supported by facts. Many respectable individuals, who well knew his conduct and character, give
a very different testimony. Chiala laid wait for
Bowana, met him in a sequestered place looking after
his cattle, and murdered him in cold blood. Chiala

* Ab. 81—12.

never held the rank of a chief among the Tambookies.
He was a heemrad or counsellor of Bowana, and consequently a subject of that chief, and it was to support
his authority that Bowana called on Macomo to assist
him against a subject who had cast off his authority,
and who had placed himself at the head of a band of
plunderers, which it was the duty of the colonial government to have assisted in suppressing.   Macomo
therefore was punished in reality not for attacking our
allies the Tambookies, (though no such alliance existed)
but for supporting their rightful authority against a
rebel.   Had the colonial government been sincere in
its reasons assigned for punishing Macomo, it ought to
have inquired into the conduct of Chiala, and have
punished him for his treacherous murder of Bowana—
but no inquiry was instituted, and no notice taken of
the affair.   Macomo did *not* pursue Chiala's people
into the colony; *they fled into the neutral territory,*
and if there were any of the Boors there to be annoyed
by this incursion they ought not to have been there,
as it had been declared by the heads of the colonial
government, that Gaika consented to the neutrality of
the territory on the condition that it should never be
given to the Boors, and that they should not be suffered to inhabit it.   Macomo was the son of Gaika,
the Kat River was the territory of Gaika; Macomo
was selected for that very place, because his father
and sovereign could depend upon him as the most
efficient person he could select to prevent depredations
on the colony.   Macomo attacked Chiala by the desire of his father and sovereign Gaika, to support his
own father-in-law Bowana, against Chiala, who had
injustly attacked him, and robbed him, Bowana, his
sovereign, of his cattle, and who shortly afterwards

justified all that had been said and done against him
by Macomo, by the perfidious murder of Bowana."[*]

It is perhaps unnecessary to notice the hypocritical
excuse proffered by the colonial party, that the taking
away of cattle from the Tambookies by Macomo,
would drive them to the alternative of plundering the
colony,—indeed it is almost incredible that Captain
Stockenstrom should have ventured to urge such an
absurdity; for if that were a reason for punishing
Macomo, did we not when we plundered him, and
drove him out of house and home, reduce him to this
very " alternative?" and was not our crime to him on
a larger scale, the crime of which he had been guilty
towards our dear allies and friends the Tambookies?
But enough has been said on the subject, to prove,
with superabundance of proof, the wretched shifts and
disgraceful excuses to which injustice reduces its advocates.

It only remains for us now to see the contradictory
statements of some other colonial partisans. Colonel
Wade, in a dispatch to Secretary Stanley, says, " You
are doubtless aware that the infant colony of the native
Hottentots, at the head of what is denominated *the
neutral territory*, was planted there in 1829—an experiment by his Excellency Sir Lowry Cole. The country in which these locations are placed is that from
which the Caffrarian chief Macomo was expelled in
1829, where he had been permitted by the colonial
government to reside, on sufferance, for some years;
an indulgence which he forfeited *in consequence
of the ruinous system of depredation* pursued by
himself and followed towards the colonists. [†] The

* Ab. 631.   † P. P. ii. 71.

date of this slander is January 1834. Colonel Wade
was at that time acting governor of the colony, with a
perfect knowledge of all the circumstances of the case,
having all the government documents and correspondence relating to Macomo's expulsion in his possession,
and yet he does not say one word about this frivolous
story of the Tambookies, but takes an entirely new
tack, by charging Macomo with "a ruinous system of
depredations," a charge which has already been proved
by the most solid evidence to be false and scandalous.
Sir Galbraith Lowry Cole, the governor who authorized
Macomo's expulsion, thus gives his *official* account of
the proceeding, one month after the expulsion had taken
place.   It is extracted from his dispatch to Sir G. Murray, dated June 1829... " Macomo, the eldest son of
Gaika, the Caffre chief, who now occupies the more
northern part of the territory of that people, and whose
talents, activity, daring character, *and depredations*,
have long rendered him particularly obnoxious to the
inhabitants of the frontier, in January last entered the
country of the Tambookies with a body of four hundred
men, and without any appearance of provocation or
previous notice of his intention given, commenced
hostilities.   The Tambookies overpowered, fled into
the colony, (*i.e.* neutral territory), for protection,
and at the distance of twenty miles from the boundary were overtaken by Macomo, when the whole
of the cattle, amounting to 300 head, were seized,
and several of their people murdered.   As it became a
matter of *necessary justice* to inflict punishment for this
wanton act of aggression and daring violation of
colony, (*i. e.* neutral territory), I ordered Macomo,
who had been allowed by Lord Charles Somerset to
occupy on his good behaviour, to *return* with the whole

of his people into his own country, giving him, however, two months to make his arrangements for so doing, and to collect his crops of corn ; and calling upon
him also for the restitution of the Tambookie cattle
within that period ; but as at the appointed time Macomo *shewed no disposition either to leave the country*
or to give up the cattle, *I have been obliged* to direct
the commandant on the frontier to expel him, and to
make reprisals to the extent of the *robbery* committed
by him."*

Sir G. L. Cole puts in as many pleas as he can. 1.
Macomo's " talents" had made him peculiarly obnoxious to the colony. How could Macomo help that ?
If he had " talents," and if his neighbours the Boors,
and the officials of the colonial government were not so
gifted, was he to blame for that ? 2. His " depredations" have been already disproved. 3. The Tambookie
affair, in all its statements, is garbled, irrelevant, and
frivolous. 4. Macomo was ordered " to return to his
own country." Return !—was he not bred and born
in that country ? Was not the territory his ? Had he
not inherited it from his great-grandfather Kahabi ?
How can the driving a prince out of his own dominions
be termed " desiring him to return to it ?" Supposing
Sir Galbraith Lowrie Cole were to be driven at the point
of the bayonet out of England into Scotland, out of
Scotland into Ireland, and out of Ireland into France,
would he not object to this being described as desiring
him to " return to his own country ?"

* P. P. ii. 43.

CHAPTER XIV.

Macomo's expulsion from the Kat River.

HAVING thus, not perhaps without some prolixity, fully examined the pretences for Maçomo's expulsion, we must now turn our eyes to the expulsion itself, for it is indeed a sad story.

W. Gisborne, Esq., a gentleman who was travelling in the colony at the time, thus narrates the story:— " Macomo's country ·was taken by actual violence against his will. I do not know the extent of it, but it must be many miles each way. I accompanied one of the military parties as a friend of the officers, when they were sent into it. I think the military was divided into three or four parties, who were in it for two days, going about the country and destroying the villages: and the country was so extensive that our party had no communication with any other. The other parties were sufficiently far from us not to be aware they were in the country, *except by seeing the smoke of the villages burning;* and it was only on the evening of the second day we joined them again, so that the country must have been many miles each way in extent. It was very good pasture-land at the time it was taken. It was said to be the best land in that part of the country. It was spoken of at the time as being a *very great acquisition, and the best situation for the colonists.* The

party of military I accompanied went into the country;
they met with no opposition; they found a number of
people, who immediately fled into the woods. They
captured all the cattle they saw feeding, and burnt
every village and every house which came within their
range. We had no communication with any Caffres at
the time, except with one man, who had got on the
other side of a rocky ravine while a village was burning. He called out to us in the Caffre language,
which was explained to us by an interpreter, and asked
us why we were burning his house; and it seemed difficult to make a reply;—*there was a general silence
throughout the party.*"

An army of marauders struck dumb by conscience!

" I saw," continues Mr. Gisborne, " one very distressing case, in which a hut had been burnt; the hut must
have contained a poor idiot Caffre woman, who was
also blind, and she was crawling about when we came
up, not knowing how to escape, and was burning her-
self. She was removed by the soldiers, who left a hut
standing for her, and some of the Hottentot soldiers gave
her their rations for food out of compassion." Ab. 335.

In the midst of this scene of violence Macomo did,
however, find a friend. Mr. Ross, the missionary, who
was then resident in the *chief's country, wrote an indignant letter to Colonel Somerset, setting forth the
wickedness of thus driving out the chief and his people
from their lands and habitations. It was a letter such
as is rarely addressed to persons in authority in that
realm of despotism, and it led to an angry interview
with Sir Lowrie Cole, who, in mingled wrath and fear,
accused Mr. Ross of intending to excite a commotion
by publishing the letter he had written. In spite of
the anger of the governor, Mr. Ross, nothing daunted

with the frowns and threats of authority, wrote a second letter on the same subject, and in a style equally unpalatable to those who are accustomed to see their arbitrary commands implicitly obeyed. There is little doubt that this unexpected resistance compelled the ejectors to pause in their proceedings, not indeed so as to make them undo their act of spoliation, but to change the destination of the territory they had thus unlawfully seized. The Kat River valley had doubtless been intended as a present to those insatiate robbers the Boors: but now it became expedient to mitigate the bitterness of injustice with some infusion of the sweets of philanthropy, and therefore, about three months afterwards, it was determined to make the Kat River valley a settlement for the Hottentots, and thus to stop the mouth of watchful Cerberus with some sop of humanity.

"The tender mercies of the wicked are cruel." The colony never did yet but one kind act to the aborigines, and that act is based on robbery and outrage; so that the Kat River settlement, which is a happy place of refuge to the Hottentots, is in fact a possession of most vicious title, the lawful property of another person, to whom in equity it ought to be restored. But if the difficulties should be great in effecting such a restitution, the colony should be made to bear all the burthen, however heavy, of furnishing another settlement, so ample and fertile, and in every other respect so endowed with all requisites of habitations, wood, and water, as should leave no room for complaint to the Hottentots in making the exchange.

And here, then, we pause, and in amazement and incredulity demand—Is it possible that such things should be done in these our days by the British nation? and truly we could not believe it if the whole of this cruel narrative did not rest upon evidence such as can rarely be produced in history,—the evidence of all the principal perpetrators and eye-witnesses of the mischief, the chief dramatis personæ in this deep tragedy. It is not, however, to be expected that Macomo's sufferings are to end here ; we shall find them increasing up to the year 1835 ; nor have we reason to expect, that as long as he lives he will be allowed to enjoy repose by his implacable enemies and tormentors.

And who is this man that has been so ill-treated—upon whose head these unmitigated tribulations have been thus accumulated, as if the colonial government were endeavouring to show to the admiring world the furthest point to which injustice can be carried ? We will answer this question by very copious evidence:—" Macomo was a favourite of mine," says Colonel Cox to the Committee of the House of Commons. " I confess I thought a good deal could be done with him, and I thought in some instances he had been *rather harshly treated.* I had a more favourable opinion of Macomo than of any other chief. I commanded at Fort Beaufort for seven years; I had frequent interviews with Macomo ; I thought a great deal might be done with him ; I do not attribute any duplicity to him. He has more intelligence than the other Caffre chiefs, and more might be done with him than the others. He has reason to complain ; he has been removed two or three times from his territory. I should *most certainly* have felt justified in reposing confidence in any engagement into which Macomo might have entered, as far as his personal influence went. *

" I believe," says Mr. James Read, " I believe that

* Ab. 348.

Macomo had a sincere desire to *sit down*, as he called it, and to promote the civilization and improvement of his people. I do not derive this confidence in Macomo from my own personal observation alone, but every missionary that I have met with, that had any knowledge of Macomo, spoke in the highest terms of him. The Rev. Mr. Ross resided with him three years at Balfour, and he said he found him always correct in all his proceedings, and I have not met with a military officer that has come in contact with Macomo yet, who has not given him a good character." Mr. James Read says, " I think he is a most intelligent man, an acute man, a man who tried every thing in his power to discourage thefts, a man who, if he could but *sit quiet*, as he once termed it, *would attend to the Word of God*. We have never had any cattle traced to his country; all the military officers have praised him. I heard Major Birnie say at Beaufort, on my way to Graham's Town, that if Macomo had been treated by every officer, as he had been treated by himself, Macomo might have been made much of, and this war would never have happened."*

Dr. Philip says, " My own opinion of Macomo is, that he has been faithful to the colony, and that the colonial government will not be able to find among all the Caffres a chief more deserving of its confidence, or one whose influence may be increased with more safety and advantage to the colony."†

These are published opinions, which any one may may refer to as authentic ; but on the authority of persons who have been long acquainted with this persecuted Prince, I am enabled to state, that his character,

* Ab. 494.   † Ab. 691.

considering all the circumstances of his birth, nurture, and life, is not only worthy of esteem, but of admiration; for when we remember that he is uneducated, that he is the son of a barbarian king, whose character could inspire little moral respect, that he has not been accustomed to the amenities and politeness of civilized society, has been a stranger to the restraint imposed on the passions by the acknowledged laws of morality and religion—has lived a commander of submissive vassals, amongst whom his natural abilities have given him an unusual and therefore a perilous ascendancy—has been accustomed from infancy to hear of wars and rumours of wars, and to see the majesty of force more respected than the comeliness of justice; and yet when we find such a one who has had to contend with these manifest disadvantages, behaving in all the relations of life with honour and integrity, and in spite of the most maddening oppressions, avoiding the crimes of despair without forfeiting the independence of a patriot, and still commanding, in all his troubles, the sympathies and affections of impartial friends and spectators—this is a character worthy of esteem ; and such a man is Macomo, whose name ought not to be mentioned without honour in the melancholy history of oppressed nations. It is true he has his calumniators, for calumny is indefatigably at work in the colony; and where so much violence has been going on for a long series of years, it is natural that many must have an interest in propagating falsehoods, in order to give some colour to their own evil deeds, but the facts of this narrative will be sufficient to establish the truth, and to shew the systematic aggression which has been continually in progress from the year 1812 to 1835, and which latterly has been directed against Macomo as the

principal buttress of the Caffre nation. It is established
that Captain Stockenstrom had,* for a long time before
the expulsion of Macomo, earnestly desired to drive
away the Caffre clan from the Kat River, under the
idea that the possession of that territory would add to
the strength of the colony, and complete its military

---

* Colonel Wade has, in his evidence, given much prominence
to the following letter of Captain Stockenstrom, dated November,
1833 :—

"As I informed you in my letter of the 7th instant, I proceeded to the frontier and left Lieut. Pettingall at Fort Beaufort.
We mutually explained to each other what we considered the
boundary, from the Winterberg to the Chumie, and it appears, by
some misunderstanding, the upper part of the Kat river and Gonap
has been hitherto considered as out of the colony by the military
frontier. The Cape Gazette, of October, 1819, clearly points out
what *was agreed upon* as the boundary between the colony and the
Caffres in the treaty of 1819, upon which I have always acted, not
being aware of any subsequent alteration.

"In your letter of August 28, last, his Excellency desires my
opinion as to the expediency of maintaining the boundary, established by said treaty. I humbly beg leave to state, that I think
the former, unquestionably, *the best and most natural.* If the
Caffres remain on the higher branch of the Kat river and Gonap,
where they are now in great force, they will always be extremely
dangerous to the Bavians river and Tarka division. I think also,
upon minute examination of the map and the features of the
country, his Excellency will perceive, that if any part of the Kat
and Gonap rivers be included in the colony, the whole of the
branches, up to their sources, should be embraced also, as the
ridge of high land, running from the Winterberg and the said
sources, and those of the Black Kyr and Chumie, is EVIDENTLY
INTENDED BY NATURE as a barrier between the country
watered by the several streams.—A. STOCKENSTROM."

Poor Nature! she never dreamed that the heavings of her
bosom were to be thus interpreted into oppression against her
children.

unity; that Colonel Henry Somerset, the commandant
of the frontier near that part of the country, who had
for some time been watching Macomo, declared he was
guiltless of committing depredations on the colony;
and that the neighbouring Boors, men who generally
loudly complain of the thefts of the Caffres, in order to
enrich themselves by commandos, did, in this instance,
exculpate Macomo, and even lament his removal.

These are facts which must stop the mouths of all
calumniators, and these are facts that cannot be denied.

Having therefore advanced thus far in this melancholy
story, we must pause to remember that all the wrongs
of the Caffre nation, as far as we have traced them, have
proceeded directly from the fraudulent and pretended
treaty made with Macomo's father by Lord Charles
Somerset in 1817, and afterwards improved in 1819, by
the more ingenious commentary and paraphrase of Sir
Galbraith Lowrie Cole—a verbal treaty, which was illegal
according to Caffre law, even if the purport of it had
been fully understood and freely admitted by the chief
selected to act the part of the colonial puppet on that
memorable occasion. Capt. Stockenstrom and Col.
Wade are each deeply interested in this treaty; Captain
Stockenstrom as an eye-witness, interpreter, and advocate of the transaction; Colonel Wade as having pushed
the consequences of that treaty to extremities, as we
shall presently see; now it so happens that both these
gentlemen have, in their evidence before the House of
Commons, inadvertently admitted the illegality of the
treaty; and it is important to draw the attention of the
reader to this curious fact.

Qu. " Our Government had constituted Gaika the
supreme authority of Caffreland, but the committee

wish to know whether he had derived supreme authority by any other means than by that construction which was put upon his authority by Lord C. Somerset?"

"Allow me to observe," replies Captain Stockenstrom, "*that the impression at that time* on the minds of most people was, that he had the power. The various relations between the Caffre chiefs, and the constitution of the Caffre nation altogether, has been principally elucidated since then, by the circumstance of educated men, such as missionaries and others travelling into Caffreland. At that time, it must be understood, there had been very little intercourse with Caffreland, except through the medium of unlettered peasants, and some functionaries who had merely travelled through the country, *and had not had the time or the means to inquire into the constitution of the nation, and the various relations existing between the different tribes;* so that the impression *at that time* certainly was, that Gaika had the right to do so, because I only knew of two parties of Caffres in direct contact with us, those of Gaika and Slambi."

Qu. "Whatever your impression was at that time, is it your impression at this moment that Gaika was not in such a degree the sovereign of that district as to be empowered to surrender it, save and except by the authority conferred upon him by the British Government?"

"No, CERTAINLY, HE WAS NOT THE CHIEF OF THE TRIBES.*"

This is as full and explicit as could be desired; but what might not Macomo have to say, if he heard his chief enemies make this confession? Might he not ask

* Ab. p. 47.

them, "Why did you not take the trouble to make yourself acquainted with the constitution and laws of our nation? Why trust to the ignorant and idle reports of *unlettered peasants, and some functionaries who had not had the time or the means* to make the proper inquiries? Why by terror or by trickery wrest a verbal treaty from my father, which treaty he had no power to make? If you were honourable men, as *we* could neither read nor write, and this was a matter of immense importance to us, even the loss of two-thirds of my father's territories, and the ruin of his family and of many powerful chiefs, should you not have taken extraordinary pains to act with all the precautions of justice, so that we might not have to say of you that you are *swindlers?* But instead of this you have taken every advantage that force or cunning, and your various superiorities of a civilized nation could give you over an unlettered and ignorant people, and beginning by dark manœuvres, have consummated your iniquity with violence and bare-faced spoliation. This land from which you have driven me is mine, it is mine by every possible right that can be imagined; your treaties of 1817, and 1819, are impudent forgeries, and tricks of knavery; and you are compelled yourselves now to acknowledge that my father had not the power to treat with you, but yet you act as if I had broken a treaty which by your own shewing is null and void."

Colonel Wade has confirmed Captain Stockenstrom's confession. "It must be here remarked that Gaika was, *however erroneously, at this period believed* to possess the supreme authority in Caffreland."[*]

We therefore see that the principal witnesses gave up their case.

* Ab. 279.

H

CHAPTER XV.

The Murder of the Chief Seko.

THE chronological arrangement of this narrative will now require our attention to the murder of Seko, and it may be taken as an interlude to Macomo's tragedy. Seko was a high chief, a prince of the royal blood of Caffreland, brother to Slambi and Jalusha, the uncle of Gaika, and great-uncle of Macomo. In June, 1830, he was murdered by a commando, and under circumstances which make the transaction peculiarly revolting. It appears that field-cornet Erasmus, was despatched with a party of armed Boors, to search for colonial cattle, in the kraals and hamlets belonging to Seko. They did not find what they wanted[*], but a commando never yet returned into the colony empty-handed, and they, therefore, took all the cattle within their reach. Seko entreated that the milch cows, at least, might be left, to save the females and children from starvation; and this pathetic entreaty was, after some demur, granted. Erasmus allowed him to retain the milch cows, and also permitted him to accompany the commando to Fort Wiltshire, that he might repre-

* Pringle, 325.

sent the hardship of his case to the commandant.
Seven Caffres were to accompany Seko, but they were
not to carry their assegais, and were to assist in driving
the captured cattle.

The party had not proceeded far, when some Caffres,
the proprietors of the cattle seized by the commando,
made their appearance. They saw their little property,
the hopes of their families, removed to enrich their
tormentors, and they could not be expected to behold
such a spectacle unmoved. They followed the retiring
herd to a woody ravine, and there one of these Caffres
gave a peculiar whistle, on hearing which the cattle are
trained to wheel round and set off at full speed. This
backward movement of the cattle caused by this signal,
brought the whole herd upon the armed Boors, and upon
Seko and his attendants. Immediately the word was
given to fire, and Seko, with six of his men, were shot
dead upon the spot. The poor chief, who was an old
man, feeling himself mortally wounded, was seen to
weep bitterly.* He said, in dying, " This is no joke,"
meaning in Caffre idiom, that it was a serious business;
that it was fatal. He crept into the nearest bush and
died. Six of his attendants were killed, and the seventh
though severely wounded, afterwards recovered.† The
Boors, therefore, destroyed all but one of the unarmed
Caffres, who had set out with them, who were peaceably
driving the cattle, and who were evidently under their
protection. If any one was to blame it was that Caffre,
who had, by whistling, disturbed the quiet march of the
party; but it is remarkable, that though they caught
that man, they only beat him and then let him go.
Their vengeance, therefore, was directed, in a peculiar

* Ab. 322.   † Ab. 321.

manner, against the innocent and the unarmed. Seko's
nephews, Macomo and Tyalie, declare that Seko was
not only shot, but pursued into a bush, into which
he had retreated when he heard the firing, and there
was put to death : and this is confirmed by the testimony of Peffer, one of the commando, who said in
his deposition :—" Cannot tell why these Caffres were
shot; saw Seko shot, *at least, saw him run into the
bush;* heard a shot in that direction, and immediately
saw Jan Gryling come from thence, who said, ' I have
shot the chief.' "*

The effect of this murder, of course, was to increase
the exasperation of the Caffre nation; they could not,
however, be surprised at it, for if the murder of Macomo's envoys had passed unpunished in the colony, it
was evident that any crime might be expected from the
colonists, as a matter of course.

Macomo and Tyalie had an interview with Captain
Stockenstrom, about six weeks afterwards, and expos-
tulated with him on this bloody affair.

Captain Stockenstrom was at that time commissioner-
general of the eastern division of the colony, to which
office he had been appointed in 1828. The commando
therefore, went to Seko's kraals, with his permission ;
but it is pleasing to be able to state, that we have now
reached a period of Caffre history, when this gentleman
appears the friend and protector of the oppressed. In
the affair of the treaties with Gaika, and Macomo's
expulsion, we have seen, by his own evidence, what his
views were; but henceforward we shall find that he
steadily resists the commando system, to the utmost of
his power, and heartily endeavours to check the plun-

* Ab. 322.

derings and cruelty of the colonists. Before this commando set out he gave his orders in writing, and these orders were evidently restrictive of the usual lawless power of such expeditions. These were his orders :—

"Provisional Field Commandant.—As it will be permitted to every one on this commando, to turn out such cattle as are among the Caffres, and *which he can swear to as having been stolen from the colony*, I have to order you to make known to all under your direction, that in case of doubt, *the oath will actually be imposed*, and that, consequently, those who appropriate to themselves Caffre cattle, *expose themselves to be prosecuted, as well for perjury as theft.*—Kat River, 15th June, 1830."

When Erasmus returned into the colony with his booty, he told the commissioner Stockenstrom that the Caffres had resisted the capture of the cattle ; that he had had "a severe fight" with the Caffres, and that he, in self-defence, was obliged to order the Boors to fire.[*] So strongly did he represent the affair in this light, that both Stockenstrom and Somerset thought he had done right in firing in self-defence ; and the commissioner so reported to the colonial government. Not long after this, however, he received information that Erasmus had disguised the truth, and that the case in reality was very different. In consequence of this information the commissioner went into Caffreland for the express purpose of collecting the testimony of eye-witnesses, both of the Caffres and the Hottentots who had accompanied the commando, and he soon discovered that the pretended "self-defence" was in reality something much more serious. The result of

[*] Ab. 85.

his inquiry he sent to the colonial government, having
first taken the deposition of some important witnesses;
but the colonial government took no notice of his communication, returned no answer to his letters, took no
steps to investigate the affair, and allowed Erasmus to
hold his situation of field-commandant. * This contu-
melious silence was partly to show the aversion of the
Cape Town cabinet to Captain Stockenstrom's new
office and his liberal views, and partly to shield Erasmus, who was a true disciple of the Somerset school.

Some time after the murder of Seko, a traveller of
the name of Bruce, of the East India Service, sent a
statement of the murder to one of the Cape newspapers. This caused a great sensation, and the inhabitants of the frontier petitioned the governor that an
investigation might be ordered; but this was refused. †
The door was shut at that time against all inquiry.
Five or six years afterwards, however, the door was
opened to examination by the zeal of Col. Wade, who
takes the dark stories of the colony under his generous
protection. This gallant officer having read Captain
Stockenstrom's evidence before the Committee of the
House of Commons, which was delivered 19th August,
1835, wrote to the Cape, begging them to send coun-
ter statements. "I have received," says he, "some
letters in reply to communications I sent to the Cape
of Good Hope, transmitting copies of the evidence
taken during last session." ‡ These communications
are statements upon oath of some of the individuals'
who served in the commando, Hans Jurgen Lambaard,
David Petrus de Lange, Boesak, Tamboer a Hottentot,
and others, and dated January 1836, nearly six years

* Ab. pp. 85, 86.   † Ab. 323.   ‡ Ab. 299.

MURDER OF SIKO. 151

after the transaction; though all investigation was at the time refused by the colonial government.

These statements endeavour to make the best of the affair, and to show that no one knows who gave the command to fire, that it was all confusion and uncertainty, that Erasmus immediately got the people together, and " inquired who had been firing, and for what purpose;" that Caffres were hovering about with assegais, and that there was " so much noise and dust that no one could see what was going on."

Colonel Wade gave in these "communications" March 25, 1836. It however fortunately happened that Captain Stockenstrom was still in England, and had heard of Col. Wade's documents, and their reception by the Committee of the House of Commons. He was on the eve of sailing for the Cape, and had engaged his passage, but still there was time to present his documents to the Committee, and this he did on the 18th of April, 1836. Nothing could be more opportune, for Captain Stockenstrom had by him the depositions of some of these very witnesses, taken July 1831, and it is curious to contrast the evidence of the Hottentot Boezak of 1831, with the evidence of Boezak in 1836. Boezak was servant of Erasmus. The evidence collected by the commissioner in 1831 is precisely that which has already been stated in this chapter.

There are indeed many points in the documents produced by Colonel Wade, bearing evident marks of positive falsehood. It will be sufficient here to notice one specimen. The most glaring and manifest untruth is the assertion of some of Colonel Wade's witnesses, [*] that the commando received instructions from the com-

* Ab. 303.

missioner " to bring away from Seko's kraals all the
"colonial *as well as the Caffre cattle* to Fort Wiltshire."
Captain Stockenstrom's written orders, of which he
fortunately kept a copy, entirely disprove the assertion.

The commissioner's comment on the murder is very
important :—" These unfortunate men were assisting
the Boors in driving the cattle, when they were shot
with nothing but their keires in their hands. There
could be no other inducement for this brutal conduct
*but to have a plea for the confiscation of the Caffre
cattle.*"

Erasmus brought into' the colony 2000 head of
cattle from this expedition, and under the plea of the
" hard fight" with the Caffres, the whole herd was
confiscated, and divided amongst the rapacious Boors.
The one fact, that Erasmus invented the fable of the
" hard fight" is quite sufficient to establish the gravest
suspicions.

CHAPTER XVI.

Macomo's Arrest at the Missionary Meeting in 1833.

Macomo, after his expulsion from the Kat River in 1829, retired eastward to the banks of the Chumie and Munkasana, over that ridge of ground which Captain Stockenstrom imagined *nature* had evidently intended as a barrier for the colony. This at any rate was a territory to which the colony could lay no claim by treaty of neutrality or partiality—but Macomo was not allowed to rest long there. It was to be expected that the forcible expulsion of his clan would produce reprisals, indeed it could scarcely be otherwise; so many persons could not be driven forth to starve, and be suddenly deprived of their habitations and cattle, without endeavouring to find means of subsistence either by fair means or by foul. To use Colonel Wade's words, who had no intention when he uttered them to shew the cruelty of the system he pertinaciously advocates:—
" Within six months after Macomo's expulsion, the whole frontier was again overrun with parties of marauders; the Caffres re-occupied the sources of the Kat River, from whence they had been removed; and were again expelled, but not before they had committed numerous excesses—the depredations amounted from

September 1829 to August 1830, to 2,619 oxen, and
134 horses."* This *may* be true, it is not improbable;
and considering that the commando which drove out
Macomo, took from him 5000 head of cattle, the extent of reprisals is extremely moderate; one would
naturally expect, taking all the circumstances of the
case into consideration, to hear that they seized at
least as much as they had lost: *mutatis mutandis*,
that is, placing the colony in Macomo's situation, there
can be little doubt they would have taken ten times as
many, and have been hardly content with that.

That "guilt makes men cowards," is an adage that
may be painfully illustrated by events which took place
on the eastern frontier, shortly after Macomo's expulsion. Colonel Somerset, the military commander of
that district, received various fearful reports in the
month of August, of the gathering of the Caffre clans,
preparatory to an invasion of the colony. Erasmus,
the provisional commandant, had told him that he had
heard from one Hermanns, that the Caffres were talking
"of the chiefs having called upon Gaika, to know why
he did not give orders to the chiefs and their people to
stand up—in other words, to attack the colony." This,
be it observed, was a third hearsay ; from the Caffres
concerning their chiefs to Hermanns, from Hermanns
to Erasmus, from Erasmus to Somerset; but it was
considered good evidence, and seems exceedingly to
have alarmed the Boors, and Colonel Somerset; *their
guilty consciences told them it was probable*, and they
were preparing to act as if it were true. Then one
Wienand Buizewelenhout had told the colonel that he
had "crept to the door of one of the huts of the Caffres,"

* Ab. 283, 284.

in which were assembled Eno's sons, and had over-heard them say, " they would go to war with the colony as soon as possible, that they would occupy the country to Bosjesman's River, and murder the Bastaards and Burgher Hottentots, man, woman, and child." Many other rumours of this sort did Colonel Somerset send off in great trepidation to Cape Town, and all was pre-pared for a grand massacre of Caffres or colonists ; the colonel " most earnestly recommending, that all those Caffres who had hitherto been permitted to reside in the neutral territory, should be forced to quit it imme-diately." All, however, ended in smoke, and Sir G. L. Cole, in his despatch to the Colonial Office, dated 2d September 1829, trusts " the Caffres have abandoned their hostile intentions, *if they really ever entertained any*."*

In other respects, though many of Macomo's people died among the mountains from cold and hunger, in consequence of their barbarous expulsion from the Kat River, it is certain that Macomo exerted himself to the utmost to restrain his clan from acts of vengeance, and that he bore his losses and tribulations with magnani-mity, though the indignation of the Amakosæ was wrought to the highest pitch, when the treatment of the chief and his people became known throughout the various tribes of the nation. In August 1831, Colonel Somerset, wrote a letter to Colonel Wade, at that time military secretary to the governor, complain-ing of the thefts committed by Botman's people, and acknowledging that " Macomo's Caffres had rendered him material assistance" in tracing the murderer of a Hottentot boy, whom he was seeking in Caffreland ;†

* See P. P. ii. 44—50.　　† Ab. 114.

a proof that Macomo was still willing to be on friendly terms with the colony.   In July of that year, Captain Stockenstrom also writes, that Macomo and his brother Tyalie had sent forty horses back into the colony, which they had exerted themselves to find in Caffreland,* and in the same letter remarks, " any difficulty towards a considerable reduction of our military force is attributable altogether to the ferment we keep up among the Caffres, *by depriving them of the means of subsistence.*"

In the year 1833, Colonel Wade was acting Governor of the colony, and whilst he held that office he had the satisfaction of inflicting or countenancing further injuries on Macomo, for it seems to have been a source of satisfaction to him, if we may judge from his own very ample details of his own government.

On the 7th of October of that year, Macomo was invited by Mr. Read to attend a missionary meeting, to be held at Philip Town, on the Kat River, in other words, in the very place from which he himself had four years before been cruelly and ignominiously expelled.   It is no small proof of the placable nature of this prince, that he should be able to command his feelings sufficiently to visit again those scenes which must have reminded him most acutely of his degradation and sufferings; but he determined to come; he knew that he should meet a few friends who sympathised sincerely with him in his afflictions, and he really seems to have taken a lively interest in the objects of the intended meeting.

He first made application to the military officer commanding the nearest frontier port, for permission

* Ab. 110.

to enter into what they called "the colony," that is, his own territory, stating that he wished to go to the Kat River settlement, and attend the missionary meeting. The officer peremptorily refused the permission; but Macomo, either thought there must be some mistake in the order, or was determined to see whether the Regent of Caffreland would be prevented in paying a visit to his friends, when upwards of two hundred English traders were at that time dwelling in Caffreland under his protection, unmolested by himself or any of his subjects; disregarding, therefore, the deficiency of a pass, he made his appearance at the Kat River, on the evening of the 6th, where he slept, probably at Mr. Read's house, and attended the meeting next day. He there made a speech, part of which has been preserved:

"My friends, I am very glad to meet you on an occasion like the present; the word of God has done great things for you; the word of God has brought you to life again. It was only the other day that you were like dogs and oppressed, (he was addressing the Hottentots) it is the word of God that has given you these churches, and these lands you have. There are no Englishmen* at Kat River; they are all in my country with their wives and children, in perfect safety, while *I stand before you a rogue and vagabond, having been obliged to come by stealth.* Ye sons of Gayake Kahohul, I have brought you here to behold what the word of God has wrought, (here he addressed his suite)

---

* His meaning is, that all were Hottentots at the Kat River settlement, no English amongst them—but amongst his people there were many English traders who did not, in vain, trust to the honour and hospitality of his nation; they lived amongst the Caffres and were safe, but he could not come amongst the English without being suspected, and in the guise of a rogue and vagabond.

the Hottentots were but yesterday despised and oppressed, as to-day are we the Caffres.   But see what
the word of God has done for them; they were dead,
they are now alive, they are men once more.   Go and
tell my people what you have seen and heard; I hope
ere long to witness in our own land such scenes as
these.   God is great, who hath said it, and will surely
bring it to pass.   I thank the missionaries for what
they have done for the Caffres, and I hope that they
will listen to the missionaries, and I hope that the missionaries will not get tired by the conduct of some of
our nation.   The time is coming when Caffreland will
be covered with missionaries.   I have done."

These surely are noble and exalted sentiments, noble
as abstaining from any allusion to his own territory
now possessed by the Hottentots, and exalted as re-
joicing in the comparative happiness of the once degraded people whom he was addressing, mingled with
a hope that he and his nation should some day be
thus elevated by the power of the word of God, and
the blessings of Christianity.

After the meeting, the party adjourned to drink tea,
at the infant school near the chapel, and there, whilst
they were sitting together, a patrol came down the
hill, headed by Serjeant Sandys, a favorite of Colonel
Wade, one whom he calls "a loyal man," and addicted
to brandy-drinking.*   The patrol, which was a detachment of mounted riflemen, under the orders of this
drunken "loyalist," came to the door of the infant

---

* The Committee particularly inquired into the fact of the
serjeant's drinking, and it is clearly established by eye witnesses ;
the serjeant afterwards said he was sober ; but the very speech
which Colonel Wade declares he made to Macomo, shews that he
was intoxicated.

school ; Mr. Read went out to see what they wanted, when the serjeant demanded Macomo, whom he had been sent to arrest. Macomo came out, and on inquiring what they wanted with him, the serjeant told him that he was his prisoner. Macomo assented to go with the detachment, but on attempting to step into the school-room again, the serjeant cried out "D— you, if you shall move from that spot," and proceeded instantly to load his firelock, and gave orders to his men to do the same. The patrol now dismounted, unsaddled their horses, and gave them a feed of corn, which they had brought with them.* Macomo was now surrounded by the soldiers on foot, and positively forbidden to move from the spot on pain of being PINIONED ! The indignation and disgust of the chief may be more easily imagined than described, thus standing amongst the soldiers; whilst the drunken serjeant offered him some brandy to drink, told him "not to be afraid," and said they were "old friends." In this situation they kept Macomo nearly an hour, the gaze of the multitude, and the sport of the soldiers. When the brutal serjeant offered his canteen of brandy to the chief, he proudly rejected it, and said, "This is not the first time you have insulted me in this way, but it is the first time you have insulted me in the presence of people who could bear evidence to the insult."

When they were going off, Macomo said, "I cannot go with this man ; this man will shoot me in the way : one of you missionaries had better accompany me, and see what is done to me, *for this man will shoot*

---

* See Mr. Barker, the missionary's, account of the arrest, who was an eye-witness, (Ab. 419.), and Mr. James Read's, who was also an eye-witness, (p. 593.)

me, and then say I wanted to escape, and therefore
some of you had better go with me to the post."

This was a very seasonable and prudent request, for
Macomo doubtless did not forget the murder of his
uncle Seko, or of his own envoys; and it is impossible
to say what might not have happened, if Mr. Read
had not accompanied the party to the next post,
which was eighteen miles distant. According to
Colonel Wade's account, Macomo was detained only
a quarter of an hour at the military post, and dismissed with a reprimand. Mr. Read returned home
next day.

Colonel Wade has given a very long account of this
transaction, which will be found in the Parliamentary
Evidence; but surely for his own credit, he had better
have been silent, for if there be any right feeling left
in the human heart, great indeed must be the disgust
on reading his truly odious comments on Macomo's
arrest. He contends for the sobriety, respectability,
and " loyalty" of his serjeant, but acknowledges that
he offered the brandy bottle to Macomo, and in these
indelible words, does he state the fact. " Serjeant
Sandys accosted him good-humouredly, and being by
experience well acquainted with *his propensities,* said,
' Come, Macomo, it is no use to be *cross;* here, take a
little wine, and let us ride friendly, you and I are old
acquaintance. — HOWEVER, MACOMO CHOSE TO BE
SULKY."*

* Ab. 420. Colonel Wade tells us a strange story, which, on
any other authority than his own, could not be credited. He says,
that in October, 1834, he went to the banks of the Chumie, where
he saw the Caffre kraals and villages all burning by Colonel Somerset's orders; that he had an interview with Macomo, who

I pass over all that Colonel Wade has said of Mr. Read's conduct in this transaction, his pitiful insinuations, and his spiteful inuendos;—one sentence only will be sufficient from his narrative, to show the spirit in which it is written throughout.

" A person of undoubted veracity, who attended the meeting, on discovering under what circumstances Macomo was there, pointed out the impropriety of the measure to Mr. Read, and left the place immediately on their coming out of chapel, as he so very much disapproved *of making religion a cloak for inducing this savage* to disobey laws and regulations intended for the benefit of the community."*

We need not comment on this sentence; it is peculiarly Colonel Wade's; but it is important here to note that this " person of undoubted veracity," is the Rev. Mr. Thompson, a clergyman, who had been an agent to the colonial government, as a spy upon Gaika, and was appointed minister to the Kat River settlement, and pensioned by the colonial government. This gen-

---

talked to him about his wrongs, and that he and Colonel Somerset afterwards requested Macomo to shew them a sham fight of his warriors. Macomo *obeyed*, for it could only be called obedience under such circumstances; but Colonel Wade, with his customary coarseness, says, " Macomo was out of humour and conversed but little; he was still in a SULKY STATE, and talked but little."—Ab. p. 315.

That Colonel Somerset should have requested the pastime of a sham fight, whilst the Caffre villages were burning all over the country, is almost inconceivable; it surely only could have been to shew how far they could add insult to injury. This story is mentioned here as offering a parallel passage of Colonel Wade's peculiar sentiments and language.

* Ab. 421.

tleman's name will appear again in the narrative, and it will be evident that he is such a clergyman as Colonel Wade is likely to commend, though it is not to be supposed that the sentiment about "the savage," was ever uttered by him; it is Colonel Wade's Ghemara on the Rev. Mr. Thompson's Mischna.

CHAPTER XVII.

Macomo's Second Expulsion.

WE are now approaching to the last act in the tragedy, and it is some relief to find ourselves thus far advanced towards the conclusion of the melancholy narrative.

Tyalie, the brother of Macomo, had kept his station on the east banks of the Mankasana, a stream which runs into the Kat River, and which separated him from the Kat River settlement, now possessed by the Hottentots. From this he was driven with all his people, by Colonel Wade's orders, in September, 1833. In the latter end of November of that same year, Colonel Wade drove away Macomo also from the banks of the Chumie, to which he had retired after his expulsion in the year 1829: "With myself alone," says Colonel Wade, "rests the whole responsibility of the removal of the Caffres in November, 1833."[*]

Captain R. S. Aitchison's Evidence. "Have you ever been employed in removing any of the Caffre tribes out of the neutral territory?"—"I have; in November, 1833, I was ordered to remove Macomo, Botman, and Tyalie, beyond the boundary, which I did.

* Ab. 307.

"Who was commandant of the frontier at that time?"—"Colonel England, of the 75th, Colonel Somerset having gone on leave to England."

"Who was the governor? the acting governor was Colonel Wade; after Sir Lowry Cole's departure, and before Sir Benjamin D'Urban arrived, Colonel Wade was acting governor."

"Will you state what took place when you were ordered to remove Macomo and Tyalie?"—"Colonel England sent for me, (I was about thirty miles from Graham's town) and stated that he had received Cape Town orders to remove those chiefs beyond the boundary, and that I was named for the duty. He then, as I had been a long time in the country, and understood these matters perfectly, asked me the policy of the steps, and we agreed that as it was the time of the year when the Caffre corn and pumpkins were in a forward state, that if this could be put off for a few months, *it would be an act of charity towards the Caffres.* Viewing it as I did, he did not act upon the order, but by the post of the following day wrote to say, that such being the case, he had submitted again the policy of allowing the Caffres to remain until they had reaped their harvest, and hoped it would be approved by the governor (Colonel Wade). By return of post, which was about fourteen days from that date, *a peremptory order arrived for the removal of the Caffres.* I was named, and ordered to repair to Fort Wiltshire, to take upon myself the command of that post, and to superintend the clearing of the country. The force that was then put under my charge was quite inadequate to effect this purpose by force. I sent for Macomo and Botman, and as I had known them many years, I told them, and in fact they ex-

pressed great confidence, knowing that I had never
deceived them in any way whatever, and never promised them that which I could not perform. At first,
they refused positively to go. I then pointed out to
them as well as I could the absurdity of objecting to
go : Macomo said he knew very well that I could not
force him; I said of course I must do it, but that if
he would go quietly, and advise all his people to do
the same, Colonel Somerset might be expected very
shortly, and also the new governor, and that his good
behaviour on this occasion would ensure him my support, and that I would not fail, if he went quietly, to
mention his conduct to both when they arrived.
After some hours of needless conversation on the subject, he at last said that he would believe me, and
would go, I gave him two days to complete the eva-
cuation of the country, and I then went with the whole
force I had, and did not find a single Caffre."

"Had they any property ?"—" All the corn which
was quite green, all the gardens, and all the pumpkins, and every thing was left—no animals were left."

"In this conversation that you had with Macomo,
did he claim his right to stay ?"—" No ; but he distinctly said, which we found out afterwards to be the
case, that he could not make out the cause of his removal, and asked me if I could tell him ; *and I really
could not ; I had heard nothing, no cause was ever
assigned to me for his removal;* and moreover I met
a Boor, who lived close to where Macomo was, and he
said, ' Pray what are you removing these people for,'
and I said, ' My orders are to do so.' He said, ' I
am very sorry for it, for I have never lost, so long as
they have been here, a single beast; they have even
recovered beasts for me.'"

"Then Macomo behaved in this interview between you and him very well?"—" At first, as may be supposed, he was very violent; the man was very much irritated; I could not assign any reason why he was ordered to be removed; and he absolutely stated, ' I will allow you to inquire at Fort Wiltshire, whether or not I have not sent in horses and cattle recaptured from other Caffres, which had been stolen from the colony.' "

To shorten this story of expulsion, it should be understood that in the first month of 1834, the Caffres were allowed again to pass the Gaga stream, indeed they could not be kept out, the inconvenience, distress, and want, amounting to starvation, which they endured by being forced with their herds upon other clans already too closely condensed, and in a dry season, compelled them to return into the lands out of which they had been driven: but in February, 1834, they were again driven out, and then again returned: in the autumn of 1834, there took place the last expulsion with all that conflagration of huts hereafter to be described; so that in fact Macomo and his people were for a whole twelvemonth in a constant state of alarm; the patrols were continually harassing, driving, burning, and expelling.

" Did you see any instance of great distress amongst them?"—" Unfortunately it so happened 'for them, that it was a particularly dry season: the grass, which is generally very abundant, was very scarce indeed, and also water, and they were driven out of a country which was both better for water and grass than the one they were removed to, which was already thickly inhabited. They took me over the country they were to inhabit, and I assure you there was not a morsel of grass upon it more than there is upon this room: *it was as bare as a parade.*"[*]

On the 7th of December, about ten days after his expulsion, Macomo sent the following letter to Dr. Philip, which was published in one of the colonial papers. The chief dictated it in the Caffre tongue, and it was translated into English.

" As I and my people have been driven back over the Chumie without being informed why, I should be glad to know from the government what evil we have done. I was only told that we must retire over the Chumie, but for what reason I was not informed. Both Stockenstrom and Somerset agreed that I and my people should live west of the Chumie, as well as east of it without being disturbed : *when shall I and my people be able to get rest?* When my father, Gaika, was living, he reigned over the whole land from the Fish River to the Kei, but since the day he refused †

* Ab. 9.

† In 1815, there was an insurrection of the frontier Boors against the English government. These men were Dutch-African colonists, occupying chiefly the country about Bavian's River, and the Taka. To strengthen their hands they sent an embassy to Gaika, the Caffre chief, with instructions to propose an alliance between him and themselves against the colonial government. They offered, in case of success, to leave in his possession Albany and other tracts of country west of the Fish River. Gaika declined the alliance, he knew the men he had to deal with, and would not swallow their bait. When, therefore, the conspiracy failed, and the principal leaders were hanged for high treason, the families of the traitors, and the Boors generally, bore no small grudge against the house of Gaika. The principal families concerned in this rebellion were *Erasmus,* Prinslo, *Vanderness,* Bezuidenhout, Lubascagné, Engelbrecht, *Bothma,* Klopper, Malan, De Klerk, Van Dyk, &c. It seems probable that some of the dark stories of the eastern frontier,

to assist the Boors against the English he has lost more than one half the country by them. My father was always the best friend of the English Government, though he was a loser by them. My poor people feel much their loss, not only of their grazing ground, without which we cannot live, but also of our corn, some of which is a considerable height; but all this we must abandon. I have lived peaceably with my people west of the Chumie ever since I have been *allowed* by Stockenstrom and Somerset *to live there in my own country*. When any of my people stole from the colonists, I have returned what was stolen. I have even returned the cattle which the people of other kraals have stolen; yet both I and my brother Tyalie have almost no more country for our cattle to live in.

"I am also much dissatisfied with the false charges sometimes spoken against me: pray do not the people in the colony steal as much as the Caffres? Not long ago several Boors came to us in search of those cows that were lost, and as I was afraid a commando would come, as usual, upon us, I was obliged to give them 30 head in their place. But after the farmers had left, I found the foot marks of the three cows, which had gone close by my kraal, and I found the cows at Fima's kraal, a great distance from me. This is generally the case, and yet the innocent are punished for the guilty. On delivering the three cows, I received the thirty head back again.

"Just yesterday a cow was returned that had been brought to one of my people by his relation, (who was

---

the murders of the Caffres, and the severity of the commandos, may be traced in some instances to *revenge* as much as to cupidity. Macomo seems to be aware of this.

in the service of a Boor), in order that he might take charge of it, as the property of the Boor's servant; yet we were charged with having stolen it. I do not know why so many commandos come into this country, and take away our cattle, and kill my people without sufficient reason. We do no injury to the colony, *and yet I remain under the foot of the colony.*

" I would beg the favour of your inquiring of the government for me the reason of all these things, and I will thank you.—Your friend,

" MACOMO, the chief."

This second expulsion of Gaika's sons plainly proved to the Caffres, that they never could expect peace or justice from the colony; they were wearied now with the multiplicity and severity of their grievances of which there was no hope of redress, nor any prospect of mitigation. Year after year opened to them fresh prospects of outrage, inhumanity, and insult; and now it was that they began to declare amongst themselves the necessity of taking vengeance on their merciless tormentors. The fire was now kindled; a twelvemonth more of oppression and injustice fanned the flame into a conflagration, which it was not easy to extinguish; and it is quite certain that unless an entire new system of equity shall be firmly established, by the resolute counsels of the home government, the colony will ere long be lost, and we shall be stripped of a fair and valuable possession, amidst the derision of all Christendom.

Sir Benjamin D'Urban (the Governor who succeeded Colonel Wade), in a despatch dated October 14, 1834, takes notice of the irritation caused by the expulsion of Macomo and Tyali, attributing it to the mistaken

I

severity of Colonel Wade, in November, 1833, though he omits to notice his own handiwork in this "irritation," when in the month of February, 1834, Macomo was again driven back, and with the usual accompaniments of " burning-out," though efforts had been made to spare this repetition of cruelty. " They came in February?" inquire the Committee of Captain Aitchison, " Yes."—" When were they driven out?—*By return of post*"—that is, as soon as order could come from the government.

This, Sir Benjamin D'Urban omits to state, laying the blame of the irritation on Colonel Wade. " The Caffre tribes," he says, " were, it appears, at this time stimulated by a strongly excited feeling of discontent and ill-will, toward the colony, arising from the following circumstances:—For many years past the tribes of Macomo, Bothman, and Tyali, had been *allowed* by the colonial government to reside and graze their cattle on the western side of the Keiskamma, upon the Gaga, Chumie, and Muncasana. In the November of last year (1833), the acting Governor, Colonel Wade, under the impression that this indulgence had been abused (which probably it might have been to a certain extent), ordered their immediate expulsion from the whole of that line, and they were expelled accordingly. This unfortunately happened when a period of severe drought was approaching, so that these tribes (I am afraid but too certainly) suffered much loss in their herds, in consequence: hence arose the feelings to which I have adverted, and which combined with it, *in this instance* perhaps, a spirit of retribution."[*]

[*] P. P. ii. 103.

CHAPTER XVIII.

The immediate Provocations to the Caffre War.

In the winter of 1833,* and the whole of the year 1834, the commandos were carried into Caffreland with increasing severity; the year 1834 may be described as one of unremitting plunder: the patrols were constantly making seizures of the cattle belonging to the Caffres, and every month, almost every week, they were provoking and injuring that miserable people. The Boors and farmers who had advanced into the neutral territory, and others in the eastern parts of the colony, now found that nothing was so easy as to augment their own herds without the trouble of purchase; they had but to complain to the military stations, and immediately, without examination, the

* Captain Stockenstrom, who had been appointed Commissioner General of the eastern parts of the colony, in Nov. 1827, resigned that situation early in 1833. The Cape Town Cabinet had, for some time, been thwarting him in his benevolent views, and upholding the commando system, which he steadfastly resisted; finding himself, by the too successful intrigues of the tyrannical party, incapacitated from rendering any services to the colony, he retired from office and came to England. His removal from office was the signal for reviving the commandos with a severity and violence before unknown.

patrols were set in motion, and brought back to the
complaining farmers anything they wanted; if they
could not find the cattle, which in many instances had
never been stolen, they brought other beasts instead,
and frequently at the rate of two or three Caffre oxen
for one of the colonists, on the plea that the colonial
cattle were of much greater value than those belonging
to the Caffres.   Indeed, it seems to me, that it was the
express object of some persons in the colony, about this
time, to provoke the Caffres to a war; anticipating that
the result of such a movement would end in a still
further siezure of the territory of the Amakosæ.   I can
put no other interpretation on the astonishing outrages
practised on the frontier at this period of our history,
and when I find that immediately after the war, and
indeed before the sword was quite sheathed, numerous
applications were made for extensive grants of the conquered country; it seems to me certain, that the unremitting provocations by the colonists at this time
were, in fact, a speculation to enrich themselves* with
large and fertile domains.

But let us see what they were doing in the year
1834. And here first we will take the testimony of
Colonel Wade, the eulogist of the colony, and the
opponent of the Aborigines.   " I proceeded to Fort
Wiltshire, on the 20th October, 1834, where Colonel
Somerset had promised.to meet me, and had requested

---

* Sir Benjamin D'Urban wished to make grants of Caffreland
when the war was concluded; but here he met with a firm
and unexpected inhibition from Lord Glenelg. "The territory of
the Caffres," says his Lordship in his despatch of December, 1835,
" I am well aware, is, in itself, a salubrious and fertile region,
*contrasting but too favourably with the prevailing sterility of our own
possessions;* but the great evil of the Cape colony consists in its
magnitude," &c.

Macomo to join us, and with which request he complied
on the following morning. We started at a quarter
before seven, crossed the Keiskamma into Caffreland at
a ford just above the Fort; visited Maċomo (who had
returned the night before) and the younger Botmans
at their respective kraals......soon after mid-day we
reached the Ombokino, a tributary of the Chumie.
These valleys were swarming with Caffres, as the whole
country in front, as far as the Gaga, the people were
all in motion, carrying off their effects, and driving
away their cattle towards the fords of the river, *and to
my utter amazement, the whole country around us and
before us was in a blaze.* Presently we came up with a
strong patrol of the mounted rifle corps; *the soldiers
were busily employed in burning the huts,* and driving
the Caffres towards the frontier; from these latter I
learned that they had been settled here better than a
month, during which time no patrol had disturbed
them; they had therefore built their huts, established
their cattle kraals, and commenced the cultivation of
their gardens. I afterwards ascertained that the statement was correct, no patrol having visited this
quarter during five weeks, [wonderful pause in colonial
cruelty!] On inquiring of Colonel Somerset, the
cause of this most unexpected occurrence, he said it
was a necessary consequence of the system that was
prescribed to him from head-quarters." Colonel Somerset then complained that he was expected to keep the
country clear of Caffres, but not to fire on them; that
he could not keep them out by driving them away
merely, that this "leniency" had done much harm, and
that he could not protect the colony "unless he were
permitted to have recourse to a more energetic system
of defence." He had *for months past* been requesting

for more ample powers (*i.e.* to shoot the Caffres), and that now all he could do was to burn down their houses!

"I rode with Macomo for some time," continues Colonel Wade, "*who was evidently vexed at the work that was going on around us.* He complained of the Caffres being so often permitted to enter the *colony*,* and again thrust out without any apparent cause for their removal; that they had remained during the last five weeks unmolested, and were *again* burned out (they had been burned out before) when there was no cause of complaint against them." He asked me emphatically, "when am I to have my country again?" I replied, "What country?" he said: "THIS COUNTRY WHERE WE ARE, AND THAT COUNTRY," pointing towards the Kat River settlement. I said, "You know well, Macomo, why† you were first removed from that country (meaning in 1829); latterly Tyali was removed from the Muncasana, and your Caffres from the country where you now are, because they not only stole the cattle of the Hottentots, but occupied the whole of the grazing ground with their own herds, and even drove them into the corn lands of locations." He said that was bad, and that we should punish those who did so. I asked him how we were to discover them, if the chiefs would not help us......He then asked, "but are there no thieves in the colony?" I said, "Yes, and every one endeavours to find them out, and when they are discovered they are hanged." He made no reply, and shortly afterwards rode away, saying, in a very

---

* It is quite certain that Macomo never could have said so; he never would call his own lands "the colony."

† Whether Colonel Wade meant here his slanderous charge of Macomo's thefts, or the idle story about the Tambookies, does not appear.

marked and peculiar manner, "But we are to have the lands again."

This is Colonel Wade's representation of the interview, and though it would be very important to hear from Macomo *his* account of this conversation, yet some particulars of considerable interest are reported even by the inimical pen of Colonel Wade.

Colonel Wade goes on to narrate that strange story, already noticed, of Macomo being requested the next day to get up a sham fight of his clan, for the amusement of his odious visitors. This truly unfeeling request was complied with; but, as Colonel Wade has reported with a language and sentiment peculiarly his own, " Macomo was in a sulky state and talked but little."*

To request this chief thus to amuse them with a theatrical pastime, when his own heart, and the hearts of his people, must have been sinking under the load of their deep afflictions, and when all their villages were in flames, is an inconceivable degree of cruelty and indecency. There is a sanctity in sorrow which ever commands respect, and I know not that we can any where find a parallel to this " sham fight," but by turning to the grim pranks of a Domitian or a Nero.

The conflagration of the kraals of Macomo's clan was seen by Colonel Wade on the 20th of October, but the same work was going on a fortnight after, as we hear from the testimony of Dr. Philip, who thus narrates what he saw : *—

" Leaving the Muncasana, I proceeded along the western ridge of the Chumie basin, and during perhaps a ride of twenty miles I did not find a single Caffre

* Ab. 114, 115.

kraal or hut which had not been burnt or otherwise destroyed by the military. Immediately above Fort Wiltshire, and below the junction of the Chumie and Keiskamma Rivers, I saw with my own eyes the kraals and.
huts of the Caffres burning. This was on ground that
was of use to no one. It was on the boundary of the
neutral ground (within the territory which goes by,
that name), and at a great distance from the colonists.
The people were sitting in small groups looking at their
burning habitations. Being asked why they did not.
go over the river, they said there was no grass on the
other side, and that they might as well perish by the patrols as by famine; they added that the patrols who,
fired their krals and huts had informed them that the.
next day every one of them was to be driven over the
river at the point of the bayonet. On the 5th of Nov.
1834, the day after I left the Kat River, I halted near
it. I halted near Fort Wiltshire about mid-day. Macomo hearing that I was there, came to the place, accompanied with about twenty of his men. They remained with me about two hours. On his way he had,
called at Fort Wiltshire, where he was reminded of a
demand which had been made upon him a short time
before by Colonel Somerset for 480 head of cattle, said.
to be due to the colony. Macomo stated in reply that
there were no colonial cattle among his people, that he
had always been ready whenever cattle had been stolen
from the colony, and reported to him, to recover them :
that in the course of a year he had sent back a great
number he had recaptured from the Caffres that did not
belong to them. Colonel Somerset had still urged that
the 480 head of cattle were to be demanded, but the
governor was not willing to use force till he knew whether Macomo would comply with the demand or not.

To·this the chief replied that he could only repeat
what he had before said, that he had done everything
in his power to recover cattle said to have been stolen
from·the colony: that he could be answerable for his
own people, but that he could not be answerable for
cattle stolen by vagabond Caffres in the bush.   Having
·given this reply, and being conscious that he had done
every thing in his power, and seeing no end to the demands made upon him, *he received this last demand
as a proof that his ruin was resolved upon,* for he had
just been told at Fort Wiltshire that a commando was
about to enter his country to take the 480 head of cattle, and that threat seemed greatly to add to·his
distress.

"The chief then entered upon a further detail of his
grievances, and declared that it was impossible for human nature to endure what he had to suffer under the
patrol system.

"I reasoned with him, and did all in my power
to impress upon his mind the importance of maintaining
peace with the colony.   I stated that I had reason to
believe that the governor, * when he came to the frontier would listen to all his grievances, and treat him
with justice and generosity.   'These promises,' he replied ' we have had for the last 15 years, and,' pointing to the huts then burning, 'things are becoming
worse; these huts were set on fire last night, and we
are told that to-morrow the patrol is to scour the whole
district, and drive every Caffre from the west side of
the Chumie and Keiskamma at the point of the bayonet.'
He asked *to what extent endurance was to be carried?*

---

* Sir Benjamin D'Urban had lately become Governor of the
colony.

and my reply was, ' If they drive away your people at
the point of the bayonet, advise them to go over the
Keiskamma peaceably; if they come to take away
cattle, suffer them to do it without resistance; if they
burn your huts, allow them to do so; if they shoot your
men, bear it till the governor comes, and then represent
your grievances to him, and I am convinced you will
have no occasion to repent having followed my advice.'
He was deeply affected, and the last words to me were
(grasping my hand), ' I will try what I can do.' " *

But, alas! the governor, Sir Benjamin D'Urban, never
did come to redress the grievances of the Caffres. A few
months afterwards he came as commander-in-chief at
the head of a large army to ravage all Caffreland, to
lay waste the whole country, to slay four thousand
Caffres, and to capture sixty thousand head of cattle.

Here, however, we cannot but remark the enormous
injustice of making Macomo responsible for the 480
head of cattle said to be stolen from the colony, of
which he and his people knew nothing. It was in vain
that he represented his willingness to restore, and more
than restore, any cattle taken by his clan, but that he
had no power, no ability, no possible means within his
reach to recover cattle stolen by other Caffres, over
whom he had no control, and who were entirely out
of his sight. " No matter," was the reply " you are
a Caffre, that is enough for us; we want 480 head of
cattle, and if you do not find them, we will take them.
To-morrow we will come with a commando, drive away
your herds, and then drive you and your people out of
the country."

Where, I ask, in the whole world are they doing such

* Ab. 553.

things as these? Do even the Bedouin Arabs or the
Turkoman hordes plunder in this style? They come
as professional robbers, and take what they choose;
but this sleight-of-hand rapacity, whereby we make innocent people suffer for the offences (real or pretended)
of others, and thus season the sweets of robbery with
the zest of hypocrisy, is a mixture of wickedness to be
found nowhere but in the British colony of the Cape of
Good Hope.

CHAPTER XIX.

The immediate Provocations to the Caffre War.

THE aggravations of injustice came now with rapidity on the Caffres. Whilst the patrols were destroying their habitations, one of the Caffres lifted up his assegai in a threatening attitude against the soldiers who were firing his house: he had a sick wife and a child within, and he could not see this barbarous treatment of his family, without lifting up his hand to defend them: poor fellow! it was a momentary act of anger, and certainly was not more than the wreathings of a worm under the foot that is crushing it. They seized him, however, bound him, and took him to Graham's Town, and put him in prison; the magistrate ordered him to be flogged " for assaulting a sergeant in the execution of his duty." This sentence was executed accordingly, the poor creature was laid across an ant-hill, severely flogged,* and then driven back into Caffreland. They

---

* The sufferer's name was Goobie; he received fifty lashes on his bare back, and was imprisoned in the common jail two months. He was a subject of Macomo, and on that account, probably, was thus treated. He afterwards went through Caffreland, showing his wounded back to his countrymen, and calling down their

had committed this outrage a short time before Dr.
Philip had the interview with Macomo, detailed in the
last chapter.   He found the Caffres all in a ferment at
the outrageous treatment of their countryman.   "One
of the first questions asked me," says Dr. Philip, " was,
what right had the English government to punish the
subject of a Caffre chief?   I was assured by the people
then around me, that it was the first example of a Caffre
ever having been flogged ; that the man could never
lift up his head in Society ; that it would have been
better had he been shot dead, and that when the
governor should arrive among them, he would hear of
it from every tongue in Caffreland, as one of the greatest
indignities that could have been offered to the nation.
I said every thing in my power to soothe them ; but
no people can have a keener sense of injustice in cases
where they themselves are the sufferers, or can be more
alive to what they deem national affronts than what the
Caffres are ; and I found that the arguments I used to
quiet their minds, tended only to increase their excitement to which this circumstance had given rise.   Some
of the Caffres asserted that Goobie was arrested on
what was then considered Caffre territory ; but this is
a circumstance of small consequence ; he was a subject of a Caffre prince, and he had only lifted up his
hand to protect his hut, and his wife, and his child,
who were in it."[*]

Captain Charles Bradford, of the East India Company's service, happened to be travelling in Caffre-

vengeance on the colony. (Ab. 161.) The magistrate who
ordered this outrage, ought, without delay, to be dismissed from
his office, and as much further punished as the laws of England
will allow.

[*] Ab. 552.

land at this time, and has confirmed the statements
of other persons, relating to the angry feelings then
prevailing amongst the Caffres. He was present on
one occasion at a meeting of several of the chiefs, with
their counsellors and followers. "Macomo, the regent,
was the first in rank: he spoke with great spirit and
energy, and at times with considerable dignity. He
adverted to the ill-treatment his people had met with
from the English—he indignantly complained that any
white man, whatever his rank might be, was permitted
to enter his country at pleasure, whilst he, the regent,
and other chiefs, could not cross the English boundary
for a few hours without obtaining permission from some
colonial authority. He then remarked upon a summons
he had just received from Colonel Somerset, to, meet
him with other chiefs at the Buffalo River, and of his
having refused to attend, as Colonel Somerset had not
first obtained permission to enter his country. Macomo,
then complained bitterly of the system pursued by the
British—of his having been driven from the country of
the Kat River, which he claimed as his own, till the
English seized on it and gave it to the Hottentots.
That he had even procured a missionary for his people;
he had built houses, and planted gardens—but his huts
were burned—his cattle driven off—his people shot—
that the arrival of the governor was promised—redress
was promised—all was unfulfilled. That he avoided
quarrelling with the English—his people had not
strength, had not arms to cope with the English; that
his people urged him to avenge his wrongs, but he
avoided war, he repressed the violence of the people.
They were accused of stealing the white men's cattle—
he had sent back many to the colony, (here he produced

·receipts given by Major Burney, for a quantity of cattle and horses delivered up at different times, by himself, at Fort Wiltshire.) Some Caffres might steal, but were there no thieves amongst the English?"*

These heads of Macomo's speech are valuable in one ·respect, as showing the quick sense of national, personal, and official honour entertained by that chief. He knew he was a high-born prince, and the regent of the western Amakosæ, in fact a sovereign, and he felt his full right of granting permission to strangers to enter his territory. Colonel Somerset ought most certainly to have asked permission to enter Caffreland; but an officer who had been trained up to systematic oppression of the Caffres, would probably laugh at the idea of acting as a polite gentleman towards a prince whom he had repeatedly and habitually injured.

It may be supposed that by this time matters were coming to a crisis, and that nothing but a retrogressive policy, some steps backwards towards the unfrequented path of justice, would save the colony from an incursion of their exasperated neighbours. The Caffres were waiting with great impatience to see the new Governor, Sir Benjamin D'Urban, who was daily expected on the frontier ; and it is certain that if he had then made his appearance, and had seen justice done to Macomo and the other chiefs, as it is believed he was at that time quite disposed to do, the gathering storm might have been averted, and all the long train of evils that ensued entirely prevented. As it was, the governor loitered in Cape Town till it was too late ; fresh grievances were inflicted on the Caffres, grievances which could not be

* Ab. 159.

endured, and Sir Benjamin D'Urban never came towards Caffreland till the war had broken out, and till
he had imbibed the angry passions and vindictive feelings of the terrified colony.

Early in December a patrol under the command of
an Ensign Sparkes, a youth about eighteen years old,
entered Caffreland, to take, as usual, some cattle from
the Caffres; the colony had lost four horses, but they
went to seize forty oxen; the seizure was resisted; the
young gentleman became angry; there was either a
scuffle or a fight, the soldiers fired, and a Caffre threw
an assegai, which wounded the ensign in the arm. This
was considered an enormous crime by the military; the
officers were in a fury at the wound of the ensign, and
it was forthwith decreed that the precious blood shed
on that memorable occasion, should be valued at the
rate of three hundred head of oxen, a triple hecatomb
to atone for the wound of this favored stripling. This
fine was levied on the chief Eno.* Very shortly afterwards, another expedition, under the command of Lieutenant Sutton, went into Caffreland to make another
seizure; and for that purpose was directed to Tyali's
kraal, though it was not even pretended that his people
had stolen from the colony. It so happened that Tyali
was not at home, but his younger brother Xo-xo, who
was there, went up to the patrol, followed by some attendants, and said to the officer "Why are you taking
my brother Tyali's oxen away? there is no war between
us; have you traced the track of oxen or cattle into our
country?" No answer was made to this very simple
and inoffensive question, but the musket was raised, and
the young prince was shot in the head. The patrol
rode off, driving away the cattle.

* Ab. 567.

This sanguinary outrage was the immediate cause of the war. The Caffres now considered, and most justly, that the war was begun by the colonists: they were all in an uproar when they heard of what had been done, and hurried from all quarters to the kraal where the young prince, the brother of Macomo, was lying bleed-ing on the ground. Twice he fainted away from loss of blood, and though the wound did not prove fatal, it was very serious, and for some time he was supposed to be dying. It was not the fault of the patrol that Xo-xo was not murdered. "When Tyali's brother was wounded," says the Caffre chief Tzatzo, "a mes-senger was sent to all the chiefs, and to king Hintza amongst others. When I came to Sutu, she told me that her son had been wounded, but she said, 'Go to Tyali and he will tell you all about it.' When I came to Tyali, he told me that his brother had been wounded; that when the patrol had come to take away the cattle he remonstrated, and was shot. And I asked Tyali, 'What are you going to do?' Tyali then replied, 'I have caused my missionary to write a letter to Captain Armstrong on the subject, and the answer I got was, that he had nothing to do with it, that it did not happen in his part of the country.' Tyali then said 'My missionary is going to write another letter to Colonel Somerset, requesting him to write to the officer at Fort Beaufort to know why the patrol shot my brother.' I told Tyali that was well. When I was about twenty paces from Tyali's place, I met the two missionaries, Mr. Chalmers and Mr. Wear. The mis-sionaries then asked me to go back to Tyali's place with them, to know why the patrol had shot Xo-xo. We then went, and with Tyali's permission, went to Xo-xo's hut to examine his wound. Xo-xo was shot in the head with slugs. The missionary then said to Xo-xo, 'You see the necessity of prayer; you might have been killed, and died an unconverted man.' Every Caffre who saw Xo-xo's wound went back to his hut, took his assegai and shield and set out to fight, and said, '*It is better that we die than be treated thus; life is of no use to us if they shoot our chiefs.*'" *

Tzatzoe being a Caffre chief of the royal lineage, and related to Xo-xo, must know perfectly what was the immediate cause of the war. He says distinctly that it was caused by the shooting the young prince; and he further adds that Xo-xo between his fainting fits said to the Caffres who crowded to see him, "FIGHT AWAY!"

Thus then began the Caffre war.

* Ab. 565.

CHAPTER XX.

The Commandos and Patrols.

Before we enter into the Caffre war, it will be requisite to be furnished with evidence of the nature of these commandos and patrols of which much has been said in this narrative, and by means of which the Caffres were at last goaded into a declaration of open war with the colony.

That a Boor should, on his own statement of his own losses, be able to send an armed party into Caffreland, and that this armed party, called a commando, should bring away as many cattle as were wanted, without any reference to the guilt of the parties from whom they took the plunder; that a chief and his clan should be made responsible for any cattle-marks traced near their villages, though that "nearness" is sometimes four or five miles distant; and that this system of barefaced rapine has been carried on ever since Lord Charles Somerset's pretended treaty with Gaika up to the breaking out of the last Caffre war; that it should have been carried on with the knowledge and assent of several colonial ministers, and with the sanction and indeed the express orders of divers governors of the colony; and that British officers and soldiers should have been the instruments of perpetrating this wrong, could not have been credited without the most authentic evidence—and that evidence the Parliamentary inquiry has amply supplied.

Captain Aitchison: "Please to describe a commando, how the orders are originally given, and the process?—A commando is merely a name attached to a force collected, either a regular military force, or partly military and partly civil. The magistrates in that country have power to order the farmers upon military duties when occasion requires. The commandant of the frontier or the civil authority, demands assistance from the military and the neighbouring counties, to check any inroads the Caffres may make, or to recover beasts that may have been stolen. These when collected are called a commando.

"Have you ever been employed upon these commandos?—Very frequently.

"In recovering cattle, you traced them as far as you could?—Yes; *generally* to some Caffres' kraal. *

* W. Gisborne, Esq. gives similar evidence:—

"Did you accompany any military parties for the purpose of recovering stolen cattle?—Yes, several.—When cattle had been stolen from the colonists, or reported by a Dutch Boor, or English colonist, to have been stolen, soldiers or others were sent to follow the track of those cattle, if possible. They traced them into a Caffre village, and then they demanded, from the inhabitants of the village, where the cattle were; and if they could not show the traces of the cattle out of the village, that village was held liable for them. Orders were then sent to the military on the frontiers to go to such a village and recover such a number of cattle. I went with them a number of times. *The recovery was always attempted by surprise,* for, if the Caffres had any suspicion of the attack, the party could not have taken the cattle. It was usual to arrive near the village after sunset, and lie there till the

"And if you did not find the cattle, what did you do?—We used to go to the first kraal we could, and make reprisals; with those of course we returned to the colony, and they were given over to the civil authorities to be disposed of as they thought fit. On other occasions we trace the cattle as far as we think proper, till we come to the kraal, and then point out to the chief of such kraal that the trace of such beasts *had gone through his territory*, and desired him to follow them up.

"Suppose he denied all knowledge of them?—If we pointed out that the beasts had gone through, and he refused to assist us, WE TOOK HIS CATTLE.

"But supposing, without refusing to assist you, he declared his inability to do so?—*That he could not do, because they have nothing else to do;* and it is a country where, if you once get on the trace of beasts, unless there has been a heavy rain, you cannot help following it." *

Let us then suppose the following dialogue between an English Captain and a Caffre chief, to illustrate the above evidence:—

Captain: We have lost 250 head of cattle and nineteen horses from the colony: we have followed their spoor, and find they have gone through your territory.

Chief: Indeed! There are many roads through my territory.

---

morning, and then rush into the village and capture all the cattle they could."

"Suppose any resistance were made, were the military empowered to fire?—I have no doubt the military were empowered to fire. They were always, I believe, loaded with ball, and carried ammunition with them." Ab. 358.

* Ab. 5.

Captain : You must help us to follow them, and to seize them, and if you do not we shall take what we want from you.

Chief: I know nothing of these cattle ; my people know nothing of them ; we are not thieves, and you must not punish the innocent. I cannot follow your commando.

Captain : You have nothing else to do; and you must help us to find the cattle. I hold you responsible. The country is such that having once a trace of the beasts, " you cannot help following them."

Chief : *Nothing else to do !* Then am I your servant? I have a great deal to do. I have to take care of my own herds and flocks, to govern my clan, to control and look after my people, to attend to my family, to cultivate my gardens and my corn-fields; I do not find bread comes down from heaven ready made into my mouth, and all of us have to work, and to work hard. Besides, if I " cannot help following" the beasts, then neither can you help following them ; and it is strictly true, that you who are kicking your heels all day at the barracks *have nothing else to do.* I won't go with you: You may find and take the beasts if you like.

Captain: We have been riding several miles: it is very hot and dusty ; and I find it the shortest and most convenient method to take the cattle from you. Soldiers! drive away 250 cows and nineteen horses from these kraals.

Chief : What wickedness ! What have we done to deserve this? You take away 250 cows, the calves will be dead to-morrow; and the poor children, what is to become of them? What are the mothers of my poor people's children to do without milk ? this is all we have. I call Heaven to witness against you, thieves and murderers as you are.

Captain: I must do my duty. Farewell.

This is the system which has been flourishing at the Cape for fourteen years. But we have more evidence to the point, and Captain Aitchison thus farther explains what he has seen and known :—

" Do you know any instance in which the Boors or Europeans had claimed a quantity of cattle as stolen, and it was afterwards proved that those cattle had never been stolen ?—Yes ; but not frequently. I have known Boors come and report to me that so many head of cattle had been driven off by the Caffres ; and my own patrol, in going to the house, have found the cattle in the little jungles in the neighbourhood of the place.

' And he did that for the purpose of getting compensation for their pretended loss ?—He was either too idle, or his herdsmen were too idle to go and look after them. If it should come on rain, there is the greatest difficulty in keeping the cattle from going astray, and the Hottentots get very idle in rainy weather.

" When the Boors joined a commando, were they under the authority of military officers ?—Yes.

" Could the officers restrain the Boors from acts of cruelty ?—Yes ; *but on more occasions than one* I recollect the Boors being without a military officer ; and upon one occasion I recollect a disgraceful scene took place. I was in the field, but it was about ten miles distant from me. There was another party of Boors, about 150, who acted in a parallel direction to me. These men had seized a number of cattle, and wantonly killed eleven Caffres. A short time before I left the country, I recollect having heard of some Boors having murdered some Caffres most wantonly, but I am not quite master of the circumstances. I recollect having heard of something very bad; that they had got hold of some unfortunate Caffres and fired at them in the most wanton manner, (that was in 1834, and therefore very near the breaking out of the war.)

" When a Boor loses cattle does he make application to the magistrate?—No; to the nearest military post. *The magistrate is not required on these occasions.* The moment a farmer is aware that his cattle are driven off by the Caffres, he rides to the nearest military post, and there states his grievance. That officer has directions to listen to that, and to ascertain as far as it is in his power, the truth of it. If he is satisfied of the truth of it, he sends an officer, if possible, but in many cases non-commissioned officers are trusted, &c. &c.

" Were you called upon constantly to perform duties of this kind?—Constantly. I have known junior officers to have been out FOUR TIMES IN THE WEEK upon these expeditions.

" So that it was the great business of the corps?— *The sole business of the corps.* I have been left at my own post with seven or eight men only."*

Captain Stockenstrom says, and his evidence is of the first importance :—" I have long since made up my mind that the great source of misfortune on the frontier was the system of taking Caffre cattle, under any circumstances, by our patrols. If Caffres steal cattle, very seldom the real perpetrators can be found, unless the man losing the cattle have been on his guard, and sees the robbery actually perpetrated, so that he can immediately collect a force and pursue the plunderers ;

* Ab. 7.

if the cattle be once out of sight of the plundered party, there is seldom any chance of getting them again ; *our patrols are then entirely at the mercy of the statements made by the farmers,* and they may pretend they are leading them on the stolen cattle, which may be the trace of any cattle in the world. On coming up to the first Caffre kraal, the Caffre, knowing the purpose for which the patrol comes, immediately drives his cattle out of sight ; we then use force, and collect those cattle, and take the number *said to be stolen, or more ;* this the Caffres naturally, and it always appeared to me justly, resist ; they have nothing else to live on, and if the cows be taken away the calves perish, and it is a miserable condition in which the Caffre women and children, and the whole party are left ; then resistance is usually construed into hostility, and it is almost impossible thus to prevent innocent bloodshed. It also often happens that when the patrol is on the track of the cattle really stolen, they find some individual head of cattle which is either knocked up or purposely left behind by the real thieves, *and this is really taken as a positive proof of the guilt of the kraal.* There have been instances where the farmers have gone into Caffreland with a patrol, pretending to be on the track of stolen cattle, and where cattle was taken from the Caffres on the strength of the supposed theft, and on returning home he has found his cattle in another direction, or found them destroyed by wolves, or through his own neglect strayed away, and thus men, not losing cattle at all, but coveting the cattle of the Caffres, have nothing more to do but to lead the patrol to a kraal, and commit the outrages I have described. The Caffres have frequently said to me, " We do not care how many Caffres you shoot if they come into your

K

country, and you catch them stealing ; *but for every cow you take from our country, you make a thief."* *
" A man of the name of Schepors represented at one of the military posts that he had lost thirty-six head of cattle ; upon this statement he went with a patrol up to the kraals of the chief Botman, and then forcibly took away nearly double the number of what he himself stated he had lost."†

Tzatzoe, the Caffre chief's evidence :—

" Have you known cases in which Caffres stole cattle, for which other Caffres were visited by a commando, and made to pay for the cattle which the thieves had stolen ?—Yes, I will mention one :—Southey lost four horses ; he followed the track as far as Kallaty's place. It got dark when he got to Kallaty's ; they had the track then. He slept at Kallaty's place ; it rained that night, and the track was effaced by the rain. He went back to the military post, and an officer came and took Kallaty's cattle. Kallaty said, ' How is this ? You come to sleep at my place, and I was to have accompanied you on the track ; how is it that you bring these men to seize my cattle.' Southey answered, ' *The rain has effaced the track at your place.*' Kallaty said, ' Is it my fault that it rained ; did I bring the rain ? must I suffer because the rain effaced the track ?' The horses were found at another place, but the Caffres paid sixteen head of cattle, and one assegai for four horses."

" Did Kallaty ever recover his cattle ?—No, when Kallaty found that another man had Southey's horses, he went to Mr. Southey. Southey said, ' I will not

* Ab. 83.   † Ab. 86.

give the cattle back.' But they gave the man eight head of cattle that never belonged to him."[*]

It is surprising that they did not shoot Kallaty for coming into the colony, and for troubling so great a personage as this Mr. Southey, who, by the way, seems to have been as treacherous a guest as ever violated the laws of hospitality.

[*] Ab. 578.

CHAPTER XXI.

THE English having thus commenced the war in Caffreland, by shooting Prince Xo-xo, the brother of the
Regent, the Caffres opened the campaign, on their
part, by invading the colony on the 21st of December,
1834. The affair of Ensign Sparkes was on the 2d ;
the shooting of Xo-xo, by Captain Sutton's patrol
expedition, was apparently on the 15th. After which
the Caffres could no longer be restrained by their
chiefs, but determined to take the matter into their own
hands, and themselves to pay off the long arrear of
vengeance due to the colony. There was a message
sent to King Hintza, who lived to the East, over the
Kei River, about ninety miles distant from Tyali's
kraal, and it is probable that the waiting for his answer
prevented a simultaneous movement of all the western
clans, and contributed in some degree to the safety of
the colony; for if the whole Caffre nation, headed by
their chiefs in person, had at once entered across the
neutral territory into Albany, and had, in some regular
plan of war, directed their movements for the express
object of destruction, the Boors and settlers would have
every where been sacrificed, and none but the military
would have been left to constitute "the colony." As

it was, the Caffres acted with uncertainty and irresolu-
tion ; they were determined to fight, but for several
days could not secure the assent of their chiefs, and
never to the last enjoyed their hearty co-operation.* It
was a popular outbreak, which the rulers could not
resist, and long and angry were the disputes between
the people and the princes, in the numerous councils
convened to discuss the grievances of the nation.†
Macomo feared that a war would bring down on their
heads still greater calamities than any they had yet
endured. Thus, it seems that as soon as Xo-xo was
shot, or two or three days afterwards, Tyali's vassals,
who were, of course, most exasperated with the attempted murder of the young prince, made small incursions on the boors and settlers in the neutral territory,
and every where showed a threatening and determined
aspect ; whilst the other Caffres were going hither and
thither amongst the various clans, summoning their
brethren to a national muster, and preparing for the
fight, by driving their cattle eastwards over the moun-

* It is supposed by some that Tyali (own brother of Xo-xo,
son of the same mother) aroused the reluctant chiefs to take up
arms, and that he exerted himself indefatigably to make them all
unite for that purpose. He certainly is the most martial of all
the chiefs, Macomo's superior wisdom and prudence directed the
movements of the war, but Tyali executed them.

† It is to be observed however, that *the chiefs* never held a
grand council of their order to decide on the war. The consult-
ations were between the chiefs and their people ; to have made it
a national war it should have been decided on in a convocation of
chiefs, who alone have the power of deciding on matters of this
high import. Tzatzoe distinctly states that there was no convocation of the chiefs ; if there had been, he would have been sum-
moned to attend it. Tzatzoe in his evidence goes farther than
this ; he states distinctly that he received a message from Hintza,
prohibiting him from fighting against the English.

tains, out of the reach of the enemy. As indications of
their hostile intentions, they ordered the English traders
residing in Caffreland to quit the country without delay,
and one man who hesitated to obey the order, was
burned out of his house and driven away. Colonel
Somerset wrote despatches to the Governor on the
18th, and though he there details several instances of
the angry feeling of the Caffres, he does not seem to
apprehend that a war was to break out in two or three
days' time. On the 22d he writes again, and in some
alarm at the occurrences that had taken place, begins to
reckon all the disposable force within reach, and declares it unequal to cope with the increasing difficulties
of his situation. But even then he talks in the old
style, which had become habitual to all the officers in
the colony, of demanding 300 head of cattle and 300
horses of the chief Tyali. On the 20th, Tyali sent him
a letter, intimating his desire to accommodate matters,
and evidently shewing that he had no power to restrain
his people. On the 23d, Colonel Somerset wrote to
the civil commissioner of Graham's Town, announcing
that a war had begun :—" Pray send Captain Campbell
to order the Boors up from all quarters. The whole of
Caffreland is up in arms in my front ; they attacked
Fort Wiltshire last night. Beg Captain Campbell to
order Piet Spandille's fellows out for service."

It was supposed that on the 21st about ten thousand
Caffre warriors entered the neutral territory, near Fort
Wiltshire. On the 24th, Col. Somerset writes :—" All
the farmers have fled, all their property has been destroyed, and I have no forces disposable but about
seventy mounted rifle corps, and all their horses are
done up."

Graham's Town now began to feel once more the horrors

of war ; all was alarm and uncertainty there ; military preparations were made, such as the emergency would allow, and a municipal body of tradespeople was hastily armed. The inhabitants of Graham's Town were terrified to find so few soldiers stationed there to defend them, and of those few Colonel Somerset was daily making demands to strengthen his position. The Caffres had, on the 25th, ravaged the farms within twenty miles of Graham's Town.* Colonel Somerset continued, by every post, to state his want of men, ammunition, and arms.

After this the ruined farmers and their families began daily to pour into Graham's Town from all quarters, bringing with them pitiable details of the destruction of their houses, the capture of their stock, and the murder of their friends, relations, or servants. The ravages of the province were extended far westward, so that in the first week of January straggling parties of Caffres penetrated even beyond the Sunday River, spreading the panic to Port Elizabeth, in Algoa Bay, whither many inhabitants of the districts of Albany and Uitenhage had fled with their herds and effects.† The *aggregate* of distress, as published by the committee of relief, is stated thus :—

" The total amount of live stock represented as lost by applicants to this board, is upwards of 51,000 head of horned cattle, 2339 horses, and 118,195 sheep and goats ; and, besides the loss in corn, furniture, and other moveable property to a considerable amount, 339 houses have been burned, and 261 pillaged and otherwise injured. The amount of live stock given in

* Colonel England's Despatch, P. P. ii. 126.

† Sir Benjamin D'Urban's Despatch, 21st January, 1830. P. P. ii. p. 131.

by the same applicants as saved, is 11,418 cattle, 1186 horses, 102,343 sheep and goats."

Thus, then, the colonists had at last an opportunity of tasting that bitter cup, the dregs of which they had compelled the Caffres to drink for twenty years. They knew now by experience what it was to have their houses set on fire over their ears; to see strangers drive away their flocks and herds; to be obliged themselves to escape with their lives; and to wander through the country pursued by an angry and dreaded enemy. And though their losses and afflictions could bear no sort of comparison with the losses and afflictions of the Caffres, yet the colonists could now testify, in sad experience, that " they who sow iniquity shall reap the same."

Mr. Kayser, the missionary, was in Caffreland at the breaking out of the war, and the account of his interview with Macomo, on the 22d of December,* is very

---

* On the 1st of January, 1835, Macomo sent the following letter to the governor, it may be considered as expressing the sentiments of all Caffreland—the Caffre justification of the war.

"May it please your Excellency. I take the liberty of writing to you, to inform you of the causes of the present quarrel between the Colonists and the Caffres. No one has told you how the colonists have been accustomed to deal with the Caffre people. It is true, Colonel Somerset communicates with you about the transactions on the frontier, but he tells you only one side of the story. Colonel Somerset for a long time has killed the Caffres, he has disturbed the peace of the land, and torn it in pieces, and matters are now come to such a crisis, that you alone are able to rectify them. Colonel Somerset has ruined me. This he did in 1829, when I aided Bowana in punishing some Tambookies who had stolen from the colony * * without any good reason killed one of Eno's sons in his own house. In 1830, * * came into Caffreland in search of colonial cattle and horses. At that time * * requested Feku, one of the sons of Hahabi, to come and speak to him in a friendly manner unarmed. The chief went to

interesting :—" I heard in the morning that the Caffres
had attacked Fort Wiltshire, and I considered it my
duty to see Macomo.   On the road to his residence I
met a Caffre who informed me that an order was issued
the preceding day for all the young and able-bodied
Caffres to proceed to the colony that night, to plunder
the farmers of their cattle.   On arriving at Macomo's
residence, I was informed that he was not at home, but
in the bush.   I was called by the council, which being
told that I wished to see Macomo, they said, ' It is in
vain for you to see or to speak to him, we are the persons who have begun the war, *and we can bear no longer
to see our chiefs shot*.   In times past several of our
chiefs have been shot and we remained quiet, but now
we are determined to fight.'   At last I procured a guide
who brought me to the opposite side of the Keiskamma,
on a height near the fort, where I met Macomo in the
bush, with a great body of his warriors, sitting on the
ground.   At the sight of Macomo my heart was ready
to burst, and I could not speak for tears.   As soon as I
had recovered, I asked Macomo what he did there? He
said :—

speak to him, when * * killed him without a cause. Lately * *
wounded one of the sons of Gaika. You, sir, must give an autho-
ritative word in order to settle our affairs. You alone can step
in as a peace-maker, and bring matters to a happy termination.
I wish that you would not forget that the country of Gaika was
taken from him, though he did not fight against the colony. An
English officer was wounded by the Caffres near Fort Wiltshire;
satisfaction for this was demanded, and 400 head of cattle were
immediately given to him. But when innocent Caffre chiefs are
killed and wounded, no satisfaction is given to us.

MACOMO."

Macomo was advised to write to Colonel Somerset, but he
positively refused to have any intercourse oral or epistolary with
such an enemy.

' I am a bush-buck, for we chiefs are shot like them, and are no more esteemed as chiefs.'

Kayser.—' Why do you talk thus ?'

Macomo.—' Have you not heard that one of my brothers has been shot in the head, and we do not know why he has been shot?'

Kayser.—' But you have heard the Governor is coming to set all these things right.'

Macomo.—(Very quick.) ' Where is he ?'

Kayser.—' I do not know, but we hear he is coming very soon, and you must go home with your people and wait his arrival at your residence, and then you can lay your complaints before him.'

Macomo.—' I have no home, the bush is my home.'

Kayser.—' But consider if you go on in this way, you will contradict all that your friends have written in your behalf, and destroy all they have done for you.'

Macomo.—' Oh, no ! I did not commence hostilities.'

Kayser.—' But think again of. the bloodshed and destruction that will ensue, if you persist in doing as you now do.'

Macomo.—' Yes, all that is true; great bloodshed will follow, but the fire is burning, and I cannot quench it.'

Kayser.—' You say you cannot quench it; here I am, send me, and I will try to speak for you to Colonel Somerset, who is near Black Drift.'

" Here some of his counsellors spoke to Macomo privately, after which he said to me,—

' Yes, you go to Colonel Somerset, and tell him that you found me here in the bush, BECAUSE MY BROTHER HAS BEEN SHOT IN THE HEAD.'

" I replied, ' Yes, I will endeavour to see him, but you and your people must go home to your dwelling.'

" At this several of the counsellors laughed, and said, ' No joke, no joke,' and I left them. I endeavoured to see Colonel Somerset, but could not meet with him, he having left at mid-day."

Two facts are here established by this interview—that the popular feeling dragged the chiefs into the war against their will, and that the outrage on the person of Xo-xo was considered such a provocation by the. Caffres, as to be, in fact, a declaration of war against their nation.

The messengers that returned from King Hintza, to whom they had sent an account of what had lately passed, brought back this laconic, but very intelligible interdict on the war:—" Hintza sends his word to you, and Hintza says you must not fight, for I do not fight."* But the message came too late ; the fury of the people could not be restrained, and they persisted in entering the colony in heavy columns, though they had not their chiefs with them to direct their movements, or to con- duct the attack with the counsel and discipline requi- site for such an undertaking.

In the meantime the colonial government began to collect its strength for vengeance. Sir Benjamin D'Urban† sent troops and stores from Cape Town on the 2d of January ; these were disembarked on the 11th at Algoa Bay, and immediately sent forward to Graham's Town. His Excellency landed at Algoa Bay on the 14th, and reached Graham's Town, the eastern capital, on the 20th, where he established his head-quarters. His Excellency there reckoned his "disposable bayonets" at twelve hundred, but stated that he should forthwith organize three thousand " men.

* Ab. 564.   † P. P. ii. 131.

of all descriptions, Burghers and others," reckoning much on the services of the Hottentots, whom he designates as "excellent men, and rapidly trained to war, whether on foot or horseback." Colonel Smith had been sent off to the eastern frontier on the 1st of January, to take the command of the army. On the 18th Colonel Smith thus writes to his Excellency :—" The savage enemy has already, since the 8th January, when I acted on the offensive, sustained a loss of four hundred warriors killed, and the number of the wounded must be considerable, as the Burghers fire with remarkable precision, and use the large shot, which they call lopers. I have, besides invading his own territory, driven Eno from his kraal, (he himself only escaped by stratagem), *killing two of his brothers*, one of *his sons*,* and thirty of his warriors, of whom many had fire-arms. Tyali's kraals have also been destroyed." Colonel Smith, who bears a painful pre-eminence in the bloody events of this war, displays in all his letters and despatches a degree of vindictive anger painful to contemplate. In this, his first despatch, he contemplates an extended rapine of Caffre territory. "It will be necessary," he says, "to include within our future boundary line a large portion of the country which is now occupied by the treacherous and murderous savages ;" and in obedience to this advice, which was as impolitic as it was unjust and cruel, did Sir B. D'Urban subsequently act.

Early in February Colonel Somerset† had succeeded

---

* It is not here mentioned that one of Eno's daughters and some other women were killed in this expedition, which consisted in surprising the kraals at early dawn and destroying the defenceless inhabitants. Eno himself escaped.

† Caffre War and Death of Hintza, p. 3.

in driving the invading Caffres over the Fish River, and
Colonel Smith drove out other parties stationed in the
woody fatnesses between the Fish River and the Keiskamma. On the 19th, Captain Armstrong's post on the
Kat River was attacked, "and in great force," but the
Caffres were ultimately repulsed. All this time, however, the governor had been collecting forces to carry
the war into Caffreland, not thinking it prudent to
commence active operations with the strength he then
possessed. On the 19th of March he writes:—"It is
of the most pressing importance to commence operations without further delay. On the several points on
the Keiskamma and Chumie I have already disposed
commissariat and ordnance stores for a month's con-
sumption, *and I must endeavour to finish my operations
within that period.*" His Excellency's endeavours were,
however, not crowned with success, for it took him six
months' most expensive and disgraceful warfare to accomplish his wishes.

The rest of the war, as described in the various despatches and enclosures of Sir Benjamin D'Urban
to the colonial office, consisted in chasing from one
mountain to another the retiring Caffres; in surrounding
and shooting them in their kraals, and taking away
large droves of their cattle, and vast flocks of their
sheep and goats. As a chapter in the bloody book of
battles, nothing can be more inglorious than this invasion of Caffreland; as a chapter in the great volume of
murders, few are more distressing and disgusting. It
was ridiculous, because so disproportionate a force
was, as it were, solemnly employed, in " hunting par-
tridges on the mountains," and recording their heroic
deeds with the most pompous eulogies; whilst the havoc
they committed with their artillery, and all the terrible

implements of war, on the utterly helpless and naked
population, cannot be read without the most painful
emotions.

It is, however, the characteristic of violent men to
hate those whom they have injured, and to inflict
greater injuries on those whom they so hate.

The various despatches issued in this campaign,
describe the operations of the war, if war it can be
called, in terms of exaggerated admiration and self-
applause. All the officers praise one another, and the
governor praises all the officers, with such inordinate
puffing, as would be considered too broad even for a
caricature.

Take the following specimens :—" The enterprise
was as judiciously planned, as it was resolutely and
successfully executed. The rapidity of the movement,
the promptness and gallantry with which the enemy
were attacked as soon as they were discovered have been
alike remarkable, and do the greatest credit to Colonel
Smith, and the officers and detachments employed."*
And what had these heroes done? They had taken
away 1200 head of cattle, and destroyed a village ; but
so desperate had been the fight, "that the whole had
been achieved *without any loss on the part of the
troops.*" The cattle, however, were " generally very
beautiful !"

Is it in such feats as these that British soldiers reap
laurels for their brows? The commander-in-chief,
however, does not seem to have been the least aware of
the ridicule which he was fastening on the army, by
copying the style of " general orders" issued in the
peninsular war, and applying it to this frivolous cam-

---

* Major Dalton's Notice. C. W. p. 27.

paign against sheep and oxen. It had been, however, resolved from the first, that it should be a great war, and that it should be a harvest for renown and promotions; a great war, therefore, it was made to be, though, in reality, it was as little worthy of a triumph, as Caligula's famous expedition against Britain.

From the ridiculous, however, we must turn to the tragical, and reserving the murder of king Hintza for a separate chapter, we will here contemplate some of the atrocious episodes enacted in this war.

An individual who served in the British army, in that campaign, was so shocked with some murders which he either saw, or knew to be committed in Caffre-land, that he thought it his duty to send an account of them in a letter to a friend at Cape Town, and that letter has been put in my hands, with such accompany-ing statements, as convince me of the validity of the testimony. Without giving the writer's name, I think it best to transcribe his plain and simple description of these horrors......... " After our return from Hintza's country, where we had established military posts in the new province, shortly before Fort Wellington was at-tacked, the Horse Guards at Fort Murray reported to the officer commanding the post, that they had seen a body of Caffres lurking about some gardens in the vicinity, which induced Captain * * * to proceed in that direction the following morning, with a strong patrol. When they reached the place that had been pointed out, they observed smoke issuing out of an old hut, which had not been burned down with the others, that it might be left as a refuge for an old decrepid couple, a man and a woman. I do not know whether they called on the old people to come out, but I know they never took the trouble to ascertain who the people were within; they concluded that the tenants were the enemy, and without any more ado, closed in and opened a fire into the hut, *till the blood of the old pair came running in a stream out of the door-way.* They fired two hundred rounds of ball cartridge on this occasion, which was an expensive mode of killing the poor old souls, as it must have cost three pounds fifteen shillings, valuing each cartridge at four-pence halfpenny."

" The second case I wish you to know, took place under a patrol sent out from Fort Wellington, under the command of Mr. B. of the Provisionals, which was divided, and the one-half sent in charge of Serjeant * * of the 72d, with directions to meet the officers at a given point. Sergeant * * came on a number of huts and cattle in a glen, before the whole of the Caffres could escape. One in particular, who was last of the party, and who saw no other means of averting instant death, threw his arms round a woman who was close by, and held her in front of his person, thinking surely they would not murder a woman ; the woman laid bare her breasts to the soldiers, to convince them she really was a woman. The Serjeant repeatedly urged the man to separate himself from the female, threatening to shoot them both, if they did not. This threat was conveyed to them in the Caffre tongue by a Bechuana, who knew the language ; but the poor fellow would not give up his only hope of life, and, in consequence, both man and woman were shot dead on the spot !"

The third case took place near Mr. Ross's station, by a party sent from Fort Beresford, under the command of Ensign * * * of the 72d. They fell in with a number of women and two old men, who were unable to secrete themselves, or to escape from the patrol. One of the old men was already wounded in the leg ;

him they speedily dispatched, but the other old Caffre's death was attended with some heart-rending circumstances. The soldier who was his murderer could not make his gun go off, it missed fire several times, and whilst he was again and again attempting to make his gun go off, the poor old Caffre was on his knees with uplifted hands in the attitude of a supplicant begging for his life. He was, however, at last dispatched, on the plea " *that he was still able to throw an assegai.*"

" The last case is the worst—it took place near Burnshill, by a party under the command of Ensign S., of the Provisionals, who has since been sent about his business ; but himself narrated to ——— what was done on that occasion. It appears they had fallen in with a number of women who had two boys along with them, still claiming their mothers' protection. Some of them insisted on shooting the boys, but the mother urged that they were only children, and could have injured no one, being only ten or eleven years old at the utmost. Their mothers seeing that this was of no avail, placed themselves between the party and their children, *as a hen would cover her chickens from the hawk* ; but, alas ! the same shot killed both mothers and their children, without leaving one to deplore the other's loss."

And these are the " brilliant exploits," the " noble achievements," the " rapid marches, executed with such celerity that the savages had no time to escape," which gained for the army redundant applause from the eloquent pen of Sir Benjamin D'Urban, and which have elevated them amongst the demi-gods in the fustian of his vaunting " general orders."

CHAPTER XXII.

The Murder of Hintza, King of the Amakosæ.

HINTZA lived beyond the Kei river, at a considerable distance from the theatre of war, and as he sent a message to the chiefs who lived to the west of his territory, commanding them "not to fight, because he did not fight," and as he restrained all his subjects from taking any part in the war, it might have been supposed that he would have been left unmolested by the colony; but such was not the case, he was barbarously and treacherously murdered in the British camp on the 12th of May, 1835.

Sir Benjamin D'Urban, so early as the 19th of March, manifested a spirit of determined hostility against this prince in a passage of one of his despatches, which deserves attention. "Hintza has been playing a double game. He has *received* the plundered cattle into his territory, some of his people have even *undoubtedly* joined the invaders, and his council (Heemraaden) are decidedly hostile; but he himself professes not to be so, and as far as I can discover in some communications which I have had with him during the last month, he is very desirous of holding off, to await the results of our first movements in advance, and then to act as may best suit his policy at the moment. In this perhaps *he may go farther than may be for his advantage;* because if he holds back from giving his essential assistance to the other tribes in the outset, he will weaken them, and when they are disposed of, will be left by ourselves to meet the ulterior proceedings upon our part, which, if we shall find it expedient to adopt them, I have little doubt we shall have discovered ample cause upon his, to justify our adoption." *

Many things are here to be remarked :—

1. The general tone of studied suspicion, which equally distorts the past and future policy of the Caffre King.

2. The charge of " receiving" stolen cattle is rash and ill-grounded, for supposing that " the stolen cattle" were in his territory, a fact which Sir Benjamin could only know by conjecture, how in any justice could this be a plea for these angry threats of future punishment ? The boundary of Hintza's territory is of large extent, so large that it is confessed by military men it could not be sufficiently guarded with so few as three thousand soldiers; how then could he be responsible for droves of cattle coming into his dominions across the Kei River, driven by persons who might take all the advantages of secresy offered to them by the wildness of the country, the rugged mountains, the deep ravines, and the thick forests ? Let Sir Benjamin D'Urban reflect on the difficulty of preventing cattle

---

* Caffre War, p. 11.

The last sentence of this passage is faithfully transcribed, but if it should appear obscure, it is as well here to remark that his excellency's grammar is occasionally as confused and vicious as his sentiments.

passing the border between England and Scotland; the immense line of guards it would require to be watching day and night, and then let him compare that border with the country through which the Kei River passes, and say in candour whether it was reasonable to expect that Hintza should know, or knowing, be able to prevent the entrance of cattle into his dominions?

3. Was it so great a crime, supposing that Hintza had been fully aware of the fact, (or even had expressly given his permission), to allow his brother chiefs thus to place their property in a place of safety? Who in common humanity could find fault with him for such an act? Nay, who with proper feelings could help commending him for it? Let us grant, for argument's sake, that large droves of cattle had passed the Kei River from the west with his permission, was he bound to know that they were colonial cattle? was he so deeply interested in the colonial prosperity as to examine the beasts and horses; and if he had, must he not have depended on the representations of those who brought them into his dominions?

4. Sir Benjamin D'Urban intimates that he has " had communications with Hintza, but finds him desirous of *holding off*:" in other words, his Excellency had endeavoured to make Hintza declare war against the chiefs west of the Kei; even as he had forced Mapassa to become the ally of the colony, telling him if he did not that he would be " removed" out of his country. But Hintza prudently and properly *held off*; that is, he declined going to war either with his brother chiefs or the colony; and this, either way, was a crime in the eyes of Sir Benjamin D'Urban; for, by keeping peace with the colony, it made it difficult to find a pretence for

quarrelling with him ; and by keeping peace with the
Caffre chiefs, it left Sir Benjamin to the sole management of a very tedious and troublesome campaign.

5. This "holding off," his Excellency, without hesitation, determines "was to await results, and then to
act as may best suit his policy;" insinuating, that
Hintza would join the chiefs, if he found it expedient—
a mere surmise, without a shadow of foundation.
Hintza's policy was clear and well-defined : it was to
keep a strict neutrality.

6. His Excellency, in a very confused and cloudy
sentence, hints broadly enough that he intended to
punish the neutrality, by what he called "ulterior proceedings." What those ulterior proceedings might be,
we cannot now say; the murder of Hintza probably
disordered the plans of his Excellency, and compelled
him to alter his arrangements for vengeance in that
quarter.

These remarks, by way of preface, will now allow us
to proceed with the narrative.

On the 19th of June, the governor writes another
despatch, in which it was incumbent on him to give the
best colouring he could to the death of the Caffre king.
He therefore begins by repeating his accusations of
March 19, and enlarging them. " Early as the month
of February, I had ascertained *beyond all doubt* that
Hintza had been *the original contriver and instigator
of the combination among the chiefs* of the savage
tribes in western Caffreland against the colony; .. received into his territory the plundered herds and effects
sent thither, &c."* ....

This accusation in every sense of the word is untrue,

* Caffre War, p. 15.

and it is evidently untrue by its own internal evidence; for in March his Excellency had charged Hintza with neutrality, and a desire to hold off; but now in June, a month after the Prince had been murdered, he forgets himself so much as to state boldly that he had even in February *ascertained beyond all doubt* that Hintza had orignated, contrived, and instigated the war!

The accusation was ridiculously, notoriously untrue. The war broke out before Hintza could by possibility have known of it, and when he did hear of it, he sent a message to all the chiefs "forbidding them to fight, because he did not fight."

April the 15th, Sir Benjamin D'Urban, the commander-in-chief, crossed the Kei River, and entered Hintza's territory. On the 17th, he encamped on the Gona, near Hintza's ordinary residence, though the Caffre king had then retreated up the country; and on this very natural and prudent retreat the construction is put that he had gone "to receive his share of the colonial plunder,"* as if under such circumstances, and at that time especially, he would have gone up the country for so perilous a purpose!

Several messages were sent to Hintza requiring him to meet the governor in person, in order to settle the difference between him and the colony. They gave him five days to come: a very threatening message, and such as could not fail to increase his alarm; but as the king did not make his appearance within the prescribed time, his Excellency, on the 24th, formally proclaimed war with him in the presence of one of his chief councillors. On the 24th and 25th, Colonel Smith began the war, by penetrating into the mountains near

---

* C. W. p. 30.

the residence of Hintza, "whom he very nearly surprised," and concluded that "brilliant affair" by driving off "10,000 head of beautiful cattle," part of them the personal property of the king. The sequel must be told in colonial language, which swells into a grand strain on this occasion. * "Meanwhile these movements and their results had a due effect on Hintza. The presence of this force in the heart of his country, and in the immediate neighbourhood of his residence, the narrow personal escape which he had himself experienced, together with the rapidly extending capture of the cattle, had probably convinced him of the reality of the danger which his *ingratitude and bad faith to the colony* had provoked; and that the English power, upon the distance of which he had presumed for impunity *when he insulted it*, had reached him at last. Upon this impression, upon the commander-in-chief's assurance of safe conduct for himself, and also *that no other person would be admitted to treat for him*, he came into the camp on the 29th of April, with his ordinary retinue of fifty followers, and had an immediate conference with the commander-in-chief."

This interview consisted of reading a very long written document to the Caffre king,—a pamphlet of colonial abuse—charging him with many offences, some of which have been already examined, and concluding with this pleasant peroration,—that his Excellency had been pleased to "take under his especial protection" the Fingoes,—in other words, had taken away from the King sixteen thousand of his subjects, who had fled to his territory from the persecution of a neighbouring African monarch, and were living quietly amongst the

* C. W. p. 32.

Caffres. This "especial" humbug of philanthropy will be presently examined. His Excellency further commanded Hintza to "restore" 50,000 head of cattle, and 1000 horses "to be approved by commissioners"—half of the "restoration" to be paid immediately, and half a year afterwards; and also to pay a fine of "600 good cattle" for the murder of two English traders within the territory of Hintza. "As acknowledged chief of Caffreland," Hintza was also to lay his *"imperative commands, and cause them to be obeyed,"* upon the belligerent chiefs and their dependents instantly to cease hostilities. To all this Hintza is said to have cheerfully acquiesced, and so a conditional peace was concluded between the high contracting powers.

Long might we tarry to comment on this farce of injustice, but here we will only remark, that in the enormous demand of cattle, no notice was taken of the fact, that they had already plundered Hintza of 20,000 head of "beautiful cattle," which went for nothing in this unrighteous calculation!*

The next step was to secure the first instalment, and for this purpose, as Sir Benjamin D'Urban states, Hintza "requested" permission to stay in the British camp, expressing a wish also to send for his young son Crieli (or Hhaali) the heir apparent. The young prince soon joined his father, so that both Hintza and his son were apparently voluntary hostages in the British camp.

On the 3d day of his sojourn in the camp, Hintza

---

* In the despatch of June 19th, Sir Benjamin D'Urban, distinctly states that they had captured 20,000 head of cattle in Hintza's territory "during the five days which *preceded* the treaty."—C. W. p. 19.

and his suite followed the Governor to the Debakazi, and on that day the Governor told him, according to his own account, "that he was free to leave the camp if he liked." In the course of that day's march, Colonel Somerset informed the Governor that the Caffres were murdering the Fingoes, in consequence, it was presumed by the Governor, of their projected abduction from Hintza's power. On hearing this the Governor informed Hintza he was no longer a hostage, but a prisoner!!!*

Of all unreasonable proceedings, this seems the most unreasonable. What possible claim could Sir Benjamin

* "It now became immediately and urgently necessary to stop further massacre by the most prompt measures, and I therefore signified to Hintza that this proceeding by which he had broken the treaty had altered his position; *that I held him, and all who accompanied him responsible,* and that if an immediate stop were not put to these acts of blood and treachery, they should take the consequence, and that I would hold them responsible until every Fingo was out of their country: *under this impression of personal fear* Hintza despatched messengers," &c.—Sir Benjamin D'Urban's Despatch, June 19th, 1835.—C. W. p. 18.

The governor here intimates, that he personally threatened Hintza, but he does not inform the colonial office that he *threatened to hang* his royal captive: such however was the case, as appears by the revelation of a certain Doctor Murray, who was with the army, and who was an eye-witness to all that passed on this occasion; this gentleman undertook by publishing a letter in the newspaper, to make Hintza's captivity appear a most righteous affair. It is needless to say, that he materially darkened the story by adding particulars which otherwise would have remained unknown. "His Excellency gave immediate orders," says Dr. Murray, "that Hintza, Hili, and Booko, and all the people with them, about 150 in number, should be guarded; and told them that he should keep them as hostages for the safety of the Fingoes. He desired them instantly to despatch messengers to stop the attack on the Fingoes—adding that if he found any subterfuge in

D'Urban set up to the service or fealty of these Fingoes? It was sheer robbery on his part taking them
away from Hintza; he had no more title to them than
he has to the inhabitants of Lyons or any of the subjects of the King of France; and if the Caffres were
murdering them, it was all the Governor's fault; not a
hair of their heads would have been touched but for his
officious interference, or rather his unjustifiable abduction.   But to make this affair a pretence of keeping
Hintza a prisoner, was violating not only the law of
nations, but the laws of common honesty and the decencies of civilized life.

Five days had been given to Hintza to pay the first
instalment, but those five days having elapsed, he requested that he might go through his country accompanied with a proper guard, and " by appearing among
his people make them obey him."

Sir Benjamin states also, that after much urging,
Hintza at last, and very unwillingly, sent his order
" as paramount chief" of Caffreland to all the belligerent chiefs to cease hostilities, but that he spoiled
the whole effect of the message by privately adding this
laconic hint, "Take care of yourselves for I am a
prisoner." It is probable that Hintza did do this; the
message is in Caffre style and seems genuine, and it
was much to his credit that he gave this timely warning to his brother chiefs, for what might he not expect

---

the message they sent, he would hang Hintza and Booko themselves on the tree under which they were sitting."—Commercial
Advertiser, February 20th, 1836.

It would require no slight acquaintance with colonial practice
to understand the true import of colonial language: "personal
responsibility," we see, has a meaning at the Cape which never
could have been divined in England.

would be the treatment of his noble kindred if ever
they fell into the hands of that perfidious enemy who
now kept him prisoner? Sir Benjamin D'Urban, however, uses many hard words in his description of this
transaction, abusing " the treacherous savage" with
bitter wrath; but did his Excellency never consider
that Hintza had his own interests to attend to as much
as those of the colony? Was not the country of the
captive king as dear to him as the colony to Sir Benjamin D'Urban? and why should he not warn the chiefs
to take care of themselves? Was he bound to sacrifice
his country to the dictates of an imperious intruder,
who had already stolen 20,000 head of cattle from him,
and 16,000 of his subjects, and who had turned the
sacred laws of hospitality into the odious offices of a
jailer? But again, Hintza was expected to " lay his
imperative commands and see them obeyed" —how
could he do this as long as he was a prisoner? What
value would they attach to these " imperative commands," when they saw their monarch in captivity?
Would they not naturally suspect that these " imperative commands" were the messages of Sir Benjamin
D'Urban, and not of Hintza? and would they not disregard any such message till they saw him freely presiding as a free king in the national council? His
Excellency the Governor must have known all this, but
he seems as if he were determined to disgrace himself
beyond recovery, by every sentence of his violent and
foolish despatches.

However, Hintza, under a strong escort, Colonel
Smith acting as jailer, and accompanied by his counsellor Mutini, and three other Caffres, went forth from
the camp on the 10th of May, with the professed object
of appearing among his subjects to make them obey

the " treaty," by paying the first instalment of 25,000 head of cattle. Whether Hintza made this proposal to find some means of escape, or whether the idea of attempting an escape was not adopted till the next day, when he saw that his subjects were everywhere driving off their herds out of the reach of the enemy, must be left to conjecture—but that he was justified in endeavouring to break his chains must be conceded without hesitation.*

---

* Sir Benjamin D'Urban issued a proclamation or manifesto on the 10th of May, the day on which Hintza left the camp in the custody of Colonel Smith; it is an important document.

" 1. Twelve days ago, Hintza,—the heart of his country being occupied by the troops of the king my master, his personal residence in danger, and his further *resistance* useless, came into my camp and sued for peace.

" 2. I there set forth and prescribed to him the terms upon which peace could be granted.

" 3. And on the following day, having duly considered them, he accepted them all, and solemnly ratified them, remaining himself with his son and heir, *by his own choice and free-will*, as hostages for the fulfilment of the treaty which he had ratified.

" 4. The deportment of the chief appeared so frank and honourable, that I was induced to abstain from using a power reserved to me by the concluding article of the treaty, that of 'continuing hostilities until the first instalment of cattle should have been paid,' and to secure his people from the scourge of war in the mean time; I accordingly caused hostilities to cease on the part of my troops, thereby foregoing the additional advantage which the then following up those already gained could not have failed to secure.

" 5. What return has Hintza made for all this *forbearance?*—he has deceived me throughout.

" 6. He has it is true very reluctantly complied with the 2d stipulation of the treaty, (i. e. the commands to be laid on the confederate chiefs) but the 1st, 3d, and 4th, the most important of all, are still unexecuted; and although their fulfilment has been

Where the captive king and his jailer halted on the 10th, does not appear; but on the 11th, by his desire they marched towards the mouth of the River Bashee, and came on the track of numerous cattle; " it was repeatedly urged to him, no effectual steps have yet been taken for that end.

" 7. In these circumstances I have a full and just right to consider and treat him as a prisoner of war, AND SEND HIM TO CAPE TOWN; but as I am still disposed to believe his asseveration, that his presence in the midst of his people may give him the power of fulfilling his solemn agreement, *I will abstain from doing so, and will not for the present send him out of his own country;* but it is upon the condition proposed by himself that he accompanies a division of my troops through such parts of the country as its commanding officer, Colonel Smith, may select, &c.

" 8. Meanwhile I retain as hostages according to the 5th demand of my treaty, Hintza's son Creli, and his relation Bookoo," &c. &c.

" Done at my Head Quarters on the Kei, May 10th, 1835.

" B. D'URBAN, Governor."

It is particularly to be observed that in this manifesto not one word is said about the Fingoes, though the governor in his despatch of June 19th, (C. W. p. 18.) gave that as his reason for changing the voluntary sojourn of the king in the British camp into imprisonment. The sole reasons in the manifesto for this imprisonment, are the non-fulfilment of articles 1. 3. 4. which relate exclusively to payment of cattle, (C. W. p. 35.) so that it seems Sir Benjamin D'Urban was not particularly scrupulous in stating his motives, or thought it of much importance to *appear* scrupulous in the kidnapping " a savage."

The manifesto, with the usual garrulity of its imprudent author, blabs the fact, that his Excellency contemplated sending the captive king a prisoner to Cape Town, where questionless he would have been put in the common jail, if not sent to Robben Island, the prison of the prophet Makanna, supposing even that they would have allowed him to reach his destination in safety. It is extremely probable that Hintza was threatened with this

evident," says Colonel Smith, " that the cattle from all
the kraals in the neighbourhood had been driven in the
direction Hintza pointed out; I therefore readily acquiesced in his desire to march this way." At twelve
o'clock of the night of the 11th, they continued their
march, and marched till eight o'clock next morning;
Colonel Smith testifies that " the track of the cattle was
recent and numerous," as was observed on the morning
of the 12th; this therefore was evidence of Hintza's
sincerity. At breakfast the king appeared particularly
uneasy, and said, according to Colonel Smith's account,
" What have the cattle done, that you want them? or
why must I see my subjects deprived of them ?"

At ten o'clock, on the 12th of May, they marched
onward still, and Hintza, shortly after setting out, made
this remark, " See how my subjects treat me; they
drive their cattle from me in spite of me." He then
requested permission to send his counsellor Mutini
with a message to his subjects, forbidding them to
drive away their cattle. This request was granted.
When they came to the Kebaka, they found the track
of the cattle divided, one track going up " a stupend-
ous mountain," and the other up " a very high, abrupt,
steep, woody hill." Hintza advised Colonel Smith to
follow the track up the hill, and here he determined to
attempt an escape. The Caffre king was well mounted,
the path through which the party was advancing was a
narrow cattle path, occasionally passing through the

punishment, and that to escape the disgrace and danger of such a
fate, he proposed going amongst his people in the custody of
Colonel Smith. We do not know what took place between
Hintza and the governor in the camp, and we probably never shall
know: the narrative is exclusively in the hands of his enemies,
who reveal or conceal what they choose.

cleft of the rock. When they had nearly reached the top of this steep ascent, Hintza rode off at full gallop, the guards crying out " Look, Colonel!" Hintza's flight was down a gradual descent of land to the River Kebaka. Colonel Smith spurred on his horse at full speed to overtake the fugitive monarch, and coming near him, snapped two pistols at him, but neither pistol went off. Coming still nearer, he struck Hintza on the head with the butt-end of his pistol, but still the race continued, Hintza keeping a little a-head of his pursuer. After about a mile and a half of pursuit, Colonel Smith came so near the king as to be able to pull him off horseback; but Hintza rose from the fall, threw an assegai at his pursuer, and ran off with great speed. Colonel Smith was unable to manage his horse, which ran away with him, but Mr. George Southey, of the corps of guides, came up, and at about two hundred yards distance called on Hintza to stop, or he would shoot him. The king ran on; Southey fired and wounded him slightly in the leg; still, however, the king continued running, and was then shot by Southey through the back. Hintza fell headlong forward, but springing up again, and closely pursued by Lieutenant Balfour, Colonel Smith's aid-de-camp, he precipitated himself down a kloof by the Kebaka, and, according to Colonel Smith's narrative,* refused to surrender.

* This is Colonel Smith's statement, which however is certainly not true: the colonel says, he even " lifted up an assegai," as if in all this chase, and with these severe wounds, and after falling down twice, he had kept his assegai! The fact is, that Hintza plunged into the water, and called out repeatedly for mercy, which was granted by the Hottentots, but refused by the officers.

The following particulars are from one of the corps of guides, who was an eye-witness, and who, though he himself had been a

Southey then fired, and shot the monarch through the
head: he fell down dead into the waters of the Kebaka.
A person, whose name I have, but will not publish,
lifted the head of the murdered king out of the water,
and cut off the ears, whilst one of the party cried out to
him not to do that "because it would set people a
talking;" the ears, however, were cut off, and were
afterwards taken in triumph to Graham's Town.
Another person, whose name I have, then cut off the flesh
of the chin, and took a bayonet belonging to one of the
soldiers, with which he dug out the teeth; after this
horrid butchery, this same person was preparing to cut
off the head, but seeing it too much disfigured, he de-
sisted.

And thus was Hintza, King of the Amakosæ, mur-

sufferer by the Caffre invasion, could not behold the murder of
Hintza without horror. "After Hintza had been wounded twice,
he jumped down a kraantz, and sheltered himself behind a large
stone. The first who came up to him was one of the Cape
mounted rifles, who jumped down the said kraantz, and when
in the act of levelling his gun, Hintza cried out for mercy, on
which he lowered his piece: the next that followed down was
another of the mounted rifles, who at the point of shooting, was
deterred by the supplications of the king. Immediately arrived
at the top of the kraantz the corps of guides, not one of whom
seemed disposed to go down. Hintza then stood up and cried
out to them, 'faku amapakati,' which is to say "take me as
your prisoner,' which they all heard—when Southey fired, and
blew the upper part of his head off. Thus fell the chief of the
Amakosæ, supplicating for mercy, whose death was predicted by
all, when it was known that he was at the mercy of those com-
prising the corps of guides. *Much to the dishonour of this corps,
the chief's ears were brought in triumph to Graham's Town.* The
glory of this deed has been the subject of a poem, and Southey
has been extolled as the saviour of mankind, which poem attracts
the attention of the public by being affixed to the church door."

dered and mangled in his own dominions, on the banks of the River Kebaka, on the 12th of May, 1835.

· The facts of this narrative up to Hintza's death, are to be found in the despatches of Sir Benjamin D'Urban and Colonel Smith: the barbarous mutilation of the corpse is given on the authority of private information, which may be depended on; it is the authority of one of the army, a person who was in the Caffre war, and in Hintza's territories with his regiment, when the murder took place. If such frightful crimes as these are to pass unpunished, it will be in vain hereafter to talk of the honour of the British army; the captivity and murder of Hintza will not be forgotten in history.

A feeling of shame for one's countrymen might lead one to spare any fresh exposure affecting persons already implicated in this tragical story, but the truth must be told, nor must we keep back the deplorable comment on Hintza's murder, which Sir Benjamin D'Urban thought proper to indite in a despatch to the Earl of Aberdeen: dated 19th June, 1835.

" I would rather, *perhaps*," says his Excellency, " that this event had not occurred, inasmuch as it may, however unjustly and unfairly, be made a handle of by a party at home. For Hintza, individually, he richly deserved the fate which he brought upon him, and which he had earned by a series of acts of flagrant bad faith, aggression, and injury to the colony; *having been the author and prime mover* of the horrors which so recently covered it with blood and ashes. He had, within a few days of his death, sufficiently proved what he was, and what he would have been to the last,—a treacherous, ungrateful, and cunning savage, whom no obligations could bind and no

L 5

benefits attach; and his blood, *most unintentionally shed*, has saved, in all probability, that of many of our people as well as of his own."*

* Extract from Lord Glenelg's despatch to Sir B. D'Urban :—
26th Dec. 1835.

" I cannot, in this brief review of your military operations, pass, without particular notice, the incident of the captivity and death of Hintza, or overlook the warfare waged against him and his people. After anxiously examining every word which has been written on the subject by Colonel Smith and yourself, I must avow that I am not satisfied, either that this chieftain was the legitimate object of your military operations, or that his death admits of any satisfactory justification. You charge his tribe, in your despatch of the 8th of January, with having supported the tribes on the border, but, at that time, you had plainly no evidence of the fact in your possession. That on the 19th of March he was not in open hostility is manifest from the omission of his name, in the catalogue which you then drew up of the hostile tribes. Indeed, it is evident that at that time his professions were pacific; he was desirous, as you state, of ' holding off.' It is said that his people were decidedly hostile, but of this assertion also the proof is wanting. In the predicament in which he was placed, neutrality was the wise and justifiable policy of Hintza ; nor can I perceive why he should have been censured for pursuing it. Yet I find that, previously to the 19th of March, hostilities against him were meditated....... I will not pause to inquire whether Hintza was justly detained in your camp as a prisoner, or whether he was really liable to pay with his life the penalty of attempting to escape from the detachment which accompanied him. All this being conceded, there yet remains the question, not hitherto solved, nor, as far as I can perceive, even discussed. He was slain when he had no longer the means of resistance, but covered with wounds, and vainly attempting to conceal his person in the water into which he had plunged as a refuge from his pursuers. Why the last wound was inflicted, and why this unhappy man, regarded with an attachment almost idolatrous by his people, was not seized by the numerous armed men who had reached his place of concealment, has never yet been explained. The case assumes a peculiar importance, from the circumstance that Mr.

The uncertain sorrow, " I had rather *perhaps*," &c.
—then the reason of that sorrow—" a handle to a
party at home"—the assertion that Hintza " richly
deserved to be put to death"—the angry and mali-
cious language mingled with false accusations against
the victim of Sir Benjamin D'Urban's policy — the
ridiculous mention of " benefits and gratitude"—
(Hintza's *gratitude* to the colony ! ! !)—the *accident* of
his death—" most unintentionally," &c.—the happy
results of that happy accident, all constitute a total
which we should in vain look for in any ordinary
despatches of a colonial ruler.

It will be perceived by the extract from Lord Glenelg's despatch, given in the note, that the murder of
Hintza was accompanied with circumstances which
materially darken the story, circumstances which were
concealed or mistated by Colonel Smith.   The inquiry
which his lordship has instituted can only be expected
to have one termination ; for when this inquiry was to
be arranged by persons more or less implicated in
the transaction, and when the witnesses were Hot-

Southey, who gave the death wound, appears to have been subsequently twice commended in general orders, though not indeed
with any express reference to his conduct.   It is said that
Hintza refused to surrender; but if the fact be so, of what importance was the refusal of a wounded, helpless, isolated man?
It is stated to me however on evidence which it is impossible to
receive without serious attention, that Hintza repeatedly cried for
mercy ; that the Hottentots present granted the boon, and abstained from killing him ;' that this office was then undertaken by
Mr. Southey, and that then the dead body of the fallen chief was
basely and inhumanly mutilated.   I express no opinion on this
subject, but advert to it because the honour of the British name
demands that the case should undergo a full investigation, which
it is my purpose to institute.''

tentots or soldiers, who aided in the pursuit, and who
knew too well the consequences of accusing their
superiors, and when we take into consideration the
furious anti-Caffre spirit now prevailing in the colony,
it would be unreasonable to expect that the truth
should be elicited amidst such disadvantages.

CHAPTER XXIII.

Conclusion of the War.

IT will be remembered that Sir Benjamin D'Urban, on the 19th of March, expressed his opinion, that he should finish his operations within a month, or about the middle of April; but in the last chapter we have seen him carrying on the war in the farther Caffreland so late as May, without any prospect of enforcing the peace for which he was daily becoming more anxious. We have seen that Macomo, Tyali, and the other belligerent chiefs, succeeded in avoiding the enemy and protecting their cattle, whilst Sir Benjamin D'Urban, not to come away empty handed, was reduced to the dishonest necessity of plundering King Hintza, and of making him pay the penalty of other people's offences. Macomo and the confederate chiefs, having a thorough knowledge of the country, and having the wishes of every inhabitant of the country on their side, contrived to elude the pursuit of the enemy, always having such information of the movements of the British forces as enabled them to decamp in time, and to move headquarters from one mountain to another, from one forest to another, with a rapidity and precision of action that quite baffled the skill and vengeance of their enemies. It is conjectured that Macomo had under his command an army of ten thousand warriors, and it certainly is to his credit as a general, that under such circumstances he should be able to furnish provisions for his troops, and so to arrange all things requisite for so large a force, that the spirits of his men never failed to the last, and that at the end of the war he should be able to muster fifteen hundred cavalry in good condition. The difficulties of his situation were very great, as would be conceded by all military men, and yet he emerged from them with an eclat that would in a European warfare have gained him no little military renown.

Sir Benjamin D'Urban *was the first to make propositions of peace.* On the 4th of May, the governor then being in Hintza's territory, sent instructions to Colonel Cox, to effect, if possible, an interview with the confederate chiefs, to induce them to surrender themselves on certain terms, and to propose terms of peace.* The instructions were as follows:

"If the people of Tyali, Macomo, &c. will come into any of our divisions with their wives and cattle, and give up their arms, they shall be protected, and retain the cattle they shall bring, not being colonial. With regard to the chiefs themselves, if they come in, (any one or all) and deliver themselves up, *unconditionally*, it may be stipulated that their lives shall be safe, and that they shall be personally well treated, but that the terms to be ultimately granted to them must depend on his Majesty the King of England, whose decision they must in the meantime wait.

"Head Quarters, East of the Kei, May 4th, 1835."

* Ab. 334.

In obedience to these instructions, Colonel Cox had an interview with the chiefs Macomo and Tyali, on the 12th of May, the day on which King Hintza was murdered, and though this fact was not known in the Caffre camp, they had already received Hintza's message conveyed to them four or five days before, and which told them "to take care of themselves, for he was a prisoner." The chiefs came to the interview attended by a hundred warriors, Colonel Cox brought with him one officer and two Hottentot orderlies;* the meeting took place about a mile distant from the English camp. Colonel Cox endeavoured to persuade them to accept the terms proposed by his excellency the governor: he was very anxious that the chiefs should come into the English camp; but he also stated that one of the final measures of the governor was to make the clans then 'at war with the colony pass over the Kei, and for ever renounce the country they now occupied. It seems, by Colonel Cox's statement, that the chiefs were not unwilling to come into the camp, but their counsellors and warriors would not allow them; they considered, and rightly, that the princes would not be safe in such keeping. The interview however passed off without any exasperating language, all was conducted with civility and good manners on both sides, but it ended without effecting the object which the governor desired.

Colonel Cox attributes the failure of the projected peace chiefly to the message of Hintza, and though it doubtless had great weight with the Caffre counsellors, yet it is also certain that the terms offered were such as they resolved not to accept, and that by continuing

* Ab. 346.

the war they secured a more advantageous peace at last.

Had Macomo and the other chiefs come into the English camp, we may not unreasonably conjecture that the habitual treachery of the colonial policy would again have displayed itself in some dark deeds—that the captive princes would, perhaps, have been sent off, like the prophet Makanna, to Robben Island, amongst the felons of the colony; or that when Hintza's death became known, it would have been a signal for some stroke of violence; and that under some pretence of preventing escape, the chiefs would have been despatched, and their memories loaded with accusations of "treachery, perfidy, and ingratitude," amidst the thanksgivings and congratulations of the pious and loyal colonists.

In this period of the war, however, when Sir Benjamin D'Urban had gained nothing but some cows, and not even those from the real enemy with whom he was fighting, did he thus set forth his conquest in a grandiloquent proclamation :—

" Whereas in the months of December and January last, the Caffre chiefs Macomo, Tyali, &c., ... *with the concurrence and countenance of Hintza*, paramount chief, did, during a period of established peace and amity between the chiefs and the colony, *without provocation*, or any previous notice of war, suddenly break into the colony frontier, &c. ....

" And whereas, with the troops of the king my master, I have *defeated*, chastised, and dispersed the chiefs and their tribes, overrun and *conquered* their country, and thence penetrated into that of Hintza, compelling him to sue for peace, and accept the terms of it which I had offered, and which he has ratified.   And whereas it is absolutely necessary to provide for the future security of the colony against such *unprovoked* aggressions, which can only be done by removing these TREACHEROUS AND IRRECLAIMABLE SAVAGES to a safer distance. I now, therefore, in the name, and on the behalf of his Britannic Majesty, do hereby proclaim and declare that the eastern boundary of the colony of the Cape of Good Hope is henceforward extended eastward to the right bank of the river Kei. From the aforesaid country, which they have lost by the operations of the war which they had so wantonly provoked, and which they have justly forfeited, the above-mentioned chiefs, Macomo, &c., with their tribes are FOR EVER EXPELLED, and will be treated as enemies if they be found therein.

" May 10, 1835. " God save the King !"

It would be waste of time, after all that has been said, to detect the numerous misstatements of this proclamation ; one only we may notice as being a rare instance of self-contradiction and self-confutation; for if we compare the " unprovoked aggressions" of this proclamation with Sir Benjamin D'Urban's despatch of October 14, 1834, we shall there find the same author making this statement:—" The Caffre tribes were at that time stimulated by a strongly excited feeling of discontent and ill-will towards the colony, arising from the following circumstances." Then follows a notice of the expulsion of Macomo and others, in 1833, by Colonel Wade: after which, Sir B. D'Urban continues:—" This unfortunately happened when a period of severe drought was approaching, so that these tribes (I am afraid but too certainly) suffered much loss in their herds in consequence. Hence arose their discontented feelings, and which combined with it, in this instance perhaps, a spirit of retribution." So soon could the governor forget his own words.

In spite of this proclamation of conquest, the war continued without intermission; and on the * 10th of

---

* On the 17th of July, certain inhabitants of Graaff Reinet, voted at a public meeting a "loyal" address to the governor, the principal object of which seems to have been to persuade his excellency to put down Mr. Fairbairn's paper—at least that seems to be a reasonable interpretation of the following sentences " ...... It is with deep humiliation that we perceive, that this colony contains a small number of mistaken or factious persons, *capable of misrepresenting* the objects and tendency of the beneficent measures of your excellency, or incapable of justly appreciating them......It is painfully evident that the same spirit of partial philanthropy *which seeks gratification in untrue statements of the colonial and of the savage character*, has a direct tendency to give an undue stimulus to the desires or the pretensions of the savages, and has been actively and successfully exerted in rendering nugatory the imperfect means of defence against external enemies afforded by arraying the armed inhabitants or commandos, &c. &c......"

To this address Sir Benjamin D'Urban responded with a faithful echo, in his peculiar style...." Whatever may be the real and ultimate object of this perversion of facts and of inferences, which I too have observed with painful astonishment, its manifest and immediate tendency is—at home to deceive and mislead his Majesty's government and the people of England, by making the ' worse appear the better cause,' and so to shut the sources of sympathy and assistance there against the sufferers here — in the colony, to paralyze the operations and impede the success of a war, not of choice, but of stern necessity, and waged, if ever war was waged *pro aris et focis*..........I will not conceal my conviction, that the support thus extended to the cause of the enemy, and the reprobation lavished upon that of the colonists—as recklessly maintained—as industriously disseminated—having been communicated to the savage chiefs, have supplied an encouragement which has acted as an incentive to re-animate among them a spirit of resistance which had been well nigh extinguished ; *has*

August, three months after the first unsuccessful attempt to bring the Caffre chiefs to terms, Colonel Cox again received a "confidential communication" from the Governor, relative to a second conference with the chiefs. "I received instructions from his Excellency," says Colonel Cox, "to offer to the chiefs the *modified terms* he intended to grant to them; that he did not intend to turn them over the Kei altogether, but he intended to grant them a portion of land in what was their own country. In consequence of that *I sought this conference.*"*

The Caffre chiefs who now had been for nearly three months acquainted with the murder of Hintza, would not, of course, trust themselves in the camp of the enemy; Colonel Cox was therefore obliged to meet them himself, and to trust to their honour, for he went amongst them with only two or three attendants, and found himself in the midst of six thousand warriors, under the command of Macomo. The conference was of long duration, and Macomo in the course of the conversation said two or three times, "Who made the war? We did not begin the war." He said this in a very significant manner; "but," says Colonel Cox, "as it was irritating to discuss the subject, and as he

prevented a submission which they had been about to make, and has consequently been a main cause of their recently renewed and obstinate hostilities."

His Excellency must indeed have been pushed hard for an excuse for his protracted campaign, to lay the blame of it on newspapers—as if the Caffre chiefs could not understand their own interests without the help of "the faction" in the colony. Sir Benjamin D'Urban's answer to the address is dated 17th August, 1835.

* Ab. 351.

had an immense force, and we were in his power, *I thought it unnecessary* : the object was to make peace."

And in general terms the peace was agreed on, though it was understood that the details were open for future discussion, as Colonel Cox was not instructed to name the extent of territory which the chiefs would be allowed to hold. This led to other conferences, and, after some delay, the peace was concluded at Fort Wiltshire in a meeting of the governor with the chiefs, which took place early in September ; for up to that time the war continued on both sides with undiminished activity. Macomo and Tyali, about the 10th of August, acted even on the offensive, and sent out parties to make reprisals in the colony ; "they even ventured upon inroads along the old colonial border, carrying off some cattle from the Fingoes on the one side, and from the farmers of the Kat River on the other." *

The treaty of peace was signed on the 17th of Sept.; †
the chiefs on their part agreed to become subjects of the king of England, obey the governor, and to live in submission to the general laws of the colony,—to deliver up all the muskets in their possession,—to call in immediately all the detachments of the Caffre army engaged in " predatory excursions,"—to refuse harbour or refuge to any person or persons, of any nation, that had been guilty of any crime or offence against the colony : the chiefs also were to execute the office of magistrate under the British crown, if required.

The governor agreed on his part to grant certain accurately defined territory to the chiefs, naming all the boundaries with precision ; and that the English laws " would not apply to or interfere with the domestic

---

* C. W. p. 100.   † C. W. p. 95—98.

and internal regulations of the tribes and families, nor with their customs, in so far as these do not involve a breach of the above cited laws." *

There are many other items in this strange treaty, which, besides terms of agreement, contains numerous miscellaneous topics of threats to the chiefs, and praise of the governor; scolding them for their crimes, and praising him for his humanity and generosity—describ-them as prostrate suppliants suing for mercy, and himself as a clement conqueror, yielding to their prayers. He tells the chiefs, moreover, that if they take up arms against the king, or commit murder or rape,

* It appears to me that this part of the treaty never could have been executed, and that one of two results must have taken place,—either that the chiefs of Caffreland must have been reduced to cyphers, and consequently, all Caffre law abolished, or else that the English law never could have been established. It was the object of Sir Benjamin D'Urban, which he candidly acknowledges in one of his "confidential" notes to the colonial office, to annihilate the power of the chiefs; this, however, was neither sincere nor prudent policy; it was deceiving the chiefs and their people, who knew not the incompatibility of Caffre and English law, and it would unquestionably have soon led to another outbreak of the exasperated tribes. In the Appendix will be seen a letter of Colonel Smith to Umhala, in which the colonel not only interferes with Caffre customs, but in language the most arbitrary and humiliating: if in the very short reign of English law in the Adelaide province, the colonial authorities treated the chiefs with this studied indignity, we may easily conjecture what would have been the sequence of such a mode of government continued for a few months.

It would be easy, by offering some advantageous treaty to the chiefs, to secure the suppression of witchcraft in Caffreland—this we ought first of all to endeavour to effect, for till that dreadful scourge of the nation is abolished, the poor people can never be much elevated above their present condition.

or set houses on fire, or steal cattle, horses, sheep, goats, *or other property*, they will be in danger of suffering "death itself."

We need not perhaps pause to examine more particularly the items of this absurd treaty, which displays as much ignorance of the laws of England, as of the laws of nations; for as it has been set aside by the Colonial Office, and has been severely criticised by Lord Glenelg; it has already become waste paper, and may be transmitted to that "limbo large and wide," where other "indulgences, dispenses, pardons, bulls," are very properly located.

These matters being so arranged, the great chiefs of the confederacy, in due form swore allegiance to his Britannic Majesty, near King William's Town, on the Keishkamma, in the month of November. Colonel Smith presided at that ceremony, which seems to have been very impressive. Macomo brought into the field upwards of twelve hundred cavalry, and Colonel Smith appeared in military pomp, attended by several ladies, and numerous spectators. All who were present admired the dignity and grace of Macomo, who voluntarily kneeled on one knee in taking the oath of allegiance, and in his speech and all his movements carried himself like a high-born prince, and a well-bred gentleman. He and his brother were dressed that day in European costume. Colonel Smith gallantly paid Macomo the following compliment: " Macomo, I have admired your character as a soldier in the bush, you have been a bold and determined enemy, and I have every confidence in the sincerity of your expressions of your attachment to my King and Governor." And thus ended the Caffre war.

CHAPTER XXIV.

The abortive Vagrant Law of 1834.

THIS narrative would be incomplete if the attempted
vagrant law of 1834 were left unnoticed; it is an epi-
sode of oppression, which was fraught with the utmost
peril to the colony. The deplorable condition of the
Hottentots has been briefly noticed in the second
chapter; it is there shewn that those miserable beings
who were held in service by the colonists, were in the
lowest state of degradation and distress, suffering the
evils of slavery in a form more severe than could any
where else be found, and in every respect so cruelly
treated, that they would probably have been soon exterminated, if the 50th ordinance and the order in
council had not seasonably appeared for their salva-
tion. That order was a declaration of rights to the
Hottentot race, declaring them free men, and placing
them on the same footing precisely with the rest of his
majesty's free subjects in the colony. The 50th colonial
ordinance was passed by General Bourke, then the
acting governor of the colony, on July 17th, 1828, and
this was ratified by an order in council in January
15th 1829, with this very important clause: "That it
should not be competent for any governor, or other

colonial authority to alter or abrogate any of its provisions."

Mr. Pringle thus describes the effect of this righteous
act :—" On the promulgation of the emancipation ordinance, a prodigious clamour was raised through the
colony, in which a very large proportion of all classes
of the white population joined, including persons high
in office, who ought to have evinced a very different
spirit. The absolute ruin of the colony from this
measure was loudly and confidently predicted; it was
asserted that the fields would lie untilled, and the
flocks go untended, for want of labourers and herdsmen, and that the white inhabitants generally would
be reduced to ruin from the cause, and by being
plundered by marauding hordes of Hottentot banditti:
for it was assumed, as a result not to be questioned,
that no Hottentot would work unless compelled by
coercion, and that the whole race would betake themselves to a life of idleness, vagrancy, and robbery,
when no longer held in servitude by compulsory laws.
The *retrogression* of the race into *barbarism* was
affected to be deplored; and the whole of these calamitous consequences were ascribed, in terms of no
measured vituperation, by a swarm of pro-slavery
pamphleteers and journalists, to Mr. Buxton, and "the
saints" at home, and to Dr. Philip, Mr. Fairbairn, and
a few other meddling mischievous hypocrites in the
colony."

The appearance of the order in council of January
1829, compelled these raging slave-drivers to submit to
that which they could not remedy, and now began, in
spite of the wrath and spleen of the colonists, the
amelioration, or rather the transformation of the Hottentot people;—they were changed from brute beasts

into men; their employers could now no longer oppress and torment them, the yoke of bondage was
broken; they were free men, and as free labourers could
demand lawful hire for their services; they were under
the protection of the laws, and could bring actions
against those who injured them, and teach their tyrannical masters that the rod of despotism had fallen from
their hands. The effects of the 50th ordinance have
been all that could have been wished, and more than
could have been expected: the Kat River settlement,
(though the territory for that settlement was taken by
an act of flagrant rapine) has been a refuge for a
happy people, who have their farms, their gardens, their
houses, chapels, churches, and schools; who cultivate
the land with success, and cost the government nothing
but the salary of the clergyman, which had better be
discontinued.

When the act of emancipation was passed in England, it became manifest to the colonists that after the
expiration of the apprenticeship there could be no more
forced labour in the colony; for having first seen the
Hottentots escape from their clutches, they were now
doomed to lose also the services of 30,000 slaves; so
that unless some means could be devised to perpetuate
slavery, in spite of the 50th ordinance*, and the act of

---

* The following constitute the 2d and 3d articles of this important ordinance, and embrace some of its principal provisions.
   "Article II. And whereas, by usage and custom of this
colony, Hottentots and other free persons of colour, have been
subjected to certain restraints as to their residence, mode of life,
and employment, and to certain compulsory services, to which
other of his Majesty's subjects are not liable: be it therefore
enacted, that from and after the passing of this ordinance, no
Hottentot or other free person of colour, lawfully residing in the
colony, shall be subject to any compulsory service, to which

M

emancipation, they must henceforward be reduced to the necessity of hiring the labour of free men, and foregoing the pleasures of oppression, the most difficult perhaps of all sacrifices to make.

In this emergency, a friend came forward to assure them that their case was not hopeless, and that means might yet be devised to perpetuate the reign of opptes-sion. That friend was the acting governor, Colonel Wade, who in a circular, published in Cape Town, dated 7th January, 1834, thus endeavoured to cheer the drooping spirits of the sons of tyranny. "As regards the fears and apprehensions which are, I am aware, entertained on the following points, namely, the entire substitution of the authority of the magistrate for that of the master, during the period of apprenticeship, the difficulties which may occur in procuring a suffi-ciency of labourers to cultivate the farms, and the losses to which property may be exposed from the depreda-tions of the idle and dissolute during that period, you

others of his Majesty's subjects therein are not liable; nor to any hinderance, molestation, fine, imprisonment, or punishment of any kind whatever, *under the pretence that such person has been guilty of vagrancy*, or any other offence, unless after trial in due course of law; any custom or usage to the contrary notwithstanding.

"Article III. And whereas doubts have arisen as to the com-petency of Hottentots, and other free persons of colour, to pur-chase or possess land in the colony; be it therefore enacted, and declared, that all grants, purchases, and transfers of land, or other property whatsoever, heretofore made to or by any Hot-tentot, or other free person of colour, are and shall be, and the same are hereby declared to be, of full force and effect; and that it is, and shall and may be, lawful for any Hottentot, or other free person of colour, born, or having obtained deeds of burgher-ship in this colony, to obtain and possess by grant, purchase, or other lawful means, any land or property therein, any law, custom or usage to the contrary notwithstanding."

will not fail to impress upon the proprietors that the legislature has not abolished the domestic authority of the master, or decided upon the emancipation of the slave, without at the same time providing for an efficient stipendiary magistracy, and for the frequent and punctual visitation by the special justices of the peace, of the apprenticed labourers within their respective districts; and also for the enactment of laws for the prevention and punishment of insolence and insubordination on the part of the apprentices towards their employers, of vagrancy, or of any conduct on the part of the apprenticed labourers injuring or tending to injure the property of their employers; and the proprietors *may further rest satisfied*, that long before the period of the expiration of apprenticeship arrives, OTHER LAWS WILL BE ENACTED, having in like manner for their object the prevention and punishment of vagrancy after that period, *and for securing a sufficiency of labourers to the colony*, by COMPELLING not only the liberated apprentices to earn an honest livelihood, but all others, who being capable of doing so, may be inclined to lead an idle and vagabondizing life."

This doubtless calmed the agitation of the colonists, as they knew that they had friends in the Legislative Council,* whose abilities were equal to the task of devising some trick to frustrate the emancipation both of slaves and Hottentots, if only their courage were equal

---

* The legislative council is appointed by the government in England, on the recommendation of course of the colonial government. The members of this council, of whom five are official, after two years' sitting hold their seats for life; their debates are carried on with open doors. In the discussions on the vagrancy law, about ten members of the council seem to have been present.

to their subtilty. Their friends *had* the courage, and
consequently, in the early part of May, 1834, appeared
the following draft of an ordinance in the colonial
newspapers:—

"Draft of an ordinance proposed by the Governor
of the Cape of Good Hope, to the legislative council
thereof, for the better suppression of vagrancy.

"Whereas, the laws at present existing in this colony
are insufficient for the suppression of vagrancy, and
whereas it is necessary to make further provision for the
apprehension and correction of vagrants; be it therefore
enacted, by the Governor of the Cape of Good Hope,
with the advice and consent of the legislative council
thereof, that every field-cornet and provisional field-
cornet shall, on the 1st of January (*i.e.* 1825), make a
return of all inhabitants then resident, or being within
his jurisdiction according to schedule annexed.

2. "And be it further enacted, that every field-
cornet, &c., may, and hereby is required, to apprehend
all persons found within his jurisdiction, *whom he may
reasonably suspect of having no honest means of subsistence, or who cannot give a satisfactory account of
themselves*, and bring them before the magistrate within
the district for examination.

3. "And be it further enacted, that every magistrate
shall examine such persons so brought before them, and
also any persons who may have knowledge of their
usual place of residence, occupation, or mode of obtaining their livelihood; and it shall be lawful for every
magistrate, *if it shall satisfactorily appear to him that
such persons, so brought before him has no honest
means of subsistence*, to employ him in making or
repairing public roads, or upon other public works,

until they find adequate security for their good behaviour, *or until some respectable person shall agree to
take them into service,* or until the magistrate shall be
satisfied from their behaviour, or from other circumstances, that they will of themselves enter into some
service or employment, whereby they may obtain an
honest livelihood.

  4. " And be it further enacted, that if any person,
after he has been so apprehended, shall make his escape
before he shall have been regularly discharged, and
shall be convicted thereof before any magistrate, he
shall be imprisoned and kept at hard labour for a period
not exceeding twelve calendar months."

Dismissing then this technical language, the ordinance contemplates that the field-cornets, &c., may
arrest any person whom they choose to suspect of having no honest means of subsistence, or who could not
give a *satisfactory* account of himself, bring him before a magistrate, and then state their suspicions ;
and if the magistrate concurs in these suspicions, or
professes not to be satisfied with the account given, he
may for any length of time adjudge that person to
slavery, by either condemning him to the public works
or binding him over as a forced and unpaid labourer
(*i.e.* slave) to any " respectable" person that might
want such a commodity, and if the condemned person
attempts to run away, he may be sent to prison for a
year—and if he again attempt, for another year, and so
on, from his " respectable" master to prison, and back
again, to the end of his life.

  All this monstrous power in the hands of the field-
cornets and the magistrates, persons directly interested
in finding slaves, by hook or by crook, persons who

have been nursed in slavery, and who have deprecated
its abolition as the greatest possible calamity to the
colony.

But we have not yet fathomed the depths of this plot
against the liberties of his Majesty's subjects. The
appearance of the draft of the ordinance for the suppression of vagrancy, created of course the utmost consternation amongst the Hottentots, whilst the main
body of the colonists received it with acclamations of
joy. The few philanthropists who are to be found in
the colony, exerted themselves to prevent this ordinance
becoming a law, and pointed out to the colonial government, that it was contrary to the provisions of the 50th
ordinance, and that no alteration could be made in that
law, till such time as his Majesty in council should
consent to declare the 50th ordinance cancelled. On
this the legislative council took the opinion of the
judges of the colony, and the answer from those functionaries was in these words:—" No law that may be
framed for the suppression of vagrancy can be carried
into effect, in respect of Hottentots and free persons of
colour, owing to the 50th ordinance, which enacts,
that such persons shall not be subject to any hinderance, molestation, or imprisonment of any kind
whatever, under the pretence that such persons have
been guilty of vagrancy, *unless after trial in due course
of law*."

On the authority of this decision the legislative
council proceeded to remove this obstacle, by inserting
a clause in the draft, repealing the 2d clause of the
50th ordinance, and thus having cleared the ground,
they proceeded with consummate skill to spin the cob-
web of slavery.

They met in council again on the 25th of August, and having solemnized their feelings by prayer,* (for the council seems, according to the old adage, always to begin mischief IN NOMINE DOMINI) they drew out the law thus:—" That all persons *not having wherewith honestly to maintain themselves, and being without any lawful employment whereby they may honestly earn the means of subsistence,* who shall wilfully live idle, shall be deemed and taken to be wilful vagrants, and shall thereby commit an act of wilful vagrancy."

This, in other words, declares unemployed poverty vagrancy, though that poverty might be perfectly innocent of any crime, though no alms might have been solicited, no act of the beggar's life committed, and no offence given to any human being. Strip this of technicalities, and what does it say to the victims of this legal iniquity? " You are a poor man, you have no money, you are not working just now, you have not a master, therefore you are a vagrant; we take you and condemn you to the public works, or to some ' respectable' colonist; with him you shall stay and perform forced labour, and if you run away, we will clap you in gaol for a twelvemonth, condemn you to forced labour again, and defy you to escape out of our clutches."

The Hottentot replies — " No; you cannot do so; there is the 50th ordinance, and there is the order in council."

---

* Legislative Council, Sitting No. 22. Monday, 25th August, 1834.

" The council met pursuant to adjournment, and his Excellency the governor took the chair: *after prayers* the minutes of the preceding council were read and confirmed.—And be it further enacted," &c. Ab. p. 749.

The legislative council answers—" We have repealed the 50th ordinance, and said prayers—so go to your old house of bondage, you vagrant Hottentots."

But the legislative council, in this pious session, signalized itself in a memorable manner: It enacted, " that the digging and gathering roots, or the natural produce of the earth, or wild honey, or the searching for, taking, and killing game, or any other wild animal of any kind soever, without permission obtained, *shall not be deemed or taken lawful employment.*" The college of Jesuits, and all the Brothers of the Sodality of " the sacred heart of Jesus," could not but applaud this well-worded clause: mark the phraseology, " *shall not be deemed* lawful," *i.e.* " shall be deemed unlawful," and therefore shall constitute the crime of vagrancy with all its terrible consequences, according to this ordinance.

To see the full force of this clause, it should be understood, that the poor Hottentots, and more especially in these days of oppression, were often too glad to dig up bulbous roots in the open fields to satisfy the cravings of hunger—and that, being moreover a very patient-enduring people, and for the most part indigent, they are in the habit, when they take their journeys through the country, (and immense long journeys they will take on foot to see their friends and relations,) to dig up certain nutritious bulbs, or to apply to nests of the wild bees for their simple meals. There are in the colony vast districts of open land, thousands and tens of thousands of acres, in which wild game abound, and which no one can claim; the road often leads through these wildernesses, and nothing is so common as that a traveller should destroy the wild game of the country, which may happen to cross his path—the hare, the springboke, antelope, or other animals, which are well known in the zoology of South Africa,—but if the poor Hottentot were to be seen shooting a partridge or an antelope in the wilderness, he is by this clause declared a vagrant, and so is converted into a slave.

The person who framed this clause was an adept in Arachne's art; he knew the places exactly in which to spin the venom of his bowels; he knew the practices, the habits, the poverty, the endurance, the patience of the Hottentots; he knew that they will undertake a pedestrian journey of more than five hundred miles,* to bring home a cow, or to see a friend, and to recover some trifle of personal property, which, to a rich colonist, would appear mere refuse; he knew, that either from economical habits or real poverty, they will, in these journeys, sustain themselves on roots or wild vegetables, or the honey comb; that they will, with their bow and arrow, sometimes bring down a partridge or a wild deer, and thus come to the journey's end; and return home again, satisfied with such cheer as nature has prepared without grudging on her bountiful table. But no, said this legislator, if you do any of these harmless things, you shall, through my vagrant traps, fall into the pit of forced labour. 1 have laid such a web that you cannot escape; your feet must be entangled.

It would be quite superfluous to analyse the other voluminous decrees of the twenty-second and twenty-

---

* "The Hottentots have frequently a very trifling object for their journey, as we should consider it according to our views: for instance, they may go a distance of 500 miles, and they may have one bullock to get in that quarter, which may be worth 2l. they will undertake a journey of 500 miles to fetch such a bullock." Evidence of Hans. P. Hallbeck, Moravian Missionary. Ab. 344.

third Session, extending to thirty-five clauses, all of
them more or less savouring of oppression. When the
legislative council had finished its labours of law-mak-
ing, it put forth certain resolutions, to convince the
world of its piety and benevolence. Never was there a
more nauseous exhibition of hypocrisy than in these said
resolutions. They declare that " the communication of
Christian instruction to the coloured population of the colony in general, is a paramount act of duty"—they anticipate with great joy " the gradual diffusion of the blessings of civilization, and of moral and religious knowledge amongst the Hottentots"—they recommend fresh
grants of lands for Hottentot locations—they quote
that " true Christian philosopher, Mr. Wilberforce"—
they even concur with Dr. Philip, in his statements of
the degraded condition of the Hottentots, before the
appearance of the fiftieth ordinance, though they themselves had just repealed that ordinance !—they protest
that they do not seek any legal restraint on the liberty
of the people of colour—they quote Dr. Vanderkemp,
and a second time do they quote Dr. Philip—and so
they come to the end of their humane exertions, in all
the odour of sanctity and the fragrance of philanthropy.

They begin with prayers, and they conclude with
love.

We need not be surprised that persons* engaged in

_____

.* To what extent Colonel Wade may be implicated in the
elaboration of the vagrant law I know not: that he generally
countenanced and encouraged it, is quite certain by his circulars,
and by his own comments on the vagrant law before the committee
of the House of Commons; in which he has pleaded for it in his
usual style. (See Ab. 290.) It is also quite certain that he was
as much in love with the 50th ordinance, and as much imbued
with the principles of philanthropy as the legislative council; for

this dark plot, should seek to veil it with all imaginable artifices. But that they should venture on this strain of exaggerated cant, so glaring as to be absolutely ridiculous, is matter of astonishment. There is a point beyond which hypocrisy, like flattery, cannot proceed without injuring itself, and to this point, and far beyond it, the legislative council of the colony of the Cape of Good Hope boldly advanced in the resolutions which conclude the vagrant law.

It would be difficult to describe the terror which the progress of this ordinance of slavery excited amongst the persons against whom it was aimed; there was a universal sensation amongst the Hottentots that they should, in a very short time, be brought back to the frightful state from which they had now, for five years, been liberated. They saw through all the tricks and stratagems of the elaborate law; they perfectly well understood its cruel intentions, in spite of the pious

thus does he speak of these matters: "I do not consider it requisite to enter into any detailed history of the state of utter degradation from which the 50th ordinance was *intended* to rescue the Hottentots and other free persons of colour. Suffice it to say, that from all I have been able to learn, the state of the slaves was a thousand times preferable in every point of view to that of this unhappy race, who, amounting at the very least to a fourth part of the whole free population of the settlement, were held in the most degrading thraldom by their fellow-subjects, at the same time that both Dutch and English governments over and over again admitted, and by the strangest of all *inconsistencies*, omitted it *in the very proclamations* and ordinances in which their compulsory service was provided for, that the Hottentots were a free people." (Ab. 287.)

The effrontery of this passage is inimitable. Colonel Wade entered his protest against Sir B. D'Urban's disapprobation of the vagrant law, which fact, coupled with other circumstances, seems to prove that the measure was his especial favourite.

and philanthropic varnish with which it was liberally
coated ; they knew perfectly well, that in a few years
every Hottentot in the colony would, by virtue of this
law, be either rotting in jail, or languishing in bondage,
and many of them prepared to quit the country, and to
flee any whither—to the Caffres, or to the wilderness—
rather than submit to their ancient yoke. The feelings
of the coloured race will best be seen in some of the
letters of the missionaries, who are the only protectors
of the oppressed in these periods of tyranny. Mr.
Barker, the missionary at Theopolis, writes :—" My
opinion is, that this law will nullify, in toto, the fiftieth
ordinance, bring us back precisely to where we were
previous to its enactments, and bring upon us all the
annoyance we suffered from the old system. One of its
first effects, after the excitement created by it, will be
a reduction in the price of wages. Eve y field-cornet
and deputy-field-cornet will bring his share of the
Hottentots he may have caught, or that may have been
caught for him, to the market, at a reduced price.
None will give higher wages for the people than those
at which they can hire them from the local authorities
of the district, because those who have Hottentots, well
know that if Hottentots refuse the wages offered to
them, they have only to let them go, and after they are
gone secure them on the road, and carry them to a
field-cornet, where they will be obliged to submit. This
is not all. The vagrant act having made vagrants of
all the people not in service, the misery occasioned by
a reduction of wages must be followed by a law of
passes—the one must follow the other. When this
enactment shall come in force, Hottentots, and all people of colour, must have passes in their own defence,
or they will be liable to be secured and carried away by

any white that may meet them on the road. (The granting of passes would also be in the hands of persons who were on the look-out for their victims.) Let this ordinance be passed into a law, and every Hottentot, on Sabbath or Saturday, at church or market, who has not got a pass, will have some one or other ready to put a halter or reim about his neck. On the principle that one mischief is sure to make way for another, reduced wages and passes must be followed by the apprenticing of the children, for how can the children be supported and have food, if their parents earn nothing for their labour? After this law has passed, we shall hear a great deal about the perishing condition of the Hottentot children; the humanity of government will be appealed to; and after having deprived the Hottentots of the means of supporting their children, government must repair the mischief it has done, by reducing the wages of the Hottentots, a fact that it will endeavour to keep out of sight, by taking the children from the hard-hearted Hottentots, and giving them to the kind-hearted Boors!"*

Dr. Philip, the superintendent of the London Missionaries, wrote several admirable letters on this subject, which appeared in the colonial papers, pointing out the mischief of the intended law. He also addressed memorials to the governor and council, from one of which the following extract may be taken as an epitome of the whole :—" That the practice of forcing the Hottentots into service will ultimately deprive them of any pecuniary remuneration for their labour, take from them the means of providing for their families, and bring them and their children under the necessity of

* Ab. 732.

stealing or starving. That the masters not having that
interest in the wives and children of the Hottentots, as
they had in the wives and children of their slaves, and
feeling himself under no legal obligation to provide for
them, to save them from starving, the proposed ordinance, should it be enforced, must shortly be followed
by another for apprenticing the children, as under the
old Hottentot system; and thus, as one error leads to
another, the system of forced labour, by reducing the
wages of the labourer, will entail upon those unhappy
people the worst of evils, slavery; evils that will have no
end but with the lives of the people, or the extermination of the race."*

In one of his newspaper letters, Dr. Philip writes :—
" No one acquainted with this colony can be at a loss
to determine against whom the provisions of this ordinance were intended, which subjects to heavy penalties
such as gather wild honey, or dig bulbous roots on
government ground ; and those who cannot satisfy any
one who may arrest them on suspicion of vagrancy, as
to their mode of subsistence for the three preceding
days. It is curious enough to see a law that confounds
all moral distinctions, that punishes a man as severely
for digging bulbous roots, collecting wild berries or wild
fruits, as if he had committed an atrocious crime, pre-
faced with so much about religious instruction, and so
many professions of tenderness for the natives, and of
concern for their improvement. How nauseous do such
professions become, when we see them mixed up with
the provisions of such an act ! Who are to be judges
of the ' wilful idleness' of the coloured classes ? How
are the wilfully idle among the slaves, when they shall

be freed from compulsory service, to be compelled to labour? Who is to support their wives and children when employed in this compulsory labour? Suppose they still refuse to labour, are they to be tied to the wheel of a waggon, and flogged by their masters? consigned to the wretched prisons, which are to be seen in so many parts of the colony, fed on rice-water, put upon the tread-mill, or herded with felons upon public roads? The annals of oppression will exhibit nothing beyond this. Any law in this colony that would attempt to compel the wilfully idle to labour, would be a law which would give back to the masters the whole of the slave population, under a law more cruel and dreadful in its operation, than the old slavery law of the colony; because the masters having no interest in their lives beyond their immediate services, they would have no check on their avarice ; and yet, the legislative council tell us, with matchless simplicity, that this is to be done ‘ without infringing the civil liberty of, or exposing to the slightest risk of oppression, any class or individual of his Majesty's subjects.’ ”*

In proportion, however, as the coloured race and their friends were thrown into consternation at the approaching calamity, were the slave-driving colonists thrown into transports of joy. So eager were they to recommence their old reign of oppression, that they chose to interpret¹ the appearance of the draft of the ordinance as a good and valid law, and began forthwith to set at work their engines of mischief. Those low and morally degraded people, far lower than our lowest constables in England, the field-cornets, began to assert that the fiftieth ordinance was now repealed ; that the

* Ab. 761.

Hottentots were no longer free labourers; that they
could not choose their masters, nor go about the
country without passes; that they would now be taught
better manners, and soon find out who were their masters.   The poor Hottentots hastened with alarm to the
missionary institutions, for the field-cornets boasted
that if they did not go to their friends very soon, they
would no longer be free to go to them at all.*   At
Pacaltsdorp, a missionary institution, two hundred
Hottentots† and upwards made their appearance within
a week after the publication of " the draft;" they fled
like the frightened antelopes to their refuge, when the
roar of the lion is heard in the forest.   In the months
of June and July, the magistrates and field-cornets

---

* Ab. 731.

† Mr. Helme, the missionary at Zuur Braak, writes on the 2nd
of June, that upwards of one hundred and fifty Hottentots had fled
to his station to escape the lash of the new law. (Ab. 742.)
One of the passes which the field-cornets thought proper to
issue at this period may serve as a specimen of the rest.

"Permit to pass the free Hottentot, Cobus Pieterse, for two
days, to Dysel kraal, to fetch Adanuria.
19th July, 1833.   (Signed)   " J. Rensberg."

"Permit to pass again for two days to Pacaltsdorp.
21st July, 1834.   (Signed)   " J. Rensberg."

If the law had been in operation (or perhaps without waiting
for its completion) and if the bearer had by any accident been detained on the road for more than two days, the field-cornets, "or
any other person within five miles of the place near which the
act of vagrancy had been committed," would have seized the
unfortunate traveller, taken him to the magistrate, procured his
condemnation as a vagrant, and so have become possessed of him
as a forced labourer, without wages, as long as he chose to keep
him in that condition!

begin to insist upon the Hottentots having passes, or to use their own expression, "no one must dare to leave the place without a pass,"* although the vagrant law was only at that time a sketch, and though it had not even received the last polish of the August sessions, so eager were these wicked men to lay hold of their victims, and so accustomed were they to see iniquity framed into a law !†

Hans Peter Hallbeck, the Moravian missionary, and now the Moravian bishop, in his evidence before the

* Ab. 734.

† Mr. Boyce, the coadjutor of Mr. Shrewsbury, is already so notorious in the affairs of the colony, as to be scarsely able to sustain the weight of any additional notoriety ; it is nevertheless requisite to let the public know the full merits of the Wesleyan Missionaries in South Africa, and therefore it must here be recorded, that in the anniversary meeting of the Albany Wesleyan Missionary Society, held in the New Chapel at Graham's Town, on Monday, February 22nd, 1835, Mr. Boyce uttered the following sentiments : " I respect the freedom of mankind as much as any man, and I detest oppression and wrong with as deep-rooted a hatred; but still I maintain—*and would that my voice could be heard in the council chamber*—that this colony requires the interference of the legislature to save us from those serious evils which threaten it from the prevailing vices of the bulk of the population—*the coloured class.*" There can be little doubt of the meaning of the words, the italics (which are those of the Graham's Town Journal) show clearly enough that the reverend orator was casting a longing lingering look on the vagrant law, and that he was invoking its resuscitation in the council chamber.

The editor of the Graham's Town Journal is a Wesleyan, and he of course agrees with Mr. Boyce, for thus is it written in that Journal. (Sept. 15th, 1836.) " On many important points, such for instance as the state of vagrancy, the members of council have shewn an independency of mind, *and an unflinching determination of purpose*, which is extremely creditable to them, and which cannot be too highly valued."

committee of the House of Commons, says:—" The
effects of the vagrant law would have been a great hurt
to the Hottentots, and to the farmers too.   I had got,
just about the time when the vagrant law was in progress, an application from near Cape Town, for Hottentots to come to the harvest.   I was afraid to tell it to any
Hottentots, until I knew what became of the vagrant
law, because I questioned very much whether they
would have it in their power to return home again;
and for that reason, I wrote to the gentleman again,
telling him my apprehensions, and he was so aware of
it, that he wrote back and gave me the opinion of one
of the officers in Cape Town, in order to satisfy my
mind that no vagrant law could be carried, and therefore I might be easy.   But if I had received another
answer, and had been told that there would have been
a vagrancy law, our Hottentots would not, under such
circumstances, have ventured to go so far from their
homes into another district, because they were under
apprehensions of not being allowed to return home
when they had done their work.   As far as I can
judge, from the circumstances in which I have been
placed, I am of opinion that the vagrancy law would
have brought down the Hottentots to about the same
situation in which they were ten or twelve years
ago."*

' The coloured people being thus fully alive to the
danger of their situation, bestirred themselves to present memorials and petitions against the proposed
vagrant law: memorials were sent to the colonial
government from Bethelsdorf, Pacaltsdorp, Theopolis,

* Ab. 341.

and the Kat River settlement; that from the Kat River contains a passage too pathetic to be omitted. "Many of your memorialists, residing from infancy in the district of Graaf Reinet and Somerset, testify that they had no food from the farmers but the offal of their cattle and sheep; no houses except miserable sheds of straw and turf, that they were open to every blast of wind and showers of rain; no medicine when sick; no covering but the sheep-skin kaross, and no wages but one cow or heifer, and from two to four or six sheep per annum; and frequently on leaving the service of the farmers, even these were detained, and wages when paid in money did not exceed twelve rix dollars per annum: that the proposed act for the suppression of vagrancy, is more unjust in principle, and will be more cruel in operation, than any vagrant act in any other country, and your memorialists consider it as more to be dreaded than a law that would punish vagrancy with hanging: because such cruelties would be exercised on a few only, whereas this law will subject almost the whole race, men, women, and children, not residing at a missionary-institution, or on the Kat River, to a condition compared with which extermination would be mercy."

And true it is, that it would have been far more merciful to pass a law making vagrancy a capital felony; for in that case, as no one would have had any interest in putting the law into execution, it would have been a dead letter; but by the law then preparing, it was intended to hand over the Hottentots as slaves to the colonists, who would have a direct interest in finding or making vagrants by any means they could invent, and thus reap a rich harvest of oppression, under the

pretence of checking a crime which had no existence,
and which this law created and invented for the purpose of punishing it with bondage.

The missionaries beheld the danger of the coloured
race with the deepest grief; they would have greatly
betrayed their trust, if they had not in such an emergency exerted themselves to the. utmost to avert the
impending calamity; apathy would have been criminal,
and indifference treason. All that could be done by
human means, within the limits of the law, and that
law administered in a despotism, they effected; but
being ministers of the Christian religion, they put more
confidence in the merciful protection of the Almighty,
than in their own exertions—they felt it was now time
indeed to invoke the arm of Omnipotence, for it was
peculiarly a season, which is called in scripture, " a
time of need." Under this impression Dr. Philip, as
superintendent of the London Missionaries, wrote a
letter to Mr. Read, the missionary pastor of the Hottentots at the Kat River settlement, recommending him
to set a day apart for a solemn religious service, in
which the feelings of himself and his people might be
expressed in prayer. Mr. Read, in the simplicity of
his heart, wrote a letter to Mr. Thompson, (the government Dutch minister of the settlement, and the friend
of Colonel Wade) inviting him to attend this service;
it certainly was an act of Christian courtesy to send
such an invitation, and every one would have thought
that Mr. Thompson, as a brother in the Christain
ministry, and interested in the happiness of the colored
race, would have either come forth as a fellow-helper
in the common calamity, by joining the suppliants on
this occasion, or would at least have congregated his
own people for a similar act of devotion. But not so,

Mr. Thompson, who had been sent to the Kat River to oppose Mr. Read, and who had collected a small congregation among the Bastaards (of the mixed European and Hottentot blood) by impressing on their minds, that as they were superior to the Hottentots, owing to the colonial blood that flowed in their veins, so they ought to belong to the Dutch church, the venerable institution of their fathers, rather than to a Hottentot missionary conventicle. This gentleman persuaded the Bastaards, greatly to their discredit, to sign a counter-memorial, which had been circulated amongst them by Captain Armstrong, the favored instrument of Colonel Wade, by whom he had been appointed to the magistracy of that district for purposes altogether colonial. Not contented with this stroke of servile zeal, Mr. Thompson betrayed the confidence placed in him, by transmitting Mr. Read's letter to Colonel Wade. "I would feel much delicacy," says this government pastor; "in treating the correspondence of any person in this way, had I given any encouragement to it on my part, but as the communication was gratuitous on the part of Mr. Read, unsought for by me, and even contrary to what, if he had any discrimination and modesty, he must have been aware my sentiments were on the subject, I do not consider myself guilty of any breach of confidence in making it public."*

---

* Ab. 318. This letter Colonel Wade gives in his Evidence. "Dr. Philip considers this law of such a nature, that he has written to all the missionaries, recommending them and their congregations to hold the 18th day of this month (August) as a day of humiliation and prayer to Almighty God, that it may please him to arrest the pending evil. In this letter to me, he says, 'Mr. Thompson I hope will join you and make the same known to his people to do the same.' I do not know

What, then ! if a letter is written in confidence, but
has not been "sought for," it may be published, and
for the express purpose of doing injury to the writer?
Mr. Read had paid the government pastor too high a
compliment ; he thought he must surely enter into the
feelings of the colored population in this emergency:
he supposed him to be a person of humane and com-
passionate feelings ; a pious christain minister, who
must at that time have been beholding the coming storm
with grief and apprehension ;—but he was mistaken—
colonial politics had infected Mr. Thompson's heart ; he
had none of these fears and apprehensions ; he wished to
please the rulers, and in the eagerness of his political
feeling, he betrays the confidence placed in him, knowing at the time, that the publication of this letter could
not be otherwise than injurious to the missionaries,
and of course illustrative of his own superior qualities
as an obedient servant of the colonial court.

And mark here the relative situation of Mr. Thompson, and the London missionaries at the Kat River !
Mr. Thompson, the paid stipendiary of government,
has a church and a scanty congregation, chiefly, if not
exclusively of the Bastaard race; he *had* also one infant school, supported by Captain Stockenstrom's
liberality, "but that support being withdrawn, the
school was dropped."[*] Mr. Read and his son had a
congregation of two thousand persons, twelve schools,
and a normal school for native teachers ; there were
seven hundred pupils in these schools, and all supported by voluntary contributions through the missionary society.   When, therefore, Mr. Thompson

whether you will be able to favour us with your company, otherwise we shall be glad to have your assistance and prayers."

[*] Ab. 590.

stretched forth his hand to injure his brother, by publishing his letter, it is impossible not to contemplate
the relative position * of the stipendiary priest and the
missionary—it is impossible not to suspect that some
personal motives may have been mixed up with his
zeal as a loyalist towards the colony.

* It is curious to read Colonel Wade's commentary on this
text. "I remained five or six days at the Kat River post,
visiting the Hottentot settlement and country in the neighbourhood. Many of the locations were in a promising state, and the
general appearance of the whole was very gratifying, but *I was
assured by those who could not be mistaken,* (i. e. Mr. Thompson)
that latterly the settlement has lost ground, and that the Hottentots, NOT THE BASTAARDS—very many of whom had exhibited
at the commencement an energy and an anxiety to improve that
had not been expected from them, *had again fallen off,* and had
become idle and restless, and discontented, and also that the
internal tranquillity of the settlement had been destroyed by the
mischievous introduction of party feeling and political discussion."
[Who were the schismatics in this case? the people of the Kat
river were of one heart and one mind till the government act,
passed against the missionary, sent Mr. Thompson thus to sow the
seeds of division among a united people.] "In fact the settlement
is divided into two parties, the Bastaards and the Hottentots; the
Bastaards looking altogether to Mr. Thompson as their spiritual
guide, and the Hottentots to Mr. Read." Ab. 316.

Colonel Wade, whose notions on cause and effect are throughout his voluminous evidence strangely perplexed, has with much
energy stated that Mr. Read and Dr. Philip "excited the
Hottentots to discontent," by "improper interference, by writing
memorials to the legislative council, and by getting up political
meetings;" as if the Hottentots would have received the vagrant
law with gratitude but for this "interference!" The committee
did not allow this nonsense to pass unnoticed; they asked the
gallant colonel, whether the law itself did not cause the agitation,
without any help from the missionaries? A question to which
Colonel Wade did not think it requisite to return any answer.
(See Ab. 317.)

Mr. Thompson has, indeed, been much praised by Colonel Wade, and his loyal act in betraying Mr. Read has been much commended ; but it is, peradventure, as little a proof of merit to be praised by Colonel Wade, as to have been the author of that letter which has received his commendations.

The results, however, of this affair have been truly disastrous ; when the Caffre war broke out, and the Kat River settlement was attacked by the Caffres, Mr. Read and his son were ordered to Graham's Town by Sir B. D'Urban, and detained there contrary to their wishes on frivolous pretexts. To various solicitations for permission to return to the Kat River his Excellency refused, and though repeatedly urged to give his reasons for this refusal, " he merely stated that his refusal was grounded upon *some information he had received from the Kat River*, and from other collateral sources," *

What that " information" was, it is easy to conjecture ; the Thompsons and the Wades, and all the disappointed advocates of the vagrant law had been at work, and it was determined amongst the clique, that the Hottentots should be deprived of the services of their friends the missionaries, and the whole people there kept under the police-eye of a more subservient "spiritual guide."

Up to this hour the Messrs. Read have not been allowed to return to their pastoral charge, to the inexpressible grief of the poor Hottentots, who feel this deprivation as the greatest affliction, and who would hail the return of their revered friends, pastors, and protectors with a joy, such as we who do not know the pe-

* Ab. 593.

caliar circumstances of that simple people, their deep sense of gratitude, and their warmth of affections, can scarcely imagine.

Andrew Stoffel, the Hottentot examined by the Committee of the House of Commons, may here be introduced as an interesting witness. "They press us now just as you would put a newspaper in the press and press it down. I have been asked what this pressure is; I say, the Hottentot has no water; he has not a blade of grass; he has no lands; he has no wood; he has no place where he can sleep; *all that he now has is the Missionary and the Bible*; and now that we are taught, the Bible is taken away from us, and they want to remove the missionaries from us: and there is another law, the vagrant law, that they want to oppress us with; a law that presses down the Hottentots. They have already removed my missionary, Mr. Read; I had twelve schools, and these schools have come to nothing."

"How have they removed the Bible from you?—There is no one now that gets up on Sunday to speak and to explain the Bible, and to preach to us."

"Have you not got your Bibles as you had them before?—If you had no English preachers in the country, what would you do with the Bible?"

"Do you mean to say that the substance of your complaint is this—that formerly the Hottentots possessed the land, the wood, and the water; but that the Europeans have taken possession of their property, and have therefore reduced them to destitution?—Yes, that is the substance of my complaint; and what the English nation sent us, was the missionaries; *and we have all resolved to die with the missionaries at the institutions; they are our only friends.*"

N

" Do they feel towards the missionaries great affection for the instruction they have given them, and the
protection they have been the means of affording them?
—Yes; I love the missionaries; but the missionaries
tell us to ascribe all to the people of England, *and I
love the people in this country also.*"*

It is to be hoped, if the colonial government shall
persist in its unrighteous and despotic policy in the
affair of the Kat River settlement, that a superior power
will speedily interfere and restore to these poor people
their best friends, with imperative orders that the peace
and harmony of people and pastor shall no more be
disturbed, and that the missionaries shall never again
be removed until they have been found guilty of violating the laws.

The vagrant law having been duly concocted in the
legislative council, was sent to the colonial office in
England for approval, where most happily it received
a veto, and thus came to nought.   Had the catastrophe
been otherwise, it is far from improbable that the Hot-
téntots, who were the most efficient soldiers in the Caffre
war, might have taken a very different view of their duty
or interest in that memorable struggle, and by either retiring from the colony or assisting the Caffres, have contributed to render the campaign of 1835 more disgraceful than even now it appears in the page of history.

Sir Benjamin D'Urban, who assumed the reins of
government whilst the vagrant law was under discussion, did not see the necessity of its enactment, nor
contribute to its progress.

The acting governor, Colonel Wade, † who preceded

---

* Ab. 588.

† It ought to be generally known that Colonel Wade is one of

Sir Benjamin D'Urban, may, if he chooses, claim all the honour of having engendered that hideous abortion of a legislative monster.

the new poor-law commissioners; though it remains to be proved that this sort of recompense has been merited by the promoter of the Hottentot Vagrant Act.

CHAPTER XXV.

The Results of the Caffre War.—The Conclusion.

THE general results of the war may be thus described in the words of Sir Benjamin D'Urban :—" In the course of the commissioners' progress in the census of the tribes of Gaika and Slambi, they have ascertained that their loss during our operations against them has amounted to four thousand of their warriors, and amongst these many captains; ours, fortunately, has not on the whole amounted to one hundred, and of these, only two officers. There have been taken from them also, besides the conquest and alienation of their country, about 60,000 head of cattle, almost all their goats, their habitations every where destroyed, and their gardens and corn-fields laid waste. They have been, therefore, chastised, not extremely, but perhaps sufficiently." * In addition to these great things, his Excellency might have added the murder of the king, the murder of many women and children, and the wanton destruction of several stores of corn ; in short, as com-

* The Quarterly Review (No. CXXV. p. 5.) well remarks that this is " a cool statement :" Lord Glenelg's criticism on this cool statement must not be withheld. " I am bound," says his

plete an *attempt* at extermination as the worst of the colonists could desire. *

Then the newly vanquished country, having been thus well baptized in blood, received a new name; it was, in true courtly style, called "THE PROVINCE OF QUEEN ADELAIDE." A map was drawn of this Adelaide province, and in it were inserted various forts with appropriate names—"Fort Wellington," "Fort Beresford," "Fort Murray," "Fort White," &c. &c. &c. Then there was a "King William's Town," a projected metropolis for Queen Adelaide's province; and, in short, it was determined that this new territory should for ever perpetuate the loyalty and magnificence of the victorious governor, and that new cities should arise in the wilderness, amazing future travellers with their opu-

lordship, "to record the very deep regret with which I have perused this passage. In a conflict between regular troops and hordes of barbarous men, it is almost a matter of course that there should exist an enormous disproportion between the loss of life on either side. But to consign an entire country to desolation, and a whole people to famine, is an aggravation of the necessary horrors of war, so repugnant to every just feeling, and so totally at variance with the habits of civilized nations, that I should not be justified in receiving such a statement without calling upon you for further explanations. The honour of the British name is deeply interested in obtaining and giving publicity to the proofs that the king's subjects really demanded so fearful an exercise of the irresistible power of his Majesty's forces."

* Take another instance of the barbarities of the war, from a letter by Colonel Smith. "The whole of the country has been most thoroughly traversed, upwards of 1200 huts, new and old, have been burnt, immense stores of corn in every direction destroyed; 215 head of cattle of all sorts captured, several horses, and nearly 2000 goats have fallen into our hands;" and these calamities heaped on a people whom Colonel Smith describes as "flying rapidly" before the invading army.

lence, the density of their population, and the grandeur
of their architecture.   But so perishable a commodity
is human greatness, that whilst the historian of these
vast events is humbly endeavouring to record them,
all has vanished away : the castles have proved to be
" castles in the air," and have disappeared ; the forts
are unfortressed ; the metropolis, with its triumphal
magnificence, is no where to be found; all is gone, and
has not left a trace behind.

That all these mighty plans, however, might be duly
executed, commissioners, and engineers, land-mea-
surers, and land-surveyors came into " Adelaide Province," to partition the new territory, and to arrange
all things to the satisfaction of the conqueror.   One of
these plans was to extend and perpetuate the system of
plunder.   " Large tracts of the conquered country,"
writes the governor, in one of his " confidential" notes
to Lord Glenelg, " are still vacant for the occupation
and speculation of Europeans ;" * and Colonel Cox, in
his evidence tells us, " That many applications had
been made to his Excellency for assignments in the
new territory," a month or two after the war was concluded.   His Excellency was anxious to grant lands to
a large amount, but he waited the decision of the home
government ; a singular act of prudence in the conqueror, who seems to have enlarged his ideas of power and
patronage the longer the war continued, and never to
have entertained a moment's suspicion that his Majesty's ministers and the people of England would have
disapproved the follies, extravagancies, and excesses of
the war.

On the 5th of November, 1835, his Excellency re-

* C. W. p. 102.

commends the appointment of resident agents with each
of the great families of the Caffre nations, "to replace
the commissioners when their labours shall be finished."
He has "good hopes of the efficiency of the gentlemen
he means to appoint," and he intends to fix " a superintendent agent of the whole" at Graham's Town, with
a salary of £500 per annum, whilst each of the agents
is to receive £300 per annum. The superintendent is
also to have an interpreter and a clerk—salary £200
per annum. * These salaries his excellency states, will
be requisite " to induce gentlemen of adequate character and ability to undertake the duty." This an-
nouncement of patronage had been preceded by something still more magnificent; his Excellency had already recommended the Earl of Aberdeen to appoint a
lieutenant-governor at Uitenhage, with a salary of
£1000 per annum, "a house, secretary, &c." The
et cetera of this plan would have required examination,
if the plan had been adopted. Many very serious and
alarming creatures may be contained in the bowels of
that mysterious Trojan horse, *et cetera.*

The person † whom Sir Benjamin D'Urban recommended for this new office was Colonel Smith, who had
just returned full of glory, and loaded with thanks from
the last scene in king Hintza's life.

These then are the great things of the war: on the
other hand, however, we must contemplate the disgraces
of the campaign. The troops began to act on the offensive the first week in January, the war was not concluded till autumn. Sir Benjamin D'Urban was the
first to sue for peace; the confederate chiefs refused his
terms, and they did not lay down their arms till he had

* C. W. p. 88.   † C. W. 59.

materially altered his first propositions, or rather till
he had quite renounced his original plan of driving
them over the Kei River. If Macomo had held out
two or three months longer, the Governor would have
been utterly unable to continue the contest. The
daily expense* of the war was enormous, and the
home government issued peremptory orders to the
Governor to bring the war to a conclusion. " I perceive, with deep concern," says Lord Glenelg, " from
the public journals of the colony, as well as from private letters, that so lately as September last your
operations were not concluded, and that you were still
on the frontier; that the Caffres were pressing their
depredations with increasing boldness into the colony,
and even to the neighbourhood of Graham's Town . . . .
You will receive as a most decided and positive injunction, the directions which I now convey to you, to bring
these hostilities to a conclusion by the earliest possible
period.   They must not be protracted for a single day
with a view to revenge or conquest." The Governor,
with all his troops and artillery, with every possible
advantage that can be imagined against an unarmed
population, (for such the Caffres were when we compare
their assegais with cannons and muskets,) could indeed

---

* " I do not think it convenient to discuss the propriety of the
payments which you report yourself to have made for the
clothing, the pay, and the gratuities of the Hottentots, and of the
burgher force enrolled and serving with your army, until I shall
have received that complete and detailed report of all the expenses of the late contest, which it will, of course, have been your
first care on your return to Cape Town, to prepare for the information of the Lords Commissioners of the Treasury : *their Lordships await the report with no common anxiety.*"
Lord Glenelg to Sir B. D'Urban, 17th February, 1836. C. W.
p. 109.

occasionally put the inhabitants to the sword, drive away cows and sheep, and burn down cottages, but the main army of his opponents he could not subdue, nor could he prevent them from retaliating on the colony so late as September. It is the recorded opinion of experienced officers, that if the Caffres had been supplied with arms and ammunition, they would have kept their ground in the mountains, and glens, or in the woody hollow of the Fish River,* and that all the troops brought into the field by the colony would have been unable to dislodge them; but even without arms and ammunition, if the Caffre chiefs had been informed of the certain disapprobation which the war would have to encounter in England, they might have utterly baffled their enemies, by merely acting on the defensive a few weeks longer. Great was the surprise expressed by the neighbouring nations of the African continent, that the Caffres could make so long a resistance; all the tribes to the north of the colony felt a strong interest in the progress of this unequal contest, for it was obvious to them, that if Caffreland were vanquished, and cleared of its population, their turn would come next.† When Moshis and other chiefs who live three hundred miles to the north-east of the colony, knew of the proclamation which annexed Caffreland to the colony, the intelligence produced a most unfavourable impression upon their minds, and every one seemed to feel for himself and his tribe, as if the counterpart to that which had happened to the Caffres was awaiting them. They said, "there was no standing against the white man." Soon after this, however,

* Journal of Geographical Society, vol. v. p. ii. pt. 317.

† Dr. Philip's Speech at a special meeting of the London Missionary Society, 10th August, 1836.

they found the Caffres were not subdued, and on hearing of the formidable resistance they were making, the chiefs then said, " Well, God is with the right." The spell is now broken, and the northern tribes have learned that the white man is not invincible—unless we speedily adopt a new system, and firmly adhere to it, we must expect to be humbled even more than the French have been at Algiers; it is the extremity of folly to expect that we can pursue our march of aggression and plunder, and not at last become the unpitied suicides of national immorality.

Sir Benjamin D'Urban had the satisfaction to receive from all parts of the colony the most flattering marks of approbation and applause. Numerous and loyal were the addresses voted him at public meetings; the colonists seemed at a loss to find terms of eulogy sufficient to express their delight in the conqueror, who came from the field of glory not only with sixty thousand cows for distribution, but with sixteen thousand Fingoes, " whose services as labourers would be eminently useful to the colony," and with a pen in his hand by which he would be able to make grants of hundreds of thousands of acres lately belonging to " the treacherous and irreclaimable savages."

These addresses Sir Benjamin D'Urban, in his infatuation, sent home to the colonial office, without having discovered the mischievous nature of such incense; for it is difficult to read these pompous productions of fustian and hypocrisy, without perceiving that the idol of such addresses must be lowered in the opinion of all unprejudiced persons. Take the following specimen from the inhabitants of Graaf Reinet:—
" It has been the misfortune of all the measures hitherto adopted for the protection of this colony from the

savages, that the great principle of national justice, which combines protection of the innocent with punishment of the guilty, could not be invariably or successfully observed. It has been our good fortune that your Excellency's wisdom has devised a mode of removing this stigma from our intercourse with savage men; and exhibited in a form, which even the most savage understand, such a striking contrast between the justice and mercy of a Christian state, and the exterminating wars of the native tribes, as well as teach a lesson which must speedily induce more distant hordes, instead of crowding upon our boundary for the advantages of plunder and the security of impunity, *to count only the benefits to be derived from our institutions and our friendship*, and to respect our justice as much as they have been taught to dread our power."[*]

The worshipful corporation of Mudfog, in its most palmy state, could never have surpassed this touch of eloquence.

In a similar style of solemn nonsense do all the other addresses fumigate his Excellence, sometimes mixing piety with adulation, and generally enlarging upon two topics, "the merciful forbearance" of his Excellency, and "that great act of philanthropy and humanity whereby 15,000 Fingoes were released from oppressive thraldom, and placed under the benign protection of a Christian Government." Here then a word seems due to this "great act of philanthropy." We have already seen in what manner Sir Benjamin D'Urban became possessed of these same Fingoes, by stealing them from king Hintza; but it remains to be seen that some earthly motives were mixed up with the nobler

* C. W. 80

instigations to this philanthropic theft. In describing this transaction, Sir B. D'Urban says, " This supply of hired servants, and especially for all farming purposes, will be of the greatest benefit to the community, *for they are well known to be excellent for that purpose;* and it will be *more than useful* at this present moment, when the recent levies have necessarily converted into soldiers so 'much of the Hottentot population hereto-. fore employed in these populations. They will, more-over, assuredly become, with a little seasonable support and management, the best militia for that tract of country, which for the last twenty-five years has been the vulnerable part of the colony, to the entrance of the savages, from the nature of the ground, full of woody ravines, of which it consists, and which is their vantage ground."[*]

The abstraction therefore of these subjects of king Hintza would prove not only useful to the colony, but " more than useful;" it would recompense the colonists for their disappointment in the matter of the vagrant law ; it would furnish them with hired servants, when Hottentot servants were scanty, and would enable the government to select the " best militia" that could be found for the time, place, and circumstances.

---

[*] C. W. 16. In this last sentence his Excellency may confidently defy all criticism ; it is an array of words that effectuall resists analysis.

Lord Glenelg's sarcastic remark on the affair of the Fingoes is highly amusing. " I must frankly confess that I am quite unable to perceive the slightest accuracy in the comparison which you instituted between the liberation of these people and the great national act of negro emancipation. In the one case we liberated the slaves of our enemies at the cost of their owners, in the other case we liberated the slaves of British subjects at the cost of the national revenue." C. W. 70.

There was something, then, more than mere philanthropy in thus bringing 16,000 Fingoes under " the benign influence of a Christian government."

It is probable that the Fingoes soon began to discover the real nature of this " benignity," for they very shortly returned of their own accord to their old masters, preferring the persecution of the Caffres to the philanthropy of the colonists.

Amongst the adulators of the Governor, the Wesleyan Missionaries in the colony, Messrs. Shrewsbury and Boyce, take a very conspicuous station; they tell his Excellency, " that amidst the distressing events of the Caffre war, they are consoled with the reflection, that so far as the colonial government is concerned, it has been conducted *in accordance with the principles of justice and mercy*," and with many odious phrases of piety — odious when prostituted to such ends — extol the humanity and clemency of the devastator of Caffreland. But this is a painful subject, and has already been much noticed elsewhere; it will not therefore be requisite to linger on this theme, by commenting on Mr. Shrewsbury's six articles of vindictive punishment, which he sent in a letter to Colonel Smith, recommending the most cruel and inhuman treatment of the conquered Caffres. It is to be hoped, that the Wesleyan body will remedy the disorders of their South African Missions, and take decisive steps to break through that very suspicious* friendship which exists between

---

* Sir Benjamin D'Urban, in one of his despatches, quotes the opinions of the Wesleyan missionaries in his favour, as a sort of shield against Dr. Philip, whose disapprobation of his conduct he seems to anticipate, and whom he indicates by name. His Wesleyan friends who had comforted him with very sweet incense, he thus describes: " Mr. B. a very humane and very excellent

the tyrannical party in the colony and Wesleyan Missionaries—a friendship which is glaring and undeniable
in the large volume of " Aboriginal evidence," exhibit-

clergyman"—" Mr. S. a most benevolent and humane clergyman."
Colonel Wade, in his evidence, pays the Wesleyans many com-
pliments, and assures us that they have "conferred incalculable
benefits on the Caffres." There is one however of their body,
whom the gallant colonel "regrets to state belongs to the Wesleyan mission;" this person is Mr. Kay, and as he has published a very valuable volume, ' Researches in Caffraria,' which
does not at all utter colonial sentiments, but takes the side of the
oppressed, we need not be surprised at this "regret." Another
missionary, however, who had written in praise of the murderous
attack of the colony on the Ficani, (Ab. p. 410.) and whose
general sentiments are altogether colonial, is in high favour.

Major William B. Dundas, of the royal artillery, whose evidence before the committee of the House of Commons, is highly
entertaining, loves and admires the Wesleyans.—" They have
done wonders, more than possibly could be expected from people
in their situation; I have the highest opinion of them and their
usefulness—I was almost in daily communication with them,
their works, their acts, and their discretion bear me out in my
opinion, and the influence they seemed to have over the Caffres in
restraining depredation and plunder *to a certain extent.*"—" In
the north of Caffreland there are some Wesleyans, excellent and ·
good men, they have done every thing they could do, *yet they
have done nothing*, the seed has fallen on unfruitful ground, and
nothing has been effected." (Ab. 142.) A very sad account of
these "excellent and good men." But it appears that the Wesleyans, in order to blacken the Caffres, represented their missionary exertions amongst them as altogether useless. Sir B.
D'Urban, says "that they acknowledged to him, with reluctance,
that in the course of their long and diligent labours, although
they had been as they hoped successful in the conversion of
many Hottentots and Fingoes, they could not flatter themselves
they had made a salutary impression *upon one of the race of
Caffres.*"

Now as we cannot possibly suppose that Sir B. D'Urban
coined this statement, we must of course give the whole honour

ing the Wesleyan Ministers as servile instruments of an odious government, and as praised and admired by certain persons, whose published sentiments are to the last degree reprehensible.

The Wesleyan ministers are just now in high favor with the colonial government, basking in the full sunshine of vice-regal approbation, but the sooner they change their position, and retire into the shade, the better will it be for their characters as Christians and missionaries, which is sadly suffering by the present arrangements.

Before this narrative is drawn to a close, we have to notice an act of violence connected with the Caffre war, which will illustrate in a peculiar manner the despotism and misrule which prevail in the colony. Jan Tzatzoe, a Caffre chief of the royal lineage, is possessed of lands on the Buffalo River : he is ruler of the tribe of the Tindees, having about two thousand subjects under his control. In his youth he was put under the care of Dr. Vanderkemp, and embraced the christian religion, of which he is occasionally an assistant preacher, endeavouring to convert the Caffres to the faith of Christ. When the Caffre war broke out, he was placed in very trying circumstances ; his own nation did not attack him, for they respected his moral character not less than his attributes of hereditary chieftain ; and this immunity the colonists chose to interpret into something very suspicious. They came around him and told him he must take up arms against

of the fable to the missionaries who had wilfully deceived him : they knew very well that they had many converts amongst the Caffres, and especially the chief Kama. There seems no loophole for them to escape from the charge of a deliberate and injurious falsehood in this matter.

the Caffres, for that if he did not they should consider
him 'a rascal.' In consequence of their importunities
he resolved to join the English in the contest, raised a
company of four hundred warriors, and went out to
fight on the side of the colony. When the war was
over, Sir Benjamin D'Urban rewarded this ally of the
British nation *by seizing his territory!*—So it is—but
as such proceedings are in England, at least, a novelty,
it will be desirable to state the circumstances in the
evidence of Tzatzoe himself, before the committee of
the House of Commons.

"What were the circumstances which led you to
unite with the English in opposing the Caffres?"—
"The settlers said, 'if you remain neutral you are an
enemy, you are a rascal.'"

"Did you consider yourself as commanded by the
Government to assist against the Caffres?"—"Yes."

"What did you suppose would have been the consequence to you, if you had refused to assist the English?"—"I thought that if I had not gone against
the Caffres, the English would have said that I was
engaged with the other Caffres against the colony.
The common talk in Colonel Somerset's camp, was,
'how is it that the Caffres do not attack you; it is a
dangerous position that you hold standing neutral.'"

"What is your reason for visiting this country?"—
"I came to see this country about these things, and
about my place which has been taken from me."

"Has any portion of your land been seized by the
government?"—"Yes."

"Did your own residence and the mission premises
stand upon the ground that has been taken away?"—
"Yes; the house that Colonel Smith occupies was

Mr. Brownley's, *and my house is their stable at present.*"

"What reason did they give to you, who were an ally of the British government, for taking away your land?"—"There was no reason that I know of, for they did not speak to me to tell me why they took my country."

"Do you consider it was a very great hardship that they took your land, you being at that time fighting on their side?"—"Yes."

"Did you ever complain of the hardship you suffered by their taking away your land?"—"No."

"Why did you not complain?"—"I did not complain because the town was built without my being consulted, and a place was appointed me to live in without my being consulted. Then I said, I will stay near the town, but the governor said, 'No, you must go to a greater distance from the town:' and I thought to myself, *this is enough.*"

"Do not you think that the governor would have done you justice, if you had made your complaint known to him?"—"*No; he would not have done it, as he took the ground from me without having any right to it.*"

"How came you to think that the government in England would be more ready to do you justice than the government at the Cape?"—"Because from the time of Dr. Vanderkemp, to this time, the missionaries used to tell us that the good people, and right people were here, and that justice was here."

"Did the governor know that he was building on the land that belonged to you?"—"Certainly: he must have known it."

"In what manner were the governor's orders, as to your removal from your residence, communicated to you ?"—"When I came there the governor was building the fort, and he asked me 'Where do you want to stay?' When the governor said that, I said to myself, the governor it seems is taking my land from me; I said, I will stay at that little river. The governor said 'no, it will be too near the town.' Then I said, I will go to the Dreby, where Botman and Macomo live. The governor said, 'I will see, when every thing is done and settled.'"

"Did the governor speak to you face to face ?"— "Yes."

"Did the governor give you any compensation for the loss of your buildings ?"—"No."

"Did you ever make any application to the governor for redress ?"—"Why should I go back to the governor, if he takes my things from me ?"

"Were the lands from which the governor removed you cultivated lands, or lands in a state of nature ?"— "He took my piece of ground that I had cultivated, and my garden, and my trees."

"What did he give you in exchange ?"—"Nothing."

"In what condition was the new place which the governor appointed you, cultivated or uncultivated ?" —"It is a wilderness." (Ab. 580.)

Here then we have as precise and accurate a statement of this flagitious act of spoliation as could be desired; but what must be the state of things, and what the state of principle, when governors, representing the British crown, dare to commit these excesses, which unquestionably are not practised in the absolute despotism of the Russian autocracy?

Shall the day of justice never dawn on the British colonies?

———

As we have now come to the end of this painful narrative, we pause to ask what henceforward is to be devised as a preventive remedy to these disorders?

The first point seems to be, to make the people of England thoroughly acquainted with the acts of military violence, and the freaks of arbitrary power which are perpetrated in South Africa, and to give publicity to all those facts which may tend to display the true state of society now existing in the colony of the Cape of Good Hope.

The second point, is to take Lord Glenelg's despatch to Sir Benjamin D'Urban, dated 26th December 1835, as the groundwork and foundation of the superstructure of equity, henceforth, we hope, to be reared, and to be brought to perfection.

But to effect this, we must first of all turn our attention to the instruments with which the work is to be accomplished; and as the government of the colony of necessity partakes largely of the autocratical elements, and as vast prerogatives are consigned to the hands of*

* There are some persons to whom a colonial representative assembly appears to be the only remedy for existing evils: such however is the vicious state of society in the colony, that we may be certain the evils would be greatly aggravated by such a remedy. Never let there be a representative legislative assembly in the colony, unless a large majority of the representatives are of the coloured race. The Boors and settlers must be completely outnumbered, in the proportion of two to one at least, before such an experiment could be attempted with safety. The atmosphere of the colony is at present saturated with the elements of tyranny.

one man, it is above all things requisite that the vice-regal ruler should be one, who not only can be made, by constant watching, to accommodate himself to the principles of good government; but one, who of his own free choice decidedly prefers a wise, just, and beneficent sway, to an arbitrary and oppressive dominion. It would indeed be possible by reiterated commands from the colonial office, to direct the governor to avoid certain specific evil measures, or to adopt certain specific good ones, but it is quite beyond the power of his majesty's ministers to infuse sound principles in the unsound mind of a governor, or to eradicate from the inward source of action the corrupt, confused, or mischievous maxims which a vicious disposition, or an evil education have already brought to maturity. In vain will it therefore be, to seal up in government despatches the most wise, humane, and just regulations, if neither wisdom, humanity, nor equity are component parts of the viceroy's character; for though he will, as a soldier, do what he is ordered, yet he will do no more—he will obey the letter, and disregard the spirit of his instructions—and in all the minute details which must be left to his discretion or good will, he will fail when the master's eye is not watching; and all the opportunities of doing good, or preventing mischief, he will pretermit in ignorance, or avoid in disgust.

Let not then this ill-fated colony be ruled any longer by mere military men; they are a real scourge to South Africa; for though they bring with them sometimes a high pedigree, and sometimes a character for military prowess, yet neither the peerage nor the army list can in any way qualify unfit persons to govern mankind. The science of government, and especially when applied to such materials as exist in the colony, does not

consist in brute force; and though for purposes of
violence it may be absolutely requisite that an army
should be governed on the principles of arbitrary power
and slavish obedience, yet when such principles are introduced into civil polity, they create only confusion,
misery, and ruin. Such, however, have been the principles that have hitherto prevailed in the colony; the
governor has always been a military man, and his one
idea of government, his simple theory of wisdom, has
been to reduce society to the servile condition of a
regiment, in which, from the colonel to the corporal,
arbitrary orders are arbitrarily executed, without question or hesitation, or are enforced, if need be, by the
vindictive severity of a court martial. How woeful,
how despicable, how disgraceful is the history of the
colony of the Cape of Good Hope! See the list of the
viceroys that have acted their part in the drama of
empire! not one of them has shewn himself qualified
to take the reins of that government which family connexion, or the favor of the Horse Guards have entrusted to his guidance. There has been a Lord
Caledon, a juvenile patrician, of good intentions, of
whom it is pleasing to say, that he did not wish to do
any harm, and that, for a governor of the Cape, is no
small praise—but he soon fell into the hands of the old
adepts in the colonial school, and under the guidance
of the colonial secretary, issued edicts, which to use
the mildest language, *conferred no blessing* on the oppressed aborigines. There has been a Lord Charles
Somerset, whom to mention, is to mention the type of
bad governors; who for seven long years sat as an
incubus on the colony, and in spite of high rank and
the resolute protection of the home government, barely
escaped at last an impeachment, which if it had been

pressed, would surely have been too weighty for all the barriers that the aristocracy could have raised in his defence.

Then there has been a Sir Rufane Shaw Donkin,[*] whose talents for government may be contemplated by any one that chooses to look for them, in the evidence taken before the commitee of the House of Commons, on the state of the Aborigines; and as the portrait is chiefly drawn by Sir Rufane Shaw Donkin's own hand, it is of course not executed in unfavourable colours. Then there is Sir Galbraith Lowry Cole, whose praise this narrative has imperfectly set forth; but if any further inquiry into his talents for government should be thought requisite, the reader must refer to the Anti - Slavery Reporter, where they will find Sir

---

[*] Sir Rufane Shaw Donkin's ideas of justice are pretty obvious by the questions he put to Dr. Philip, in the committee of the House of Commons.

Sir R. Donkin—" Do you think it *possible*, however much it may be to be lamented, to prevent enlightened Europeans who settle in a country from ultimately driving out and exterminating the unenlightened inhabitants?" Dr. Philip—" I most decidedly think it practicable to prevent it."

Sir R. D.—" Are you aware that in America it has been *distinctly proved*, and recognised by the chief person of the state, that the natives must be driven out, and yield to the increasing colonists?"—Dr. P.—" I do not at all agree in that opinion."

Sir R. D.—" Have you ever read M. De Tocqueville's account of the manner in which the enlightened Americans are gradually exterminating the natives in their country?"—Dr. P.—" I have never read the book, but I consider the Americans highly censurable for their conduct to the natives." (Ab. 559.)

He that can gravely ask if it be *possible* to prevent " enlightened" European settlers from driving out and exterminating " the unenlightened inhabitants" must have strange notions of the *light* of the Christian religion.

Galbraith Lowry Cole figuring in the government of the Mauritius, and legislating for slave-drivers, in a manner not soon to be forgotten. Next there is Colonel Wade, who, in the same volume of evidence, has also drawn his own portrait at full length. Colonel Wade commiserating the unemancipated Hottentots—Colonel Wade issuing a circular preparatory to the vagrant law—Colonel Wade presiding over the birth of that said vagrant law—and Colonel Wade entering a protest in the legislative council against the Governor, who disapproved that vagrant law, will not soon be erased from the grateful remembrance of the Aborigines.

And then we have Sir Benjamin D'Urban—the victor Sir Benjamin D'Urban, crowned with a load of laurels—the great general, and the still greater writer of despatches—the devastator of Caffreland—the applauding historian of king Hintza's death—the spoliation of the allies of Great Britain—the remover of landmarks—the builder of fortresses, the founder of cities—the beloved of Boors, and the admired of Methodist missionaries!

And who next? Alas! shall Great Britain, that realm of power and wisdom, that island, super-eminent in glory and grandeur amongst the kingdoms of the earth, on whose vast dominions the sun never goes down,—shall England, imperial, haughty, illustrious England, never send forth more joyous specimens of her intellectual and moral excellence, than these king Logs or king Cranes, for her unhappy colony? Shall all that pass by this settlement, for ever point the finger of scorn against our glaring misrule, our ceaseless oppressions, our insatiate aggressions? Shall we never begin to be wise and good? Shall no ray of justice ever penetrate the density of this darkness,—darkness that may be felt—and shall this mighty province never lift up her head, bowed down with the yoke of her doleful satraps? If these men must be elevated and enriched, let them be so in their proper spheres. Promote them in the army list; make them Generals; give them companies; stuff them with regiments; saturate them with pensions, and gorge them with sinecures; cover their breasts with stars and crosses, with garters and saints, with dragons and thistles, but give them not colonies to desolate, nor mankind to devour, and do not turn them forth from the Horse Guards to inflict intolerable evils on the human race.

The very first step, therefore, towards a better system, is to entrust the government of the colony to civilians, and to pass over the Knights Commanders, Knights Companions, and other dignitaries of the Horse Guards; for, though amongst military men, one here and there, and that as a sort of monster, may be found, who, to the science of a swordsman, might add the wisdom of a statesman; yet, certain it is, that nine-tenths of the military order are not only useless, but injurious in provincial governments, serving no other purpose, than to foment wars by injustice, and to execute them in cruelty, and to extend a system of boundless spoliation, which must at last terminate in the decline and fall of the British empire.

The object hitherto has been to establish, as much as possible, a military dominion in the colony : the object to be aimed at ought to be precisely the reverse ; to keep aloof from all temptations to the exertion of force, and to remove to a distance the implements of aggression. So easy would it be to establish an harmonious sway amongst the neighbouring tribes, by pacific mea-

sures, and by manifesting a real disposition to do them
good, that troops would soon become useless, little
more than the ornaments of authority, though their
services might, perhaps, be acceptable for some time to
come, to keep in check that generation of violent men
within *the colony*, who, having once broken forth into
rebellion, are again exhibiting their seditious tendencies,
now that their ancient sway is in danger. There are
many, very many colonists who are elbow-deep in
blood,—men, who for many years have been engaged in
commandos, and who have been accustomed to destroy
Bushmen, Hottentots, and Caffres, as they would destroy vermin! They have been bred up in the pesti-
lential atmosphere of slavery; their ideas have been
formed in a school of tyranny, and they can neither
speak, think, nor act, but under the impulse of their
habitual feelings. These men, in some districts, are
all powerful, and it is they who must be repressed and
taught the wholesome discipline of general justice and
moderation. It is for them chiefly that an imposing
array of soldiers might be useful, not, it is to be hoped,
for any actual collision, but to inform them that there
is a force at hand superior to their own.

The Caffre nation will next demand the serious attention of the colonial government; for it is in this
quarter that the safety and prosperity of the colony are
to be established. If Lord Glenelg had not compelled
the conquerors to disgorge their acquisitions in the last
war, and if the Boors and "other respectable settlers"
had been allowed to occupy the large tracts of land
reserved for them by the munificent governor, to the
east of the Keishkamma, we should soon have had
another war, and perhaps another seizure of territory as
far as Port Natal; but the accumulated vengeance of

o

the barbarian nations would certainly prove too powerful for us at last, and after spending immense sums of
money in fruitless campaigns; after squandering mil-
lions in the service of the rapacious colonists, we should
be at last driven out of our South African possessions,
and be recorded to all generations as baffled spoliators
and discomfited oppressors.

As, therefore, we may not, and, indeed, cannot
dislodge the whole Caffre nation to please these " highly
respectable Boors and settlers," we should endeavour
to convert them into friends rather than to torment
them into enemies. And here it is most fortunate for
our interests that we have such neighbours as the
Amakosæ; it is fortunate for us that we have not to
contend with the Arabs of northern Africa, and the
fierce tribes of the central regions, who know not how
to forgive, and never forget an injury. Our neighbours
are a placable and good-natured people; they have not
imbibed the sanguinary doctrines of the false prophet;
they are strangers to the warlike creed of the Ko-
ran, and, though courageous and determined when
thoroughly excited, they have no inclination to go to
war. Nothing would be more easy than to convert the
Caffres into most valuable friends; and if there were
no pleasure in making the attempt, if there were no
satisfaction in conquering them by kindness, the policy
is so obvious, that one would think even military governors would at least have tried the experiment.

There are some few points to attend to under existing circumstances, and though doubtless these points
will not be forgotten in other quarters, where many
other propositions of matured wisdom, founded on the
principles of justice and humanity, will be duly propounded, yet we may venture to offer the following

suggestions which the narrative itself seems to have dictated :—

1. The wrongs which the house of Gaika have sustained at our hands are great : they have a full right acknowledged * by the home government, to all the neutral territory. Every inch of it has been taken from them by force or fraud. Now, it would be difficult to restore all this country to its lawful owners, yet still they have a right to it; and considering all the numerous injuries they have sustained in addition to loss of lands—the burning of their villages, and that repeatedly—the immense plunder of their cattle—the violent deaths of their subjects—and the grief, vexation, and alarm which has been their portion for many years, owing to our injustice and inhumanity, it is incumbent on us to *purchase* this territory ; and for this purpose, it would seem but justice to recommend the payment of 20,000*l.* to the House of Gaika—chiefly to Macomo and Tyali, to be laid out for their benefit in building for them on their own lands, houses, chapels, and schools; in assisting them in agriculture, and in aiding them in their very laudable wishes to elevate the moral condition of their people.

This having been effected, a formal cession of the neutral territory, in consideration of the money so expended for their benefit, would be. signed by the chiefs, and all feelings of irritation for past injuries would be buried in oblivion.

The sum of 20,000*l.* would, indeed, be a poor payment to Macomo and his brothers for the injuries they

---

* See Lord Glenelg's despatch, where the acknowledgment is made several times that the Caffres have been driven out of their lawful possessions, which we have unlawfully seized.

have sustained, and if it were increased tenfold it would
hardly compensate for their losses and tribulations;
but as any attempt at recompense on our part would
surprise them, the effect produced would be incalcu-
lably advantageous.

2. The other great chiefs, three or four in number,
should not be forgotten, though much smaller sums
would be required for them,—unless, indeed, we should
undertake to render justice to the house of Slambi,
which, by continued acts of plunder, from the year
1812 down to the present hour, we have completely
ruined. A fair estimate of the damages of Slambi's
sons would amount to a frightful sum; and although
these princes will never recover a tithe of their damages,
yet certainly the British government should endeavour
to confer upon them some benefits. Jan Tzatzoe has
an unanswerable claim for damages sustained in the
case of his unlawful ejectment, and it would seem difficult to refuse them on any other plea than such as
superior force usually urges.

3. The government should establish, endow, and
sustain a school for the children of the chiefs,
either within the Caffre territory, or close to the border. The chiefs should be treated with respect as
long as they respect themselves: their entrance into
the colony on peaceable missions or friendly errands
should be received with courtesy and hospitality. The
military officers should be strictly enjoined to treat
them as chiefs, and the magistrates, field-cornets, &c.
made to understand that their rank is to be respected.

4. No Englishman should go into Caffreland without permission obtained from the ruling chief of the
district; this prohibition to be general for all ranks,
from the highest to the lowest.

5. The colonial government should carefully abstain from interfering with the missions in Caffreland; the government has continually been meddling in spiritual matters, sometimes protecting and tolerating, but more commonly tormenting and harassing. If the missionaries violate any law, let them be punished by all means; but if they live peaceably and quietly, attending to their religious duties, then—*let them alone;* that is all that is demanded—*let them alone* : they ask for no stipend, they require no government-pay; their only prayer is, that the hateful paw of the colonial government may not invade the sanctuary. The government has its own clergy, whom it may pay or protect as much as it chooses, but the missionaries desire neither pay nor protection—they only require neutrality, a very cheap and simple boon to demand.

6. Protectors of the Caffre tribes should reside with the principal chiefs, and by the chiefs should be selected. No treaty with the Caffre nation should be ratified, that had not first been reduced to writing, in the Caffre, as well as the English and Dutch languages. Drafts of these treaties should first be published in the colonial newspapers, two months, at least, before ratification; and every possible precaution should be taken to make the chiefs acquainted with the full import of the treaty, that it might be fully discussed in the national councils. The chiefs should be furnished with official seals, and every treaty should be signed and sealed by *all* the ruling chiefs of Caffreland. After these formalities the treaty should be sent to the home government for approval. No military man should be allowed to decide on the pretended infraction of a treaty by the Aborigines.

It will be further essential for the peace, prosperity,

and happiness of the colony, that the violent and lawless habits of "the Boors and other respectable settlers"
should be restrained.* This a good governor would
find the most difficult part of his duty : it requires,
however, but firmness and prudence to keep these men
within bounds, and to lay down such rules for their
restraint, as would at last compel them to submit to the
majesty of the law.   We hear of these men going forth
by hundreds into the north, beyond the colonial boundaries ; and this, their emigration, is partly to avoid
the effect of the emancipation act, by removing their
slaves beyond the reach of the law; partly to take
possession of boundless estates, without paying for
them ; and partly to live unrestrained by any master.
If it were only the loss of such subjects we would

* The colonial government is in this respect more feeble or
worse principled than the Dutch government 150 years ago : in
the year 1693, the council resolved " that the cattle trade with
the Hottentots was strictly forbidden to private persons, and no
one was allowed to go beyond Hottentots Holland, Rodezand or
Oliphant's pad to the Sousequas, Hessiquas, Obiquas, Griquas
or Namaquas, under pain of confiscation of waggons, cattle and
every thing found in possession so offending, who should in addition be fined 60 rix dollars, *and be confined in chains for one year
in the public works.*"   A little of this wholesome discipline would
soon effect a cure in the vagrant disorder of the Boors.   Again in
1727, " the cattle trade with the Hottentots was once more prohibited, on account of it having appeared that the colonists compelled them to trade, and thereby caused their poverty ; and
therefore that those trading with them or giving them the least
trouble, or doing them the least injury, *should forfeit their goods,
waggons, and cattle,* and be moreover punished as disturbers of
the public peace, and enemies to justice and liberty."   P. P. i.
15. 17.
  Let the government carry out these ordinances, and all will be
right.

gladly make a bridge of gold for them to escape for ever into the wilderness; but as they take their slaves with them, and spread havoc and destruction amongst the northern tribes, whose territory they invade, it is incumbent on the colonial government to punish these real vagrants, by taking from them their slaves and servants, by declaring forfeit all their colonial possessions, and by proclaiming them outlaws, both within and without the colony; and thus leaving them to the reprisals of the tribes whom they have irritated, unprotected by English law, and stripped of all the privileges of British subjects.

And, lastly, every endeavour must be made to elevate the remnant of the Hottentot race, by granting them locations in other parts of the colony, besides the Kat River settlement, and by leaving them unmolested where they are now settled.

A proclamation, in the Cape Town Gazette, should solemnly assure the Hottentots and the coloured race that there will be no attempt to bring them back to a state of slavery, by any vagrant ordinance, or any other contrivance of any description; that the laws already in existence are sufficient for the peace of the colony, and that those only will be punished who having broken the existing laws, have been found guilty after trial, in due course of law. It is requisite to give a feeling of *security* to the coloured race; they that live in constant dread of an earthquake will never build a substantial house.

We have no hesitation in saying, that a policy based on humanity and justice, and carefully purged from the doctrines of force, would speedily be followed with the happiest results, would remove the fear of invasion from the borders, would convert angry enemies into grateful friends, would surround our South African possessions with moral bulwarks, more impregnable than mountain fastnesses and military posts, and change a land of violence and mourning into a kingdom of tranquillity and peace.

₊ If we wished to make a rough estimate of the losses sustained by Macomo alone, we must put down in the account 300,000 acres of valuable land in the Kat River settlement; and at least 20,000 head of cattle taken in the various commandos and wars, so that if the cattle were valued so low as 1*l*. per head, the account is very serious against the colony. But to this we must add the loss of kraals destroyed by fire, the loss of corn, garden stuff, &c. &c. : the deaths of multitudes of vassals, and a life of distress and terror which never could be redeemed by any payment.

The losses sustained by the brothers of Macomo, and by the families of Hintza and Slambi, may be thus glanced at, but cannot be estimated.

Jan Tzatzoe's territory contains about 103,000 acres.

APPENDIX.

No. I.

Civil Government.

Salaries, ...	£23,601	0	0	
Contingencies, . . .	4,216	0	0	
				£27,818 0 0

Judicial Department.

Salaries, ...	30,736	0	0	
Contingencies, . . .	2,742	0	0	
				33,478 0 0

Revenue Department.

Salaries, ...	15,497	0	0	
Contingencies, . . .	5,650	0	0	
				21,147 0 0

Schools.

Salaries, ...	1,912	0	0	
Contingencies, . . .	463	0	0	
				2,376 0 0

Medical Department.

Salaries, ...	1,955	0	0	
Contingencies, . . .	2,777	0	0	
				4,732, 0 0

Pensions.

Civil, ...	4,683	0	0	
Military, ...	760	0	0	
				5,443 0 0
Convicts and Prisoners, . . .				6,606 0 0
Jurors and Witnesses, ...				2,138 0 0
Public Roads, Bridges, Ferries, . .				2,276 0 0
Public Works and Buildings, . .				8,654 0 0
Remittance to Colonial Agent in London,				3,755 0 0
Advances for the Public Service, . .				242 0 0
Miscellaneous, ...				640 0 0

Total Expenditure, . .	126,889 0 0
Commissariat Department for the Army, .	155,000 0 0
	£281,889 0 0

Some of the pensions for such a government and such a population seem to be flagrant instances of jobbing.

PENSIONS.

Sir John Truter, late Chief Justice, with a reversion
of 300*l.* per annum to his wife, . . £600 0 0
Colonel Bird, late Colonial Secretary, . . 600 0 0
Sir Richard Plasket, late Secretary, . . 500 0 0
Walter Bentinck, late Auditor General, . . 500 0 0
Mrs. D. Alexander, . , . . . 300 0 0
Mrs. Sheridan, ... 300 0 0
A member of the *late* Court of Justice, . . 100 0 0
Ditto, ... 100 0 0
Ditto, ... 100 0 0
Ditto. . . . . . , . . 100 0 0
Mr. Denyssen, late Fiscal, ... 400 0 0
Late Collector of Tithes, ... 200 0 0
Late Sequestrator, ... 200 0 0
A pension to a person not named, . . 150 0 0
Ditto, ... 150 0 0
Ditto, ... 150 0 0
Ditto, ... 150 0 0
Ditto, ... 150 0 0

The total of the pensions I do not find; the above are a specimen. One phenomenon is remarkable in the pension-list, besides the largeness of the grants, the happy state of idleness which these pensioners enjoy—" late secretary," " late tythe-collector," " late sequestrator," " members of late court of justice." Fatigued with their operations, these favored dignitaries soon retire from the scene of their toils, to enjoy a wealthy beatitude in the Elysian pastures of the Cape Pension-list.

*** The colonial government has raised a loan of 35,000*l.* in the colony, to defray some of the expenses of the late Caffre war.

No. II.

ENGLISH GOVERNORS OF THE COLONY OF THE CAPE OF GOOD HOPE.

J. H. Craigh, 1st September, 1795.
Earl Macartney, 23d May, 1797.
Sir Francis Dundas, (Lieutenant-Governor), 22d Nov. 1798.
Sir George Young, 18th December, 1793.
Sir F. Dundas, L. G. 20th April, 1801.
Jan. Willem Jansens, 1st March, 1803. Dutch.
Sir David Baird, 10th January, 1806.
Hon. H. G. Grey, L. G. 17th January, 1807.
Du Pré, Earl of Caledon, 22d May, 1807.
Hon. H. G. Grey, L. G. 5th July, 1811.
Sir John Francis Cradock, 5th September, 1811.
Hon. R. Meade, L. G. 13th December, 1813.
Lord Charles Somerset, 6th April, 1814.
Sir Rufane Shaw Donkin, Acting Governor, 13th Jan. 1820.
Lord C. H. Somerset, returned 1st December, 1821.
Richard Bourke, L. G. 8th Feb. 1828.
Sir Galbraith Lowry Cole, G. C. B. 6th May, 1828.
Colonel Wade, Acting Governor, August, 1833.
Sir Benjamin D'Urban, January 14, 1834.

No. III.

MURDER OF HINTZA.

By Lord Glenelg's desire, the Horse Guards issued an order for a military inquiry into the murder of Hintza. The court of inquiry, in consequence of these orders, met at Fort Wiltshire, on Monday August 29th 1836, and continued its labors of investigation for several days. The members of the court were the Honourable Lieutenant Colonel Hare, K. H., 27th Regiment, *President*: Major Macpherson, of the 27th Regiment, Major Tripp, of the 98th, Captain Amsnick, of the 27th, Captain Fawkes, of the 27th. The Graham's Town Journal has published some of this evidence, commenting on the extracts which it has thought proper to divulge, in its usual spirit of party fury and falsehood. The evidence of Dr. Ford is too important to be omitted :—

By the Court.—" Your name is mentioned as a person who is likely to give us some important information about the mutilation of Hintza's body."—"I saw the body of Hintza after it was carried up the hill some distance. Mr. Puleston, of the 75th Regiment, led me to the place where he lay, and to which it had been conveyed by Colonel Smith's orders; he conducted me to some Caffre huts, and pointed to the body, saying, 'there it lies,' and immediately left me as the bugle sounded. I then proceeded to examine the state of the body; as well as I recollect, I first turned it on its right side, and in consequence of seeing blood flow from the back, I examined the wounds, which were as follows :—The top of his head was completely shattered, a ball, I suppose, having passed through from ear to ear; the bone of the arch of the head was broken to pieces; the foremost part of the scalp was hanging over the face, and the back part fallen into the base of the scull: the brains were all out. I next observed the laceration of the chin, and on examining more closely I found a fracture of the symphysis of the jaw, that is, the lower jaw, where the two wings of the lower jaw-bone unite or grow together. I then examined the wound in the back—as well as I recollect, it was in the left side, on the back part; the ball had entered there, and I did not see any mark of the egress of the ball. I looked in front, and I supposed it had lodged in the body. There was a small quantity of blood flowing; there was also a wound in the calf of one of his legs: I examined the bone to see if it was broken, but it was not. During this examination the advance-bugle sounded for the troops to march, and I hurried off as fast as I could. I was sure there were a good many Caffres in the neighbourhood, and I had a considerable distance to ascend the hill; I mounted my horse and rejoined the troops. Two days afterwards, on returning from the Bashee, when about five or six miles from the place, Colonel Smith sent to the rear for me, and asked me if I knew the place where I had last seen the body, *as he wished to look at it*, to see whether the Caffres had taken it to bury. We rode together, but I did not recognize the place until we had passed it about half a mile. This I mentioned to Colonel Smith, and he deliberated for a moment, and said he was too anxious to get on to Mr. Finn, and his party, to lose time in returning, therefore, we went on and did not again see the body."

By the Court.—" Did you observe if the ear or ears were cut off?"—"THE LEFT EAR WAS OFF, but it not being a matter of any interest to me, I did not turn the body to look at the other."

As the Graham's Town Journal had with frontless audacity, repeatedly declared that the mutilation of Hintza's body was a calumny, although it was a public notorious fact, much boasted of and rejoiced in, till the appearance of Lord Glenelg's despatch, it was particularly imprudent in that paper to publish Dr. Ford's evidence. This the editor perceived after a while, and, therefore, gave out that the loss of Hintza's left ear was not by amputation, but by the blow of the musket ball. Dr. Ford destroyed that subterfuge in the following letter:—

To the Editor.

" Fort Wiltshire, September 19th, 1836.

" SIR.—An incorrect report of part of my evidence before the Court of Inquiry, having appeared in the last number of the Graham's Town Journal, and which might tend to excite a belief that I had given an evasive answer; I request you will have the goodness to have the error rectified in your next number. I allude to the last question, and my reply to it, *both of which have been wholly misstated.* The question, as *proposed to me by Colonel Smith*, was in the following words, or nearly so:

" 'Can you state if the ears were cut off, or might its removal have been caused by a ball which entered the head?'— My reply was—No, *it could not have been the consequence of the ball*, as the opening made by it was some little distance above the situation of the ear. I am, &c.

W. M. FORD,
Assistant Surgeon, 72d Highlanders."

Barrow, the celebrated South African traveller, has in his second volume, published " articles of instruction," proposed by one of the landdrosts, to regulate the conduct of those who went out in commandos against the Bushmen and Caffres—and these articles, he thinks, will shew in a striking manner the cruelty of the commandos.

Article 1.—No unnecessary cruelty to be exercised on the prisoners, on pain of exemplary punishment. Article 3.—On conquest of any kraal, the huts are not to be set on fire, as usual; as there is every reason for supposing that, *to this practice alone,* the burning and plundering of our farm houses are to be ascribed. Artilce 4.—THE DEAD CARCASSES OF THE ENEMY ARE NOT TO BE VIOLATED, as has usually been the practice of the evil disposed part of the commandos, by cutting them with knives, lashing them with waggon-whips, and hacking them with stones: as such conduct tends only to exasperate the enemy, and induces them to commit murder.

Barrow comments thus on the articles,—" I should not have ventured to give the fourth article of these extraordinary instructions as authentic, had it not appeared before me as an official document." Little did that enlightened traveller imagine, that in the year 1835, the fourth article might be issued as an official document.

George Southey, the person who shot Hintza, has given *his account* of the affair before the Court of Inquiry; but he had better have been silent, for this is his version of that " untoward event :"—

" I again called out to Hintza, who was running, to stand, but he took no notice; and Colonel Smith said, '*fire again Southey;*' I did so; Hintza fell, but was soon upon his legs again, and kept on the same course down the hill with great speed, and rushed into the bush. I continued the pursuit, and ran a full mile on foot. I came to the edge of the bush just after Lieutenant Balfour had arrived there, *and where Hintza had just before gone in.* And, gentlemen, should I not have been wanting in my duty, and deficient in the courage of an Englishman, had I not followed him? Lieutenant Balfour and I leaped down the bank together. I went up the stream, and Lieutenant Balfour down. We had proceeded some little distance—too far to be seen by each other in such a thicket, and it was impossible for me to be seen by any person on the outside of the bush. While going on near the edge of the water, I heard an assegai touch a stone or rock on which I stood, and quickly looking round, I saw a Caffre's head, and an assegai uplifted so near me, that I had to spring back to make room for my gun. I fired AND SHOT A CAFFRE WHOM I AFTERWARDS FOUND TO BE HINTZA."

No comment is requisite on such an exculpation.

No. IV.

THE WESLEYAN MISSIONARIES AND SIR BENJAMIN D'URBAN.

The flattering and courtly address of the Wesleyan Missionaries, Messrs. Shrewsbury and Boyce, to Sir Benjamin D'Urban, on the conclusion of the Caffre war, is to be seen in the *Parliamentary Returns*, No. 279, 'Caffre war and death of Hintza.' The answer of Sir Benjamin D'Urban to these gentlemen has not yet been published in this country:—it is as follows:

"I thank you, Gentlemen, for the kind feeling towards me which pervades the address that you have done me the favor to deliver me: *the prayers of good and holy men are beyond all price*, and, therefore, assuredly I rejoice that I have yours. It is a source of unfeigned satisfaction to me, that the pious, humane, and enlightened body of the Wesleyan Mission, are convinced of the wantonness, cruelty, and ingratitude of the late Caffre aggression against the colony—of the consequent justice of that cause which I have been called upon by my office to avenge; and that I have discharged that painful though necessary duty, *in accordance with the principles of mercy*. It is very gratifying to me, that you should attribute to me arrangements beneficial to any of the members of the Wesleyan Mission, which, as I know by long experience, are such continual benefactors to mankind, have well deserved of my hands, whatever it may have been permitted me to be the instrument of in their behalf: and I entreat you to believe, that in endeavouring to be so, my sincere satisfaction has gone in hand with my duty. Again, gentlemen, I thank you for your prayers and good wishes for me and my family, and I return them to you and yours collectively and individually, with every sentiment of sincerity, regard, and esteem.

17th June, 1835.   B. D'Urban.

"To the Reverend W. J. Shrewsbury, Chairman;
the Reverend Mr. Boyce, Secretary, and the
Members of the Wesleyan Mission, assembled
in Graham's Town.

In July 1835, a Wesleyan preacher had been insulted whilst preaching in the open air: the methodists complained of it in a memorial to the governor, and received the following reply:—

"I have not failed to deliver to the Governor the document

which you placed in my hands, and I am commanded by His Excellency, (in having the honour to acknowledge it) to assure you that no testimonial could have been necessary to convince him of the upright, pious, and exemplary conduct of the Wesleyan missionaries, since a long experience *of the virtues and religious services of that body here,* and in other countries, has justly impressed His Excellency with the highest opinion of their unaffected piety, loyalty, and *pre-eminent utility,* &c. &c.

Government House,   J. E. Alexander, A. D. C.
  July 30th, 1835.

It does not, therefore, seem possible to increase the intensity of love existing between the governor and the methodist preachers. The editor of the Graham's Town Journal is a methodist; and methodism in the colony, "rules the court, the camp, the grove."

No. V.

Copy of a Despatch from Lord GLENELG to Governor Sir B. D'URBAN.

Downing Street, 26th Dec. 1835.

SIR,—I have to acknowledge the receipt of your despatch of the 19th of June last, reporting the progress and the conclusion of the warfare in which you had been engaged for several preceding weeks with the Caffre tribes inhabiting the country to the eastward of the Cape of Good Hope.

My immediate predecessor, the Earl of Aberdeen, had the honour of signifying to you his Majesty's entire approbation of the " prompt and energetic measures which you had adopted, with the view of arresting the progress of the invaders, and of compelling them to retire within their own territory." I have to discharge the additional and grateful office of acquainting you, that the King is pleased to commend the vigour and decision with which that important service has been executed.

It is indeed true, that even success, against such an enemy, could bring little accession to the military distinction which you have acquired in other parts of the world; but it affords His Majesty high gratification to observe, that in this new form of warfare, His Majesty's forces have exhibited their characteristic courage, discipline, and cheerful endurance of fatigue and of privations.

It has also been peculiarly gratifying to His Majesty to

learn, from your General Orders, that the loss of life incurred by his forces in this service, has been, comparatively, so inconsiderable.

Having thus performed a duty agreeable on every account to my feelings, I proceed to the more difficult office of considering the origin, the progress, and the results of your hostilities with the Caffre tribes. On these subjects it was my anxious desire to address you at a much earlier period: but after the most attentive and repeated perusal of every part of your despatches, and of their enclosures, I still find myself impeded in the execution of that purpose, by the want of sufficient official information for the guidance of His Majesty's Government on this occasion. With the most ample details of all your military operations, you have not combined any clear and comprehensive explanation of the causes which provoked the irruption of the Caffres into the colony. I advert to this omission with no intention of imputing it to you as a neglect of duty. I can well understand that amidst the labours, civil and military, so urgently demanding your attention, you may not have found leisure for such a retrospect of the origin of this calamitous warfare. Thinking, however, that a correct understanding of the relations between the colonists and the Caffres for several years past was indispensable, in order to form a right judgment on the events of the year which is now closing, and having, in expectation of assistance from yourself on that subject, postponed this communication to the latest possible moment, I am at last reluctantly compelled, in the deficiency of official intelligence, to draw many conclusions from less authentic sources of information.

I have thus been led to the study of a large mass of documents, of which some are accessible to the public at large, and others have been brought under my inspection by the voluntary zeal of various individuals, who, from many different motives, interest themselves in this discussion. These researches have afforded me some advantages for forming a correct conclusion as to the causes and probable effects of the war, which I could not have found in the perusal of any reports, however minute and elaborate, drawn up by any single writer, even though possessed of all the means of knowledge so peculiarly at your command. The disadvantage of reposing my judgment on materials of this nature is too manifest to require any particular statement; while many facts are demonstrated to my own conviction, and to that of my colleagues, so completely as to exclude all reasonable doubt, I am compelled to state them without the possibility of adducing the proofs by which they are supported. Those proofs could not be intelligibly arranged within the compass of a despatch; nor indeed within that of a considerable volume. To some of them I should be extremely reluctant to make a more particular reference, because it would involve the necessity of discussing the credibility of the different witnesses, and would thus lead me into personal topics totally unbeseeming the present occasion. In some instances also, I might perhaps, however unintentionally, be violating the confidence in which some of the papers before me were written. The result, therefore, is, that I must on my own responsibility state the conclusions which I have formed respecting the origin of the late invasion of the colony, and the events which ensued. I should gladly have declined such a duty, had it been possible; but I may not shrink from it when thus forced upon me. For my own acquittal hereafter, I have caused the whole series of documents, printed ¡and written, which I have been compelled to examine, to be carefully recorded in this office. If not immediately accessible to the public at large, they will at least remain here in vindication of the opinions which I have deduced from them. In the meantime, you will, I am sure, give me credit for having studied them all, not merely with diligence and impartiality, but with a predisposition, arising alike from duty and inclination, in favour of the measures adopted by yourself, and by the various officers who have preceded you in the government of the colony of the Cape of Good Hope.

I commence with one position which is beyond the reach of controversy. Adopting the language of Lord Aberdeen, I concur entirely with him in declaring it to have been your clear and indispensable duty, "to arrest the progress of the invaders, and to compel them to retire within their own territory." Nor was this the whole extent of your duty in that critical state of public affairs; you were not less distinctly bound to take effective measures for putting down within Caffreland itself, all assemblages of men who had either formed or were in the act of forming themselves into bands hostile to the colony. You were also entitled to take effectual securities against the recurrence of similar invasions.

Passing from this preliminary statement (which may, perhaps, seem little else than the enunciation of a self-evident truth) I reach those questions which really demand inquiry, and on the solution of which the practical measures of His Majesty's Government must, to a considerable extent, depend. Thus, it is necessary to consider whether the invasion of the colony by the Caffres was provoked by such wrongs as afforded them a legitimate cause of war, or whether it is correctly designated by you as an " unprovoked aggression." If the Caffres were able to allege in defence of their hostilities any such intolerable wrongs as justified them in seeking redress by the sword, then our victory should have been followed by such ample reparation for the original injury as it was in our power to make. Having, in fact, been followed by the expulsion of the tribes from their own territory, and by other extreme measures, it is further necessary to consider whether your hostilities might not have been more limited in their range, or arrested at an earlier period.

The reasons to which I have already adverted, compel me to state merely the result of my inquiries into the origin of the Caffre invasion, unsupported by the evidence on which I rely. The conclusion, though exhibited in a few general terms, is the fruit of a long and extensive investigation. I abide by it with the greater confidence, because it has been forced upon me by proofs, of which I would gladly have resisted the pressure. But yielding to the conviction which has thus been impressed on my mind, I am constrained to admit, that in the conduct which was pursued towards the Caffre nation by the colonists, and the public authorities of the colony, through a long series of years, and which the short period of your administration could not have enabled you to correct, the Caffres had an ample justification of the war into which they rushed with such fatal imprudence at the close of the last year. This justification rests on two distinct grounds.

First, The Caffres had to resent, and endeavoured justly though impotently to avenge, a series of encroachments upon them, which had terminated in the assumption by Great Britain, first, of the dominion, and then of the exclusive possession, of all the country between the Great Fish River and the Keishkamma. To effect this object, we commenced by ascribing to the chieftain Gaika an authority which he did not possess, and then proceeded to punish him and his tribes because he failed to exercise that imaginary power for our benefit. We held him responsible for the acts of his and our own common enemy, and exacted from him and his people a forfeiture of their lands, as a penalty for the retaliation made by the chief Slambie, after the invasion of his country by Gaika and ourselves. We forced on our ally a treaty, which, according to the usages of the Caffre nation, he had no authority to conclude, and proceeding on that treaty, we ejected the other Caffre chiefs, who were no parties to it, from their country. The compact thus made was on our side repeatedly infringed. Of the country of which the dominion was acquired in order that it might be placed as a barrier between the two nations, and which, with that avowed object, had been especially devoted to be thenceforward a neutral and uncultivated waste, extensive tracts were speedily occupied, partly by British, and partly by Hottentot settlements. The Caffres, imitating our example,

endeavoured to resume the possession of some part of their
lost country. They were at times driven back at the point of
the bayonet, and either shot or flogged, if captured to the westward of the Keishkamma. At other times, their residence
within that frontier was permitted if not encouraged. But as
often as the fluctuating policy of the colonial government led
to the disapproval of this indulgence, they were again driven
back in large bodies into their remaining lands, with all the
rigour of military execution against their persons and property.
Harassed by this long series of aggressions, and the victims of
successive changes in the opinions and conduct of the local
authorities, the immediate motives of their invasion in December, 1834, would seem not very difficult to be discovered. In
the Appendix to your Despatch of the 19th of June, you state,
" the avowed object of the savages in their present invasion, is
the extension of their territory, or, in other words, the recovery
of a tract of country from which similar atrocities to those they
are now committing compelled the colonial government to
remove them, and which was afterwards formally ceded to us
by treaty." Dissenting from the accuracy of the impressions
which you have received respecting the cause of the expulsion
of the Caffres from their former possessions, and unable as I
am to attach any authority to the treaty to which you here
refer, I yet deduce from this passage a clear confirmation of the
opinion maintained by almost every other witness on the subject, that the Caffres were stimulated to this war by the belief
that they had been unjustly despoiled of their country, and by
the hope of regaining possession of it. I am compelled to
conclude, that they wanted nothing to the completeness of this
right, except the power to render their assertion of it effectual.
    2dly. The next cause of war which the advocates of the
Caffres have alleged in their defence, is, that the tribes were,
for a long series of years, harassed by incursions into their
country, which, though conducted under the express sanction
and guidance of the authorities, civil and military, of the
frontier districts, were yet, it is said, attended by a long series
of acts of injustice and spoliation in the highest degree indefensible. On the part of the colonists are alleged the predatory
character and habits of their neighbours, and the right, or rather
the duty, of retaliation for robberies committed upon the
defenceless farmers and other inhabitants of the districts of
Albany and Somerset.
    It is evidently impossible to weave into any one connected
history the long catalogue of these border forays : nor would
such a narration, if it could be compiled, answer any useful
purpose. But throughout the whole of these incidents, the
mode of proceeding against the Caffres for the restitution of

stolen cattle, was one which it is impossible to condemn too strongly as unjust, or to lament too deeply as productive of calamitous results.

It is established beyond all possibility of contradiction or doubt, that for a series of years immediately preceding the invasion of 1834, the practice on our frontier districts was as follows: A farmer who had lost, or who thought proper to allege that he had lost, any of his cattle, preferred his complaint either to the field-cornet or to the military commandant of his district. Without further evidence or investigation, either into the reality of the loss or into the causes which might have produced it, a military force, with the complainant for the guide, entered the Caffre country. Following up any tracks which he might, with whatever truth or falsehood, point out as the traces of his own cattle, they advanced to the first kraal or village to which these marks conducted them. There, without further inquiry, they demanded restitution. Innocence of the theft was not admitted by the commanders of these parties as any defence against these demands. Whoever might have been the real authors of the wrong, the inhabitants of the kraal were required to compensate the loss, whether real or pretended, of the complainant, for no better or other reason, than that he chose to ascribe to the tread of his lost cattle the marks which had been traced from the borders of the colony to that particular kraal. It was to no purpose to allege that these were the traces of other cattle, or that the real robbers had driven the cattle into the neighbourhood of the kraal to excite an unfounded suspicion against its inhabitants. Utterly regardless of these and all other grounds of vindication, the commanding officer, in the regular discharge of the duty assigned to him, enforced immediate reprisals against the kraal, driving away the cattle, and, in the event of resistance, proceeding to whatever extremities he might find or suppose necessary; extending in many cases to the burning the huts and the firing upon the inhabitants.

The injustice of such proceedings of course requires no proof. Their disastrous results are scarcely less evident. The Caffres were unavoidably converted by them into a nation of depredators. The inhabitants of the pillaged kraal had before them the alternative of perishing for want, or of imitating the conduct of their aggressors, by retaliating upon the nearest proprietor of cattle whom they could surprise or overpower. Thus the predatory spirit was incessantly receiving new force and renewed apologies for its indulgence. Insecurity, depravity of manners, and social wretchedness, were diffused throughout our whole vicinity; and our own people, though not the only victims, were necessarily amongst the chief sufferers, from the maxims which we had established and the conduct we had pursued.

If this practice of punishing the innocent for the guilty, and of assuming the existence of guilt on the bare assertion of the interested party, had occurred in insulated cases only, or at a remote time, or had been the unauthorized act of individual wrongdoers, the injuries of which the Caffre nation had to complain might not perhaps have afforded them a legitimate cause of war. But this system of reprisals appears to have been the established usage of the colonists, under the direct sanction, and with the constant co-operation, of the officers of government on the frontier. It was pursued from year to year, even down to the very close of the year 1834. I have before me the evidence of eye-witnesses whose statements in this respect derive strong incidental confirmation from the official reports which you have transmitted, and who assert that at the eve of the invasion they saw the kraals burning and the Caffre chiefs lamenting with bitterness of heart the injuries which they had sustained by the punishment of their defence-less and unoffending people for the imputed robberies of their fellow-countrymen. At the very same time I find that the principle of punishing resistance to our patrols, by firing on the Caffres who might venture to defend their own property, was acted upon in such a manner, that two of the native chiefs were wounded. And yet it is well known that the national affection for the chief is such, that an injury offered to their persons, even in war, is regarded in the light of a profanation. Of course I do not mean to assert that our troops when engaged in open hostilities with the tribes were bound to adopt their maxims, or even to respect their feelings with regard to the chiefs; I refer to those feelings only as contributing to explain the intensity of the sense of injury, and the blind thirst for revenge which the Caffres so speedily manifested.

· With such facts before me, I cannot refuse to the Caffres the benefit of this second apology for their irruption into the colony. They may indeed have been, nor can I doubt that they were, accustomed to harass the inhabitants with their depredations. But driven as they had been from their ancient and lawful possessions, confined within a comparatively narrow space, where pasturage for their cattle could not be readily found, and urged to revenge and desperation by the systematic injustice of which they had been the victims, I am compelled to embrace, however reluctantly, the conclusion, that they had a perfect right to hazard the experiment, however hopeless, of extorting by force that redress which they could not expect otherwise to obtain.

You, indeed, would deny the last of these statements. In

your despatch of the 21st of January, you denounce the irruption of the Caffres as inexcusable, for a reason which you assign in the following terms:—" I was in special negotiation with them for a new, and to them, a very advantageous, order of relations, into the details of which Dr. Philip, chief of the London mission, had personally, as well as by his missionaries living among them, entered fully with them as lately as October, 1834, with which they had expressed their satisfaction."

It is no impeachment of your habitual accuracy to say, that you have inadvertently fallen into a misconception of the facts of this part of the transactions under review. I have before me evidence the most conclusive, to shew that Dr. Philip did not, either in his own person, or through the agency of any other of the missionaries of his society, make those communications to the Caffre chiefs, with which you state him to be charged by you. Whether he misunderstood your instructions, or whatever circumstance may have occasioned it, of the fact itself there can be no doubt. He neither negotiated as the agent of the local government with the Caffres, nor even delivered any message from you to the chiefs. We are, therefore, not entitled to impute to the Caffres the fault of having burst into the colony regardless of the obligations to forbearance imposed upon them by the pendency of such negotiations as you have mentioned.

I find, however, both in the proclamation which you published at Graham's Town, and in your despatches to me, expressions, of which it is the object to show that the total and incurable depravity of the Caffres is such as to place them, not only beyond the pale of civilized society, but even beyond the range of those principles which regulate the hostilities of more cultivated nations. From this representation it would seem to follow, that in the case of such enemies there is no room for those anxious deliberations, in which I have thought myself bound to engage, respecting the justice of the cause of the war. In your proclamation of the 10th of May, you denounce these people as " irreclaimable savages:" and in your despatch of the 19th of June, you observe, that the Hottentots and Fingoes " not at all inaptly compare the Caffres to wolves, which in truth they resemble very much, which, if they be caught young, may be brought, for their own interest and gratification in the matter, to an appearance of tameness, but which invariably throw it off and appear in all their native fierceness of the woods, so soon as the temptation of blood and ravage, which never fails to elicit their natural fierceness, presents itself to their instinctive thirst for it."

It would be difficult for me to describe the pain with which

I have read and have laid before his Majesty the preceding passage. I am well aware with what prompt and earnest humanity you applied your mind, shortly after your arrival in the
colony, to the improvement of the social condition of the
Caffres; and I would venture to refer the views and feelings
expressed in the words which I have quoted, to the passing
excitement of the hostilities in which you were engaged. You
will, I am sure, concur with me cordially in reprobating the
practical consequences which in so many regions of the globe
have been enforced and palliated, if not directly justified, by
similar reproaches cast indiscriminately on the uncivilized men
with whom the natives of Europe, or their descendants, have
been brought into contact. Having classed their fellow-crea-
tres among the wild beasts of the forest, these claimants to the
exclusive title of human beings, have found little difficulty in
defending, at least to their own satisfaction, whatever measures
were necessary for the subjugation or destruction of the common enemy. Abhorrent as such conduct is from your own
temper and character, I must express my regret that you should,
even through inadvertence, have given any countenance to it
by the employment of terms alluded to; terms not used in
any careless discourse, or hasty writing, but in a despatch
addressed to His Majesty's Government for their guidance on
a practical question of the utmost importance and difficulty.

I am further constrained to record my dissent from the unfavourable estimate which you have formed of the Caffre
character. Referring to the great mass of evidence which it
has been my duty to examine, I find it replete with proofs of a
directly opposite tendency. I learn that amongst this pro-
scribed race, Christian missionaries have passed many years
respected, honoured, and secure. It is placed beyond dispute
that at the very moment when the countrymen of those missionaries were harassing Caffreland with incessant patrols and
commandos, the teachers of religion, relying implicitly on the
honour and good faith of the tribes, continued to receive kindness and protection.

In the midst of all the calamities incident to their situation
in our immediate neighbourhood, the Caffres, under the guidance of their Christian ministers, have built places of public
worship; have formed various congregations of proselytes, or
of learners; have erected school-houses, and sent their children
thither for instruction. In the meanwhile no inconsiderable
advance has been made in agriculture and in commerce. A
trade, variously estimated, but not amounting to less than
30,000l. per annum in the purchase of European commodities,
had been established on the frontier, and as many as two
hundred British traders were living far beyond the boundaries

of the colony, protected only by the integrity and humanity of the uncivilized natives.

To such a people the character of " irreclaimable savages" cannot with justice be assigned. Nor indeed, even if well founded, would this reproach come with a good grace from us, unless it can be asserted that we have, as a Government, fairly brought to the test of experiment whether they can or cannot be reclaimed.

Quitting a topic on which I have not entered without unaffected reluctance and pain, I proceed to the next argument on which you rest the vindication of your measures against the Caffres. It is drawn from the authority due to the opinion of their own Christian teachers.

In your despatch of the 21st of January you observe, that "all the missionaries on the border, men of peace and religion, concur in one opinion of the wanton atrocity of the invasion, and of the impossibility of any other remedy than that of the sword." This statement, however, was evidently made under misapprehension of the real facts of the case. I have before me the conclusive proof that the missionaries of the London and Glasgow Societies, instead of regarding the invasion as a wanton and unprovoked act, considered it as a natural re-action on the part of the Caffres against a series of extreme and intolerable oppressions. So far are they from thinking the sword the only remedy, that, on the contrary, they insist, even with importunity, on the certain efficacy of other methods, of which kindness, conciliation, and justice should form the basis.

The Wesleyan missionaries, in an address professing to be offered in the name of the whole body, though signed only by Messrs. Shrewsbury and Boyes, support your measures, and pronounced an unqualified condemnation of the Caffres. Whatever might be my own opinion of the tone and character of that address, and of the topics which its authors have selected, I should not scruple to allow to their declarations all the weight due to the sacred office which they sustain, if I had not found amongst the enclosures in your despatch of the 19th of June, Mr. Shrewsbury's letter of the 10th of January 1835. After the perusal of that document, I must plainly say that I cannot attach the slightest value to that gentleman's judgment on the present occasion. You state yourself not to have been prepared to adopt measures so severe as those which he there recommended. It was scarcely necessary for you to have taken the trouble of giving me such an assurance. Trusting that the highly respectable body to which Mr. Shrewsbury belongs will promptly disavow all participation in the opinions which he has recorded, and the counsels which he has given,

P

respecting the conduct to be observed towards the Caffres, and hoping that on mature reflection they will be retracted by their author, I spare myself the pain and humiliation of any more particular comment on the document in question.

I am not aware that in the preceding pages I have omitted to notice any one of the grounds which have been adduced in order to throw on the Caffres the responsibility of the late hostilities. It is with the utmost reluctance that I find myself reduced to the necessity of confessing that the result is very far from favorable to the character of British policy in Southern Africa.

I will now advert, though more briefly, to the progress of these hostilities.

It would be impossible to add anything to the strength and emphasis of the terms in which the ravages of the Caffres within the districts of Albany and Somerset are depicted in the papers before me. These expressions, however, advance very little beyond generalities. I find no statement from yourself, or any of the officers of your government, in any definite or tangible form, of the actual loss of life or property. That the invasion was marked by bloodshed and devastation, is a fact of which formal proof is of course unnecessary. That it was accompanied by any outrages of which, in our own incursions into Caffreland, the precedent, and therefore the apology, could not be found, is an assertion of which more direct evidence must be required. Whether, according to the laws of war, as established by our own practice in Southern Africa, the Caffres abused their belligerent rights, is a question which would merit inquiry if our own subsequent conduct is to be defended on the plea of retaliation. It is on every account material to know what was the precise loss which the settlers sustained by the invasion.

Your measures for repelling the invaders were conducted on a most extensive scale. You collected on the frontier an army of no less than 5,000 men; leaving one division for the protection of the frontier, you advanced with the larger portion of your troops into Caffreland, on an expedition, of which the success never appears to have been checked, even for a moment. The only opposition which you encountered was from disorganized bodies of men skulking in their natural fastnesses; and, after a campaign of nearly three months' continuance, your loss in killed and wounded amounted only to eighteen men. Even of that small number, some appear to have lost their lives by such a contempt for their opponents, as led to acts of almost incredible temerity. After the date of your despatch of the 19th June, I collect from other sources, that some detachment of your troops had been cut off by surprise.

When I contrast with these results the fatal consequences of the war to the Caffres, it is impossible not to be deeply impressed with the inequality of the contest, and the utter helplessness of their undisciplined hordes in an encounter with regular troops. The various General Orders published by your officers and by yourself, abound with accounts of the most formidable losses, both of life and property. I find no reference to the capture of any prisoners, but on various occasions hundreds of Caffres are noticed as having fallen. Amongst many passages illustrative of the manner in which the war was conducted by the British troops, I select for illustration the following, from a letter addressed by Colonel Smith to yourself on the 11th of June. "The enemy, although his traces were numerous, fled so rapidly, that few were killed, and only three shots fired at the troops. The whole of the country has been most thoroughly traversed; upwards of 1,200 huts, new and old, have been burnt; immense stores of corn in every direction destroyed; 215 head of cattle of all sorts captured; several horses, and nearly 2,000 goats, have fallen into our hands. The women were very numerous; and I therefore caused them to be amply supplied with beef and biscuit, and dismissed them with the assurance that the atrocities of their husbands had made them forfeit their homes, and that they must move over the Kye. They all stated that they were anxious to do so. It is most gratifying to know that the savages being the unprovoked aggressors, have brought down all the misery with which they are now visited upon the heads of themselves and their families; and that the great day of retribution, and the punishment of the unprovoked atrocities committed by these murderous savages on our colonists, had arrived."

Reading these statements at this distance from the scene of action, I must own that I am affected by them in a manner the most remote from that which the writer contemplated. In the civilised warfare of Europe, this desolation of an enemy's country, not in aid of any military operations, nor for the security of the invading force, but simply and confessedly as an act of vengeance, has rarely occurred, and the occurrence of it has been invariably followed by universal reprobation. I doubt, indeed, whether the history of modern Europe affords an example even of a single case, in which, without some better pretext than that of mere retribution, any invaded people were ever subjected to the calamities which Colonel Smith here describes: the loss of their food, the spoiling of their cattle, the burning of their dwellings, the expulsion of their wives and families from their homes, the confiscation of their property, and the forfeiture of their native country. I am, of course, aware that the laws of civilized nations cannot be rigidly applied in our contests with barbarous men; for those laws presuppose a reciprocity, which cannot subsist between parties of whom the one is ignorant of the usages, maxims, and religion of the other. But the great principles of morality are of immutable and universal obligation, and from them are deduced the laws of war. Of these laws the first and cardinal rule relating to a state of hostility is, that the belligerent must inflict no injury on his enemy which is not indispensably requisite to ensure the safety of him by whom it is inflicted, or to promote the attainment of the legitimate ends of the warfare. Whether we contend with a civilized or a barbarous enemy, the gratuitous aggravation of the horrors of war, on the plea of vengeance or retribution, or on any similar grounds, is alike indefensible. Now I must profess my inability to discover what danger could be averted, or what useful object could be attained, by the desolation of the Caffre country, which Colonel Smith has described. The inhabitants had been taught the utter hopelessness of a contest with the British force. They had learnt that, for their injuries, whatever they might be, the redress was not in their own power. As the conviction of their helplessness was thus forced upon them, forbearance in the use of our irresistible means of destruction became still more clearly the paramount duty of the leaders of His Majesty's forces.

I cannot even in this brief review of your military operations, pass without particular notice the incident of the captivity and death of Hintza, or overlook the warfare waged against him and his people.

After anxiously examining every word which has been written on the subject by Colonel Smith and yourself, I must avow that I am not satisfied, either that this chieftain was the legitimate object of your military operations, or that his death admits of any satisfactory justification. You charge his tribe, in your despatch of the 5th of January, with having supported the tribes on the border, but at that time you had plainly no evidence of the fact in your possession. That on the 19th of March he was not in open hostility, is manifest from the omission of his name in the catalogue which you then drew up of the hostile tribes. Indeed it is evident that at that time his professions were pacific; he was desirous, as you state, of "holding off." It is said that his people were decidedly hostile, but of this assertion also the proof is wanting. In the predicament in which he was placed, neutrality was the wise and justifiable policy of Hintza; nor can I perceive why he should have been censured for pursuing it. Yet I find that, previously to the 19th of March, hostilities against him were meditated.

By your despatch of the 19th of June, it appears that, as early as the month of February, you had ascertained beyond all doubt, that if not the original contriver, Hintza had been the instigator of the combination; that he had been very early referred to, and consulted by the chiefs; that he had afforded them his countenance and advice; that he had received the cattle of the colonists; that he had permitted, if not directly, many of his own people to join in the invasion, and that the chiefs had relied on his support. Still stronger convictions of these facts having been impressed on your mind, you on the 22nd of February delivered to Colonel Smith a plan of operations, which you proposed to extend to Hintza's country; and proceeding shortly afterwards to carry that plan into execution, this chief was induced to offer himself in your camp as a hostage for the performance of the engagements into which he was required to enter.

You will of course have provided yourself with the proofs on which you acted on this occasion. It may be true that the borderers had driven the cattle into Hintza's country. Nor do I doubt that every assertion which you have made on this subject was carefully weighed, and represents the facts with the closest possible adherence to the evidence which was in your possession at the time. It is not therefore without extreme distrust that I exhibit, in contrast with your statements, impressions derived not from a distinct knowledge of facts, but from the apparent presumptions of the case. Reasoning only from probabilities, I should have thought it scarcely likely that Hintza had either instigated or countenanced the war. Threatened by the Zoolah nation to the eastward, and removed from immediate contact with the British dominions, he had a few years before found in our power a support against his formidable neighbours. By engaging in war with us, he had much to dread, and little or no apparent prospect of advantage. It is evident that he was fully aware of the benefits of our alliance, and possessed judgment and sagacity enough to take a very distinct view of his own interests. On the other hand, there were many who had an unworthy but powerful motive for traducing him, as the enemy of the colonists: he ruled over a remote but fertile country, rich in cattle, and offering a far more tempting prospect of indemnity or of gain than the lands of the border chiefs.

I will not pause to inquire whether Hintza was justly detained in your camp as a prisoner, or whether he was really liable to pay with his life the penalty of attempting to escape from the detachment which accompanied him. All this being conceded, there yet remains the question, not hitherto solved, nor, as far as I can perceive, even discussed. He was slain when he had no longer the means of resistance, but covered with wounds, and vainly attempting to conceal his person in the water into which he had plunged as a refuge from his pursuers. Why the last wound was inflicted, and why this unhappy man, regarded with an attachment almost idolatrous by his people, was not seized by the numerous armed men who had reached his place of concealment, has never yet been explained.

The case assumes a peculiar importance, from the circumstance that Mr. Southey, who gave the death wound, appears to have been subsequently twice commended in general orders, though not indeed with any express reference to his conduct in this affair. It is said that Hintza refused to surrender. But if the fact be so, of what importance was the refusal of a wounded, perhaps, isolated man?

It is stated to me, however, on evidence which it is impossible to receive without serious attention, that Hintza repeatedly cried for mercy; that the Hottentots present granted the boon, and abstained from killing him; that this office was then undertaken by Mr. Southey, and that then the dead body of the fallen chief was basely and inhumanly mutilated. I express no opinion on this subject, but advert to it because the honour of the British name demands that the case should undergo a full investigation, which it is my purpose to institute.

With the views which I have thus explained of the origin and conduct of this warfare, you will anticipate the extreme difficulty in which His Majesty's Government find themselves placed respecting its result. I stated in the commencement of this despatch the peculiar nature of the evidence from which, in the absence of official intelligence, I have been compelled to derive my views of the origin of the recent hostilities; and although I have not thought it necessary to interrupt the preceding statement by a repeated reference to such considerations, I have yet written it under the full and lively impression of the inconvenience of reasoning upon such premises. The proofs which have produced conviction on my own mind, not having been made public, have escaped the scrutiny to which they would otherwise have been exposed. Neither can I expect that others will on the authority of my judgment attach to that evidence the regard which it appears to me to merit. Consequently, in advancing from the retrospect of what has occurred to practical instructions respecting the course to be hereafter followed, I find myself precluded from giving you instructions of so fixed and unbending a character as I might have furnished to you, had I been more immediately assisted and guided by your own previous investigations into the origin of the war. But the urgency of the case is such, as to forbid a further and indefinite delay. Yielding to the necessity of acting at once upon my imperfect, and it may be materially inaccurate, apprehension of the facts, the only escape which I can find from the difficulties on either side, is by devolving on you a responsibility, from which, had it been in my power; I would gladly have relieved you.

The general principles by which the British policy towards the Aborigines of Southern Africa should be governed, are obvious, and beyond the reach of doubt. The extension of His Majesty's dominions in that quarter of the globe, by conquest or cession, is diligently and anxiously to be avoided. Hostilities with the tribes in our vicinity may occasionally be inevitable for the protection of the King's subjects; but on every other ground they cannot too earnestly be deprecated. In our relations with those tribes, it yet remains to try the efficacy of a systematic and persevering adherence to justice, conciliation, forbearance, and the honest arts by which civilization may be advanced, and Christianity diffused amongst them; and such a system must be immediately established and rigidly enforced.

Thus far I am persuaded of your entire concurrence in the views of His Majesty's government. The very short period of your administration before the irruption of the Caffres had not passed without manifesting the desire of the colonial government to act upon those views in their intercourse with the border tribes. But although we are thus agreed as to principles, yet when I proceed to reduce them to a specific form, and to pursue them into those practical consequences which they seem to me to involve, a very material difference of opinion may perhaps arise between us. It is possible that you may be in possession of facts of which I am ignorant, the knowledge of which would have irresistibly dissuaded the adoption of some of those measures which I am about to explain. You may have it in your power to convince me that some of the premises upon which I have been compelled to reason are so entirely mistaken, or fallacious, as not to support my practical deductions from them. Conscious of those sources of error which are always open to persons reasoning at so great a distance from the scene of action, and to which I am on the present occasion so peculiarly liable, I cannot, I repeat, hazard the experiment of laying upon you peremptory and inflexible injunctions for your guidance in those affairs. In explaining the course which His Majesty's government propose to take, I shall proceed on the assumption that I do not labour under any such cardinal error respecting the facts of the case as would refute my conclusions. If, however, in the exercise of your deliberate judgment, and availing yourself of your peculiar means of knowledge, you shall be clearly persuaded that I have fallen into any such misapprehensions, it will become your duty to assume to yourself the responsibility of suspending, until further directions, the execution of any part of the following instructions, which you may be convinced had its origin in such misconception.

For the purpose of perspicuity I shall endeavour to separate from each other, and to arrange in order, the various practical questions which offer themselves, so far as they at present require or admit of a solution.

First, For the reasons already given, I cannot admit that the British sovereignty over the country between the Fish River and the Keishkamma rests on any solid foundation of international law or justice; yet the relinquishment of that dominion is surrounded by difficulties so many and inextricable as entirely to forbid such a surrender. It is needless to enumerate or to describe these impediments. The restitution of invaded rights in this, as in many other cases, would involve injuries more formidable than it could remedy.

Secondly, The claim of sovereignty over the new province, bounded by the Keishkamma and the Kye, must be renounced. It rests upon a conquest resulting from a war, in which, as far as I am at present enabled to judge, the original justice is on the side of the conquered, not of the victorious party. Even if there were the most powerful motives of apparent expediency to recommend this extension of His Majesty's dominions, which I cannot allow, yet His Majesty would never consent to consult expediency at the expence of justice. You will, therefore, prepare the public mind in the Cape colony for the relinquishment of the newly acquired province, by announcing that the British occupation of it is temporary and provisional only, and will be resigned by the end of the year 1836. I fix that date, as it will afford a sufficient interval for making those arrangements which will be necessary to enable the colony to recede with safety from the limits assigned to it by your proclamation.

I place this resolution on the ground of justice, because I should be most unwilling to appear to act on such an occasion on any subordinate motive. But if the conquest could be maintained with indisputable right, I should hold the impolicy of abiding by it equally clear. In this I have the misfortune to differ from you, and I must, therefore, distinctly explain the grounds of that difference.

You state that this accession of territory will be some indemnity against the expenses of the war. To the assumption involved in this statement, that an enlargement of the British dominion in Southern Africa is a national advantage, I feel myself unable to assent. The territory of the Caffres, I am well aware, is in itself a fertile and salubrious region, contrasting but too favourably with the prevailing sterility of our own possessions. But the great evil of the Cape colony consists in its magnitude; in the vast space for which it encroaches upon the continent, and the consequent extent of its boundary. We are thus brought into contact with tribes numerous and warlike, and a scale of establishment is required, both civil and military, extensive beyond all proportion to the number and wealth of the inhabitants. In a country containing more square miles than the whole of the British Islands, we have a population of about 150,000 souls. To connect these dispersed settlers by roads, and other communications, to bring them under the protection of magistrates and officers of police, to afford them the benefit of prompt administration of justice, and to shield them by military defence, are duties incumbent on the Government, but duties which cannot be performed without imposts so heavy as to excite universal and apparently just complaints, and which, even with such imposts, have never been performed but most defectively. Whence the necessary revenues for defraying the additional establishments, civil and military, are to be extracted, is a question to which your consideration does not appear to have yet been given, and to which I have directed my own in vain.

But it is said that the defence of the new frontier will be more economical than that of the Keishkamma. Much as I am disposed to rely upon your professional judgment, I must own that upon that point I feel no little hesitation in acquiescing in the accuracy of your calculations. I shall not scruple to explain unreservedly the nature of my difficulties, convinced that you will estimate them with candour, and that you will afford me the benefit of your experience and professional skill for the more full elucidation of the subject.

It is evident that the new frontier, being much more distant, is therefore less accessible from the interior than the old. It embraces a larger area, and would therefore seem to demand a longer line of defences. In the absence of any exact military survey of both, the general presumption must seem to be, that in proportion as the frontier is protracted it becomes more readily assailable. Pushing further forward into Africa, the new line of defences would bring us into contact with new tribes of uncivilized men. Amongst these the exiled Caffres must be received as intruders, and will form a band of desperate adventurers, at one time seeking subsistence by plunder in the colony, at another provoking war on its borders. Thus we shall again be brought into contact on a new line with African warfare in all its ferocity. New enemies will be acquired; new conquests must be achieved; a new frontier must be sought, and we should be engaged in a series of contests desolating to Africa and ruinous to ourselves. It would be a melancholy acquisition to exchange the neighbourhood of men who have been taught to fear our power, and in some degree to practise our social arts, and to adopt our religion, for that of fresh hordes of barbarians, who, however inaccessible to the arts of peace, may yet prove no unapt scholars under our tuition in the art of war. Nor is it possible to contemplate without emotion, the extinction of the churches which had been planted in Africa, and of the prospects of diffusing Christianity and the other blessings of civilized life in that portion of the globe.

You state, however, that for the defence of the Keishkamma frontier, the regular troops must be augmented to about 3,000 rank and file, while the increase might be considerably less if the Kye be taken as the boundary.

Now, even if on a careful and complete survey it should be established, in a military sense, that the Kye is a better boundary than the Keishkamma, still this argument of comparative ease and cheapness of defence may be open to question. Of two lines of defence, the one may by nature be stronger than the other, and consequently, if regarded simply in that view, without reference to other circumstances, may be pronounced the less expensive. But other circumstances may far more than counterbalance the difference. If the stronger frontier comprehend the larger extent of territory; if it be the more remote from the main strength and body of the colony; more remote from the resources on which it must in case of attack rely for supplies of all kinds; for men, for provisions, for munitions of war; if in all these respects, therefore, it be in fact the weaker of the two, and if at the same time it be more exposed to attack; if, for example, it should gather and dam up along its whole line a raging mass of savages, tormented by the narrowness of their limits, by famine, and by revenge, and threatening every moment to break over the mound; if these should be the relative circumstances of the two defences, it is very easy to perceive, that with all its natural advantages, the stronger may at the same time prove not only the more costly, but also the more difficult to maintain, and, therefore, be less secure. In truth, however, this argument of comparative expense proceeds on the assumption that the security of the colony can be assured only by having a force of regular troops, numerically large enough to man the whole frontier. But this, whatever line of defence be chosen, is obviously impossible. The army of England would not suffice to man, in the proper sense of the word, our colonial frontier from sea to sea. For the defence of such a frontier some regular troops are necessary, and the number already supplied is probably all that in justice to the people of this country, and to the great demands of the empire, ought to be allowed for that object. The further military defence must be sought in the enrolment of a local militia force. But even this force in its best state, and in conjunction with a sufficient number of regulars, can never be our exclusive reliance. The surest of all defences, or rather the only sure defence, is to be found in a wise system of border policy. Without this the strongest frontier that nature or art can supply is miserably weak, and with it the Keishkamma is as secure as the Kye. It cannot be too often or too importunately pressed on our conviction as a plain practical truth, that the safety of the colony, which after all is the first object, is to be derived from observing in our dealings with the frontier tribes the most rigid justice, respect for their feelings and prejudices, regard for their real interests, conciliatory kindness when it can be properly shown, and above all, an unwearied anxiety to diffuse among them the blessings of education and of Christian knowledge. Colonies which it is attempted to maintain in the neighbourhood of savage tribes on any other principles, must either be destroyed by that vicinity, or be upheld at a cost utterly disproportionate to their real value.

It remains to consider what course is to be pursued towards the people with whom we have been brought into contact. And first, in reference to the Fingoes:

I must frankly confess, that I am quite unable to perceive the slightest accuracy in the comparison which you have instituted between the liberation of these people and the great national act of negro emancipation. In the one case we liberated the slaves of our enemies at the cost of their owners, in the other case we liberated the slaves of British subjects at the cost of the national revenue. Still the act having been done, is irreversible. To replace the Fingoes in the state of slavery from which we have rescued them, would be an act altogether indefensible. These persons must, therefore, be settled under British protection, on lands to be assigned for their maintenance. The territory which would appear best adapted for this purpose, is that to the westward of the Keishkamma, from which the Caffres were expelled.

With regard to the tribes which were driven from those lands, and to those against which our hostilites had been waged, His Majesty's government cannot think it consistent either with justice or with sound policy, that they should be exiled from their ancient possessions between the Kye and the Keishkamma.

The restoration of the Caffres to the conquered territory must, however, be accompanied and preceded by such arrangements as will assign to each tribe its own proper limits.

For the due regulation of the future relations between the Caffre tribes and the colonists, as well as for other purposes of local convenience, His Majesty proposes immediately to appoint a lieutenant-governor of the eastern districts of the colony. On the lieutenant-governor will be devolved the administration of the executive government within the boundaries to be assigned to his command. It is further proposed to appoint a civil commissioner, or protector of the native tribes, who shall reside within the colony, probably at the seat of the lieutenant-governor's residence. To this officer will be entrusted the duty of protecting the borderers on either side against mutual aggressions. It will be his office to inform himself of every inroad and act of plunder committed against the colonists, and of every outrage or injury offered to the Caffres; to investigate the truth of every allegation of that nature; to report all such occurrences to the lieutenant-governor; and to superintend in person the execution of all measures which may be necessary for obtaining redress; and to take charge of all cases in which the subjects of native chiefs are brought before the colonial courts of justice. It is also intended to appoint a government agent to reside in Caffreland, with the requisite powers to make him an efficient guardian over the rights as well of the natives as of European traders.

All communications with the Caffres on what, in the absence of a more simple word, may be termed international subjects, must be carried on through the government agent for Caffreland.

The following is a statement of the principal rules which it is intended to prescribe to the lieutenant-governor and civil commissioner, for the guidance of their conduct.

1. A treaty, fixing the boundaries of the colony, must be made in writing, in English and in the Caffre language, and, being explained to each border chief, must be signed or attested by each. Copies of this treaty must be delivered to each of the contracting chiefs.

2. A separate treaty must be made, in the English and in the native languages, with the chief of every tribe to which a portion of territory is assigned within the British dominions; defining the limits of his allocation, the degree of his responsibility, and the nature of his relations with the British govern-

ment; and all other particulars admitting of specification. A copy of this treaty in the native tongue must be preserved by the chief.

3. A separate treaty must be made in the native and English languages with the chief of every tribe in alliance with us, or in any degree under our protection; defining also in each case all that can be specified in such an instrument. A copy of the treaty must be preserved by each chief.

4. The rules of mutual restitution, and those which relate to the prevention of inroads, and the redress of the injury occasioned by them, must be particularized in each of the above treaties.

5. The responsibility of particular kraals, or villages, for the acts of individual Caffres, must no longer be enforced. But

6. The chiefs must be called upon to bind themselves to make restitution of plundered cattle, on sufficient proof of the reality of the theft. They must be left to detect the offenders, or to indemnify themselves at the expense of the tribe collectively for such losses as they may sustain by being required to make these compensations. In other words, we must look to the chiefs, and to them alone, and must no longer take upon ourselves to make reprisals upon the people. The chiefs to enter into securities, or pledges, of such a nature as may be deemed sufficient, and not inconvenient for the due fulfilment of these stipulations.

7. Fairs for the interchange of commodities should be re-established at convenient places on the frontier.

8. The wounding or killing a Caffre, or otherwise injuring his person or property, will be made liable to the same punishment as if the sufferer were one of His Majesty's subjects. This of course would not apply to times of actual war, nor prevent the compulsory removal back into their own territory of any Caffres who might re-appear within the boundaries with purposes apparently hostile or fraudulent, or in opposition to any existing laws. No violence must, however, be used in effecting their removal, which is not strictly required by the necessity of the case, and for the effective execution of the service.

9. No European or Hottentot, or any others but Caffres, to be located or allowed to settle east of the Great Fish River. Those Hottentots who were placed in the ceded territory prior to the late war, and all Christian teachers, are exempted from this rule. I may observe here, that in the above rules, under the general name of Caffres, I include the Fingoes.

In aid of these general rules, it is proposed to submit, for the approbation of Parliament, a law to enable our colonial tribunals to take cognizance of and to punish offences committed by British subjects within the Caffre territory, in the same manner as if they had been perpetrated within the limits of the colony itself.

I have thus indicated in general terms the measures which it is proposed to adopt, and which are of course liable to be altered or modified on further consideration. The lieutenant-governor will also be the bearer of instructions defining the relative authority and duties of himself and of the governor of the colony. I therefore abstain from enlarging at present on those topics.

Throughout this despatch I have proceeded on the supposition that the war has been brought to a termination. Your despatch of the 19th of June would appear to encourage and justify that hope, although I perceive with deep concern, from the public journals of the colony, as well as from private letters which have reached this country, that so lately as September last your military operations were not concluded, and that you were still on the frontier; that the Caffres were pushing their depredations with increasing boldness into the colony, and even into the neighbourhood of Graham's Town. Of course it is impossible to address to you any definite instructions for your conduct, in contingencies respecting which I can form only a doubtful and uncertain conjecture. But you will receive as a most decided and positive injunction the directions which I now convey to you, to bring these hostilities to a conclusion by the earliest possible period. They must not be protracted for a single day with a view to revenge or conquest. The safety of His Majesty's subjects in the districts of Somerset and Albany is the single legitimate object with which such a contest can be carried on at all, and that object once attained, it must be immediately terminated. To maintain a considerable army for any other object, and to incur an enormous expense connected with its maintenance, is a proceeding to which the Parliament and People of this kingdom could never be reconciled. The utmost possible benefit to be obtained is insignificant when contrasted with such an outlay of the national resources at a moment when the strongest necessity exists for carrying an enlightened but strict economy into every part of the public service.

The loss of money, however serious, as on every account it is, would yet be the least of the causes of that regret with which the people of Great Britain would be affected by the continuation of these hostilities. It is a melancholy and humiliating, but an indisputable truth, that the contiguity of the subjects of the nations of Christendom with uncivilized tribes has invariably produced the wretchedness and decay, and not seldom the utter extermination, of the weaker party. This uniform result must be attributed, not to any necessary cause, but to the sinister influence of those evil passions, which, in such circumstances, find but too much to provoke, and too little to restrain them. Of all the chapters in the history of mankind, this is perhaps the most degrading. Nor is there any one great course of events on which every humane mind dwells with such settled aversion and shame, as on that which records the intercourse between the Christian States of Europe, and the heathen nations of America and Africa. I know not that a greater real calamity could befal Great Britain than that of adding Southern Africa to the list of the regions which have seen their aboriginal inhabitants disappear under the withering influence of European neighbourhood. It is indeed a calamity reducible to no certain standard or positive measurement, but it involves whatever is most to be dreaded, in bringing upon ourselves at once the reproaches of mankind, and the weight of national guilt. I do not say, nor mean to imply, that those fearful desolations which Colonel Smith's letters record, are justly liable to this censure : but thinking that we were the real aggressors, not indeed in the actual warfare, yet in the series of events by which it was preceded and provoked, I feel that if it be continued for a day or an hour longer than the necessity of self-defence plainly requires, we shall not be able to rescue ourselves from the reproach of having exerted our superiority needlessly and unjustly to crush a people, whose impotent resistance leaves room for no feelings but those of compassion.

These views I am well assured will be partaken by the generous, humane and Christian people, over whom it his Majesty's glory and happiness to reign. Sympathizing with every just and honourable sentiment of the subjects of the British Crown, His Majesty has commanded me to express his solicitude for the protection of the Aborigines of Southern Africa, and his repugnance to sanction any enlargement of his dominions of which their sufferings would be the price. You are aware that in the session of Parliament of 1834, the House of Commons especially invoked His Majesty's protection for these defenceless people, and received from the King an assurance of His Majesty's determination to act in this respect in accordance to their wishes. In the spirit of that assurance I am commanded to issue these instructions; nor will His Majesty regard his pledge as redeemed until he can present to his people the proofs of the establishment of a system of border policy advantageous alike for the Caffres and for the colony.

I am persuaded that your sentiments fully concur with my own on the general principle on which these instructions are founded; and it affords me much gratification to know, that as you have been called to the discharge of severe and unwelcome duties, so now the more agreeable task will devolve upon you of carrying into effect His Majesty's gracious intentions, which I have the honour of communicating to you in this despatch.

It only remains for me to state, that his Majesty's Government will await with solicitude the report which you will transmit to me in answer to this despatch. That report will, I have no doubt, contain as full an explanation as you can supply on every topic on which I have stated doubts and difficulties. After a deliberate consideration of it, His Majesty's Government hope to be able to issue their final instructions.—I have, &c.

(Signed)   GLENELG.

Copy of a Despatch from Lord GLENELG to Governor Sir B. D'URBAN, dated Downing-Street, 17th February, 1836.

SIR,—I have received your despatch, dated 7th November, your despatch marked "Supplementary" to and dated 12th November, and your despatch dated 22d October, marked "Miscellaneous," reporting the conclusion of treaties of peace between yourself and the chiefs of the various Caffre tribes, and the termination of the hostilities with those people.

These communications embrace many topics which, on any other occasion, might have been more conveniently discussed in separate despatches. In the present instance, however, a departure from the established rules of official correspondence was plainly inevitable; and I will therefore advert to the various subjects mentioned in your despatches, in the order in which they there occur.

1. It is very gratifying to His Majesty to receive your assurance of the continued discipline, zeal and good conduct of His Majesty's officers and troops, who have been serving under your command in the late war with the Caffre tribes.

2. Your release of the chief Bookoo, the uncle of Crieli, from his confinement as a hostage, appears to have been a well-timed and judicious measure.

3. I do not think it convenient to discuss the propriety of the payments which you report yourself to have made for the clothing, the pay, and the gratuities of the Hottentots, and of the burgher force enrolled and serving with your army, until I shall have received that complete and detailed report of all the expenses of the late contest, which it will, of course, have been your first care, on your return to Cape Town, to prepare for

the information of the Lords Commissioners of the Treasury: their Lordships await that report with no common anxiety.

4. I cannot advert to the employment of the Hottentots, without apprising you, that a rumour has reached me, that the Moravian missionaries settled at Guadenthal, and other places in the colony, complain of the very unequal share which the Hottentot members of their congregations have been compelled to bear in the burthen of the common defence, leading, as it is asserted, to the depopulation of their villages, the great distress of the women and children, and the interruption of their religious labours, to a far greater extent than in a just apportionment of the duty of military service would have fallen upon them. If in the unavoidable pressure of other topics upon your notice, this should have been overlooked, you will, I am convinced, immediately take the necessary measures for the redress of any such grievance.

5. I transmit to you a copy of a correspondence between this department and the office of the General commanding in chief; from which you will learn that under the peculiar circumstances of the case, I have approved your detention of the 98th Regiment.

6. The basis of the treaties into which you have entered with the Caffre chiefs being the subjection of themselves and their people to His Majesty, the other terms of those treaties scarcely demand a very studious attention. Between the King and his subjects no convention, in the proper sense of the term, can subsist. The rights and the duties incident to that relation must be determined by the general law, and cannot properly be defined by any other rule. But, as you will already have learned, from my despatch of the 26th December, that His Majesty is not disposed to accept the allegiance of the Caffres, or the dominion of their country, it is the less necessary for me to discuss the effect of these treaties. It remains to be seen what will be their fate: and I regret that His Majesty's ratification of them was not declared essential to their validity.

7. I cannot, however, pass over in entire silence the illustration which these instruments afford of the objections which I have already urged to the annexation of the Caffre territory to the colony under your government. They announce to His Majesty's new subjects that the penalty of death will hereafter follow upon the offences of cattle-stealing, and of setting fire to houses or other property. If this menace was not seriously uttered, it was not judicious. If meant to be carried into effect, it must involve the most alarming consequences. With minds unaccustomed to regard with any moral reprobation such acts as these, and reduced by the casualties of war to a state affording the strongest temptation to perpetrate them, the

penalty of death must appear a punishment extreme and utterly disproportionate. The infliction of it upon multitudes is impossible. The selection of few offenders to expiate the crimes of their tribe would bear the appearance of partiality and wrong; and would, by exciting resentment and other passions, tend to a revival of the late disasters. In short, I fear that the Caffres are unripe for those laws to which it is proposed at once to make them amenable.

8. Such, indeed, would seem to be your own conclusion; for I perceive that you intend to frame a distinct code for the government of the Caffres; and in the meantime to leave them under martial law. The plan has not been very fully digested; but I fear that it would be found in practice scarcely possible for the legislature of a civilized country to devise and promulgate a code fit for the government of a barbarous people. If not accommodated to their habits of thought and action, it would be at once unjust and inefficient; and if so accommodated, it must involve a compromise of many principles which we justly regard as sacred.

9. You propose a civil establishment for the newly conquered country, involving an expense of 1,600l. per annum. You are, however, silent as to the means of defraying this charge. For the present, and until the arrival of the lieutenant-governor of the eastern districts, not only the decision, but the further discussion of this plan must be suspended.

10. You further suggest an enlargement of the colonial territory on the north-eastern frontier, by embracing within His Majesty's dominions certain lands which you state to be uninhabited. This question must also be postponed until after the lieutenant-governor's arrival. It will then be necessary to consider carefully whether there may not be any prior title to the land by the occasional occupancy of the natives, and whether the probable advantage from this accession of territory is such as to counterbalance the evil of extending the limits of a colony already so inconveniently large.

11. It is stated in your confidential notes of the 17th of September, that in the territory described as Queen Adelaide's, " large tracts are left vacant for the occupation and speculation of Europeans." I cannot too distinctly impress upon you the instruction, that under no circumstances a single grant or licence of occupation be made of any part of this territory in favour of any European. Even if ultimately added to the British dominions, it must be reserved exclusively for the occupancy of the natives.

12. Your proposal for embodying a militia has been anticipated in my despatch of the 26th of December. There are few

subjects which will more deserve your own and the lieutenant-governor's early and serious consideration.

13. The single remaining topic noticed in your despatches, to which it seems to me necessary to advert, is the summary which you have given of the result of the late war. It is as follows:—

"In the course of the Commissioners' progress in the census of the tribes of Gaika and T'Slambie, they have ascertained that their loss during our operations against them, has amounted to 4,000 of their warriors or fighting men, and among them many captains. Ours, fortunately, has not in the whole amounted to 100, and of these only two officers. There have been taken from them also, besides the conquest and alienation of their country, about 60,000 head of cattle, almost all their goats, their habitations everywhere destroyed, and their gardens and corn-fields laid waste. They have, therefore, been chastised, not extremely, but sufficiently."

I am bound to record the very deep regret with which I have perused this passage. In a conflict between regular troops and hordes of barbarous men, it is almost a matter of course that there should exist an enormous disproportion between the loss of life on either side. But to consign an entire country to desolation, and a whole people to famine, is an aggravation of the necessary horrors of war, so repugnant to every just feeling, and so totally at variance with the habits of civilized nations, that I should not be justified in receiving such a statement without calling upon you for further explanations. The honour of the British name is deeply interested in obtaining and giving publicity to the proofs that the safety of the King's subjects really demanded so fearful an exercise of the irresistible power of His Majesty's forces.—I have, &c.

(Signed)   GLENELG.

Horse Guards, 27th January, 1836.

SIR,—I do myself the honour, by desire of the General commanding in chief, to transmit for the information of Lord Glenelg, the copy of a despatch which I have received from Major-General Sir B. D'Urban, reporting that he has detained the 98th regiment, which the 27th was sent out to relieve; and I am to request that you will be so good as to let me know if Lord Glenelg approves of this measure.

The letter announcing the relief of the 98th was dispatched in due course, and ought to have reached the Cape long before the 27th regiment.—I have, &c.

(Signed)   FITZROY SOMERSET.

R. W. Hay, Esq. &c. &c. &c.

Cape of Good Hope, Port Elizabeth,
15th Nov. 1835.

My Lord,—I have the honour to acknowledge your Lordship's letter of the 8th April, and thereupon I request your reference to my despatch to the Secretary of State, of which a copy was enclosed in my letter to your Lordship of the 7th instant, for the reasons which have compelled me to take upon myself the responsibility of retaining the service companies of the 98th regiment for the present, and until instructions reach me from England.

Your Lordship's letter now before me was the first official advertisement which had reached me of the coming of the 27th, and of its being the intention of the General commanding in chief that it should relieve the 98th now at the Cape Town. When it reached me at Fort Wiltshire on the 18th September, the 27th had already on the 8th arrived at Graham's Town, relieved the 75th there and along the old colonial border, and enabled the latter to join me in advance very seasonably for the service I had then in hand.

Although I had no official, nor indeed any certain, intelligence of the coming of the 27th, yet the newspapers had announced it, and the tenor of my despatches to the Secretary of State of January, February and March, (of all which copies had been transmitted to your Lordship) had, as I thought, rendered it possible that a reinforcement might be on its way; therefore, as I could not at the period afford to throw a chance away, I had sent orders that if a regiment should arrive at Table or Simon's Bay, it should immediately join me by Algoa Bay, which it did accordingly, as I have already mentioned. And even when I had learned from your Lordship's letter, that this regiment was not at all meant to be a reinforcement, but merely a relief to the 98th, I felt that I was still unable, without compromising the security of the colony, and the interest of His Majesty's service, to spare the 27th from the eastern border, or the 98th from Cape Town; and this paramount duty has compelled me to keep the 27th at Graham's Town, and on the line of which it is the centre, and the 98th at Cape and Simon's Town. But as the duties of the 98th in these latter quarters have long been too severe for its strength, I have availed myself of the apparent prospect of continued tranquillity which the first month of peace has afforded, to send the head-quarters and two companies of the 27th to Cape Town; and under this arrangement I trust to be able to await the ultimate instructions which my despatch of the 19th of June to the Secretary of State (of which copies were transmitted to your Lordship for Lord Hill) will probably have elicited.

I hope that in thus retaining a regiment which the General commanding in chief had destined to return to England, his Lordship may be disposed to regard the measure as justified by the circumstances of my position, and to prove it accordingly. —I have, &c.

(Signed) B. D'Urban, Major-General.

Major-General Lord Fitzroy Somerset,
  K.C.B., &c. &c. &c.

Downing-Street, 8th Feb. 1836.

My Lord,—I have received and laid before Lord Glenelg, your Lordship's letter of the 27th ultimo, enclosing the copy of a despatch which your Lordship had received from Major-General Sir Benjamin D'Urban, reporting that he had detained at the Cape of Good Hope the 98th regiment, which the 27th had been sent out to relieve.

To your Lordship's inquiry whether Lord Glenelg approves of this measure, I am directed by him to return, for the information of the General commanding in chief, the following answer: the reports which, on the 30th ultimo, reached Lord Glenelg from Sir B. D'Urban, of the political state of the frontier districts of the colony, and of his own position, at the time when the resolution of detaining the 98th regiment was taken and executed, have convinced his Lordship that the Major-General was justified by the exigency of the occasion in adopting a measure involving so grave a responsibility. In communicating to your Lordship this conclusion, Lord Glenelg desires to be understood as not intending to convey any opinion respecting the wisdom of the various military operations, in furtherance or support of which the 98th regiment was detained.—I have, &c.

(Signed) James Stephen.

Major-General Lord Fitzroy Somerset,
  K.C.B., &c. &c. &c.

PRINTED BY STEWART AND CO., OLD BAILEY.

New Publications and Standard Works in Theology and Miscellaneous Literature.

PUBLISHED BY

JAMES DUNCAN,

37, PATERNOSTER ROW.

NARRATIVE of a RESIDENCE in KOORDIS-TAN, and on the SITE of ANCIENT NINEVEH, with Journal of a Voyage down the Tigris to Bagdad, and an Account of a Visit to Sheraz and Persepolis, with Maps and a Plan of Nineveh, from original Observations, and numerous Illustrations. By the late CLAUDIUS JAMES RICH, Esq., the Honourable East India Company's Resident at Bagdad, author of "An Account of Ancient Babylon." In Two Vols. 8vo, 30s. cloth.

CHRISTIAN RECORDS; or, a Short and Plain History of the CHURCH of CHRIST: containing the Lives of the Apostles; an Account of the Sufferings of Martyrs; the Rise of the Reformation, and the present State of the Christian Church. By the Rev. THOMAS SIMS, M.A. Sixth Edition. One Volume, 18mo, with a beautiful Frontispiece, 3s. 6d. boards.

" Every Protestant child and young person should be generally acquainted with the outline of the history of the Church of Christ, and for this purpose we cannot recommend a better manual than that before us."—*Christian Observer.*

*** This little volume has been in part translated into the Modern Greek and Chinese languages, by the Rev. Mr. JOWETT and Dr. MILNE; and the Author has received a Letter from the Right Rev. Dr. CORRIE, Bishop of Madras, dated Ship Exmouth, 21 June, 1835, with the following intimation :—

" *I have by me, and intend to have printed, please God I arrive at Madras, the whole of Christian Records translated into Hindoostanee. This language is used by Mahomedans all over India, and understood by most Hindoos.*"

THE LAST DAYS of Our LORD'S MINISTRY; a Course of Lectures on the Practical Events of Passion Week. By the Rev. WALTER FARQUHAR HOOK, M.A., Vicar of Leeds, Prebendary of Lincoln, Chaplain in Ordinary to the King. A New Edition, compressed into small 8vo, price 6s. boards.

A MEMOIR of the LIFE and PUBLIC SERVICES of SIR THOMAS STAMFORD RAFFLES, F.R.S., &c. &c., particularly in the Government of Java, 1811—1816; Bencoolen and its Dependencies, 1817—1824; with Details of the Commerce and Resources of the Eastern Archipelago, and Selections from his Correspondence. By His WIDOW. A New Edition, in 2 vols. 8vo., with a Portrait and other Illustrations, 24s. boards

PROOFS and ILLUSTRATIONS of the ATTRI-BUTES of GOD, from the Facts and Laws of the Physical Universe, being the Foundation of Natural and Revealed Religion. By John MacCulloch, M.D., F.R.S., F.L.S., F.G.S., &c. &c. In 3 vols. 8vo., 36s. boards.

"The gifted author's name and eminence have long been well known in connection with natural science; but it now appears that all his devotion to that and other departments of human knowledge has been made subservient to this his last and ablest work, which we confidently predict will hand down his celebrity to the latest times."—*Monthly Review.*

"The information is worthy the present advanced state of science; and its calm and moderate tone is in perfect accordance with the important subjects discussed."—*Literary Gazette.*

THE BOOK of the PATRIARCH JOB, translated from the original Hebrew, as nearly as possible in the terms and style of the authorised English Version. To which is prefixed an Introduction, on the History, Times, Country, Friends, &c., of the Patriarch ; with some Strictures on the Views of Bishop Warburton, and of the Rationalists of Germany, on the same subject. And to which is appended a Commentary, critical and exegetical, containing Elucidations of many other Passages of Holy Writ. Inscribed, by permission, to his Royal Highness the Duke of Sussex. By Samuel Lee, D.D., Prebendary of Bristol, and Regius Professor of Hebrew in the University of Cambridge. In one thick vol. 8vo.

THE HOLY BIBLE, containing the Old and New Testaments, revised from corrected Texts of the original Tongues, and with former Translations diligently compared ; with Critical and Explanatory Notes. By B. Boothroyd, D.D., Editor of the " Biblia Hebraica," &c. &c. In royal 8vo., 30s. cloth.

The work announced comprises the text of the author's Family Bible and improved version, with such corrections as a repeated and diligent perusal during the last ten years has suggested, aided by the many biblical works which have been published since his own was completed. The results of the labours of the most eminent scholars and biblical critics, of past and present times, will here be found in a condensed form, by which Infidel objections are in many instances satisfactorily obviated, and the judicious English reader will be enabled to perceive the sense, coherence, and beauty of the Holy Scriptures.

BIBLIA HEBRAICA, secundum ultimam editionem Jos. Athiæ, a Johanne Leusden denuo recognitam, recensita, atque ad Masoram, et correctiores, Bombergi, Stephani, Plantini, aliorumque editiones, exquisite adornata, variisque notis illustrata. Ab Everardo Van Der Hooght, V.D.M. Editio nova, recognita, et emendata, a Judah D'Allemand. New Edition, in One Volume, on fine paper (1200 pages), price 21s. boards ; and on inferior paper, but very superior to any Foreign Edition, 15s. boards.

"The most correct Edition of the Hebrew Scriptures is the last reprint of Van der Hooght's Hebrew Bible, which has been revised by Professor Hurwitz."—*Journal of Education.*

CPSIA information can be obtained at www.ICGtesting.com
Printed in the USA
LVOW10s2102030415

433208LV00022B/593/P